Divine Humanism

Divine Humanism

Creating the Happiest Society

Frank Ignace Babatoundé ALAPINI

Copyright © 2012 by Frank Alapini

Cosmic Harmony and Happiness Publishing

E-mail: cosmicharmony12@gmail.com

ISBN: 978-0-9855888-0-9

All rights reserved. No part of this publication may be reproduced, stored in a retrieval system, or transmitted in any form, or by any means, electronic, mechanical, recorded, photocopied, or otherwise without prior written permission of both the copyright owner and the above publisher of this book, except by a reviewer who may quote brief passages in a review.

The scanning, uploading, and distribution of this book via the Internet or any other means without permission of the publisher is illegal and punishable by law. Please purchase only authorized electronic editions and do not participate on or encourage electronic piracy of copyrightable materials. Your support of the author's rights is appreciated.

The three strangest things on this earth consist in three observations:
1- *Most humans still do not have absolute proofs that a Creator God or gods exist or not; some only believe, others doubt, still others deny*
2- *Something is really wrong with the human and the world condition*
3- *Humanity has not yet found a philosophy for all to be truly happy*

However,

Anybody who understands the need for a philosophical and spiritual upgrading can use the content of this book and the one that precedes it to guide him/herself and society better than with the use of astrology passing through a global transitional period toward cosmic harmony and happiness

CONTENTS

Preface 1

Introduction 5

Part I: HUMAN NATURE AND ORIGIN 12

**Chapter 1: The human nature according
to 23 important thinkers** 13
Nineteen ancient thinkers on human nature 14
Human nature according to four contemporary thinkers........................19

**Chapter 2: The human nature according to Hinduism, the Jehovah
Witnesses, and the Unification Movement** 21
Hinduism 22
Jehovah Witnesses...22
Unification Movement...25

Chapter 3: Esotericism on human nature 28
Manly Hall and Helena Blavatsky..28
The Temple of the People..31
Rosicrucianism 39

Chapter 4: Seeker's understanding of human nature 45
Contributions of quantum physics, biology, medicine, and other disciplines to the understanding of human nature 46
Description of human nature predominantly using a philosophical, spiritual, and religious language 54
    Spirit 54
    Definition and proofs of the existence of a human spirit 54
    What is wrong with the general and special theories of relativity and why time travel appears to be only pure fiction 58
    The growth of the spiritual body 59
    Blood sacrifices of animals and Jesus versus education and good actions for spiritual growth: the place of the Holy Spirit and rituals in spirituality 60
    The question of the death and external appearance of the spiritual body 66
    Soul, mind, nous, psyche, or ego: its nature, constituents, functions, qualities, and problems 68
        Tabula Rasa? Archetypes and Prototypes? 68
        Why the mind or soul is not a brain product and is not destroyed like it at death: origin of the soul, preformationism, epigenesis, soul judgment and justice 71
        Reason, morality and virtues, laws, passions, love, goodness, evil, and freedom 83
    Reincarnation, resurrection, heaven, and hell 96

Internal nature of animals, plants, mineral, and of the
particles of quantum physics; meaning of pantheism 103
The question of twins 105
Heredity, culture, and human nature 106
Astrology, prophecy, predestination, destiny,
determinism, non determinism, and the unnecessary
character of pain 106
Definition of a human being 109

Chapter 5: On the origin of humanity 110

**Part II: DIVINE HUMANISM FOR THE ESTABLISHMENT OF
THE HAPPIEST SOCIETY** 116

Chapter 6: Secular Humanism 117
Definition 119
Beliefs and practices of secular humanism according to
Jeaneane Fowler 120
The power of secular humanism as explained by
Paul Kurtz 123

Chapter 7: Divine Humanism 126
Religious and spiritual humanisms 126
Comparison of the three traditional kinds of humanism 129
Secular humanism compared to divine humanism 130
What is divine humanism? 133

Chapter 8: Education for the happiest society: generalities 144
Definition of education 144
Environmental factors that influence education 144
Formal and informal education 145
Education as a gradual process 146
Problems of hidden education 147
Titles and curricula vitae 149
Language and education 150

Chapter 9: Spiritual science, philosophy, and theology 151
Generalities 151
Spirituality or energeticity? 151
    Comparison of spirituality, religion, and spiritual science 152
    Spiritual science defined in a few words 154
    Spiritual science, theology, philosophy, and psychology differentiated 154
    Teachings of spiritual science 156
A discussion on the "voice" of God 156
Prayer 158
    Definition and goals of prayer 158
    Some benefits of payer **163**
    Elements that support prayer including magic, alchemy, fasting, and prayer frequency 163
    Forms of prayer 171
    Meditation 173
Music 173

Worship 174
The mountain, the roads, and the elephant 176

Chapter 10: Sexuality, reproduction, and marriage 177
Sexuality 178
The Tree of the Knowledge of Good and Evil [TKGE] 180
    Five different interpretations of the TKGE 180
    Seeker's understanding of the TKGE and
    the original sin 182
Examination and assessment of various
sexual behaviors 194
    No sex at all? 194
    To have sex with animals? 198
    To be lesbian, gay, bisexual, transsexual,
    or transgender [LGBT]? 200
    To fornicate? To cheat? Group sex or orgies?
    Multiple spouses? 205
    Pedophilia? 207
    Masturbation? 207
    Pornography? 208
    Abortion? 208
    To be married and be faithful to one spouse? 208
Reproduction, family and friendship, and child adoption 211

Chapter 11: Recreation, arts, sport, media, politics, and economy 212
Arts, sport, and the media 213
Politics and economy 215

Chapter 12: Human beings and their futures 221
Individual and collective futures 221
Apocalypticism 224
Cosmic cooperation, harmony, equality, beauty, health, justice, and happiness 225

Conclusion 229

References 234

Index 237

Appendix: the philosogram 242

Preface

The Adventures of Seeker: Episode 2

EPISODE 1 of *The Adventures of Seeker* has presented the goal of the quest of a man which was to discover, a way or another, a light able to dissipate all the aspects of Darkness. The purpose of the first step of his engineering process was to make clearer the existence and nature of Mahu, Zinflougan, and their respective courts.

One of Seeker's conclusions was that Mahu is the Universal Mind or Soul that pervades all substance; an androgynous [male-female] being, cause or creator of all beings. Second, he became convinced that the highest being in the most common book of guidance is not the same when one leaves its first part for the second part. He noticed that the correct idea of Mahu is present in the second part while the first part almost all the time only talks about watchers, some very powerful, who helped Mahu bring into existence several other beings.

Third, Zinflougan emerges out of the scriptures as a god of the class of the watchers created by Mahu but who became corrupted. Seeker found out that this scriptural conclusion also made sense philosophically but requires experiential proofs as the affirmation that gods exists does. He has identified several paths of research that promise to yield those proofs.

A fourth major conclusion of Seeker was that scripturally and logically, the walker called Jesus did not pre-exist as the watcher Michael before his birth on earth and that he was sent by Mahu to help walkers on earth the way many other walkers have been sent, are sent, and will be sent. However Jesus like any spiritually advanced walker can be called a god that can even be superior to the gods of the class of the watchers or any other class.

Fifth, the Holy Spirit is the super substance, energy, matter, electricity, fire, life force, power, and part of the body of Mahu that He-She uses to create and restore. Two remarkable collective manifestations of the Holy Spirit took place at the Pentecosts, at the time of Moses and the 70 elders of Ancient Israel, and when it came down upon the disciples of Jesus. Remarkable individual cases include Hermes Trismegistus, Jesus, Moses, and many others. Seeker thinks he has received and continues to receive his share.

However, that some walkers have received the Holy Spirit does not mean they are incapable of mistakes. As many scriptures say, even watchers do not know everything and can make mistakes. Zinflougan had made successive terrible mistakes which resulted in the birth of evil. So, receiving the Holy Spirit is a thing and using it properly is another.

Seeker, based on his own experience and instructions knows that the science of physical things is not aware of these manifestations of the Holy Spirit while several religions and spiritual schools are. The later sometimes offer accurate explanations that cannot be seen in any book on physical things including medical books.

Nevertheless, several physical researchers are getting close to that truth. They research more and more about the pineal gland, the substance called DMT, out of body experiences, near death experiences, dreams, quantum physics, and so forth.

Sixth, Seeker has found out that the old religious and philosophical concept of 'I AM' is the most inclusive and describes Mahu more than any other concept including the high human notions of parenthood, fatherhood, and motherhood. In this light, many 'isms' appear to make sense completely or partially.

While he was working on the diffusion of his conclusions, Seeker decided to proceed to the next step of the light engineering. As he used to, he sent a prayer to Mahu saying: 'Oh Lord-of-Lights-and-Delights, I sincerely thank you for everything I have found so far and ask that I be able to use them efficiently in a practical way to help this earthly world that needs healing. Please continue to assist me with your Holy Spirit and guide my way towards walkers who have the same concerns no matter what their approaches might be. I'm confident that in due time your spirit of truth, wisdom, and peace will manifest in all of us so that everything be in harmony.'

'Who do you take me for young man?' Mahu replied. 'Do you think I'm fool enough to trust this task to you alone?' And He-She continued: 'Know that many are there with whom you can associate to do the job. Of course I will grant you the rest of the things you asked for, but can you come up victorious out of this new enterprise? That, we will see in a few years.'

After his prayer, Seeker went to study more of the answers that many great seekers of the past and the present has proposed and are proposing for the healing of the world and the creation of a harmonious and happy society. Then he let his heart and his mind poor out their content. He remembered his experiences and anterior studies which the Holy Spirit had helped him store. Then he meditated and used the share of reason he has received to organize the information available and bring forth new ones.

Once he has finished this second step, he found it very good and did not regret leaving the practice of medicine for a while. While he was healing walkers, Seeker had noticed that many were more troubled in their souls and minds than in their body and that this is responsible of most problems including bodily sicknesses.

That is why he decided to produce two books to help walkers heal and/or strengthen their souls or minds and prevent many diseases of the body and wars that kill a great number. The first book explains a lot about Mahu the

Source of all and the second, this one, is to help all walkers and also watchers live harmoniously and happily.

    Frank Ignace Babatoundé ALAPINI: M.D., M.Div.
    New York, April 2012

Introduction

It is fitting that a book on how to create the happiest society through the philosophy of divine humanism starts by paying homage to the four great men whose historical existence is sometime doubted but who have significantly influenced the world through the spiritual sayings and deeds ascribed to them. They are in chronological order Hermes Trismegistus, Moses, Gautama Buddha, and Jesus of Nazareth.

The story of the *Poimandres* tells how Hermes started his mission under the injunction of God: '*Go forth, to become as a guide to those who wander in darkness, that all within who dwells My Mind, may be saved by My mind in you, which shall call forth my mind in them.*'

Hermes in response went to people and told them this: '*O people of the earth rise from your sleep of ignorance! Be sober and thoughtful. Realize that your home is not in the earth but in the Light. Why have you delivered yourselves over to death having the power to partake to immortality? Repent and change your minds. Depart from the dark light and forsake corruption forever.*'

This is good news! Is it not? A God Spell long before the time of Jesus assuredly. Hermes taught that the reason of the mind is what saves from evil delivering it from problems such as ignorance, anger, sorrow, intemperance, lust, injustice, greed, deceit, and envy. He added that reason gives birth to qualities such as knowledge or truth, joy, self-control, generosity, and goodness.

To him, there are spiritual beings that associate themselves to human beings according to their time of birth and often push them to commit errors. But those beings cannot invade reason through which direct connection with God is made for true development and freedom. Now let's take a look at Moses.

Moses belonged to the Ancient people of Israel and the name 'Israel' means 'spiritual victory.' It ought to be said that several scholars suggested that the word was composed based on three majors divinities of the ancient world namely Isis, Ra, and El. Based on the biblical definition of spiritual victory, anybody can be part of that nation whether genetically related to the patriarch Jacob or not. That is why several strangers on many occasions have joined the nation of Ancient Israel in the Bible.

The God of the Old Testament who was a powerful angel told Moses: *'I am aware of the suffering of my people and have come to rescue them. I am sending you to go lead my people out of suffering.'*

What did Moses do or say? His immediate reaction was to find himself unworthy of the task and to reject the mission. But the angel finally succeeded in appeasing the concerns of Moses and gave him some energy. Moses taught not to follow demons who are gods but not God [his protective powerful angel]. Moses did not realize like Hermes that there was an all Pervading God called the Universal Mind above even the God of the Old Testament who appeared to him and others.

How is Gautama Buddha special? His story says that his spiritual quest was triggered by his first encounters with human suffering caused by aging, illness, and death. It is not said that God asked Buddha to do anything but that he took the decision to help solve humankind's problems in accord with his own mind and heart.

INTRODUCTION

Having reached an enlightened state, Buddha discovered Four Nobles Truths the mastery of which lead to a state of mind free from ignorance, greed, hatred, and so on. The synthesis of the Four Noble Truths is that suffering is caused by attachment to desires which must be severed by following the Noble Eightfold Path of right understanding, intention, speech, action, livelihood, effort, mindfulness, and concentration.

By 'desires', Buddha did not mean 'all desires' but unreasonable ones as Hermes clearly taught. At first Gautama Buddha hesitated to teach because there was so much ignorance, greed, and hatred that could prevent people from understanding him. But finally he taught people convinced that at least a few of them will understand. Among his teachings figures the notion that there are some form of spirits called devas who often direct ill intention, words, and actions towards humans.

According to the biblical Gospels, an angel informed Joseph that the mission of Jesus was to deliver people from their sins. How did he try to accomplish this? Written records indicate that he asked people to repent for their sins and turn to God for the Kingdom of God was near. Then, he started teaching how to leave a virtuous life telling inspiring stories famously known as his parables.

Latter, the scripture portrays a Jesus doubting until the end whether he should die on the cross to save humanity or not. When he decided to go through the crucifixion, his last words do not show any satisfaction of a job well done but an immense sadness, disappointment, and incomprehension of why God [the All Pervading] has abandoned him. Jesus taught that truth will set people free and he fought entities called demons.

A careful consideration of Hermes, Moses, Buddha, and Jesus shows that they have several characteristics in common. All started a public ministry centered on spiritual teachings with the will to do something about the general condition of human kind that they found unsatisfying. All emphasized truth, or knowledge, or wisdom, or reason or law and all gave guidance about negative spiritual entities.

Only Buddha did not acknowledge a Supreme God though he admitted the existence of spiritual beings. Also the supreme being of Moses was different from that of Hermes or Jesus and was inferior in comparison. Hermes found qualities and shortcomings to astrology or astrotheology while Moses was radically against. As for Buddha and Jesus, they did not give their opinions about it to the knowledge of Seeker.

The remembrance of these four pioneers is important in introducing the current work because like them, it wants to change the condition of today's world through reason, knowledge, truth, wisdom, spiritual science etc… centered on the Supreme Invisible All Pervading God and the power of His-Her Holy Spirit. Indeed, can it not be said that ignorance, lies, deceit, intemperance, violence, greed, hatred, and so on are rampant in the world today? If the answer is yes then can it not be said that it is truly possible to elaborate a teaching that could change the situation? Answering no would underestimate both human and Divine potentials.

Like Hermes, Seeker wants to stress the power of the mind. Like Moses he wants to emphasize the benefits of making and respecting good laws while working seriously so that all receive the Divine Holy Spirit in abundance. Eradicating useless pain is an aim they share.

Similarly to Buddha and Jesus, Seeker wants humans to believe in their own potentials without forgetting to seriously look for God. The three of them share the intense desire to reasonably fight diseases.

However, Seeker's work has particular aspects. First it has to be adapted to the time from the 21st century characterized by advanced technologies and a great capability to reason within the general human population.

The second particularity of his work is to strive so that it be a common venture in which constructive proposals made by others be properly acknowledged and harmonized with Seeker's. That is why he also insists on non-plagiarism and introduces old ideas and their authors whenever they exist. He is convinced that the attempt to generate the happiest society today considerably benefits from all previous attempts.

INTRODUCTION

The third particularity of Seeker's endeavor is to give spirituality, philosophy, and morality, a more scientific and united shape so that people can be at the same time as wise as Hermes, as enduring as Moses, as insightful as Buddha, and as powerful as Jesus. The real goal is to even surpass together the level of these righteous men bringing solution to what have not been successfully dealt with.

This work would be impossible to one person; but not to a big community especially when many are awakening spiritually and discovering truths which have remained inaccessible for a longtime.

Seeker was happy to notice that a contemporary thinker such as Ardavan Amir-Alsani declared that religion is the main factor determining the identity of nations and international relations in his book *La Guerre des Dieux, Géopolitique de la Spiritualité* [*The war of the Gods, Geopolitics of Spirituality*].

Amir-Aslani went as far as to say that tomorrow's war will be religious or will not be, emphasizing the strong religious nature of the American Republican Party, the growing influence of the Orthodox Church in Russia, the replacement of dictators by Islamic regimes with a background of Sharia as the result of the revolutions of the Arab Spring, and the irruption of the religious into politics everywhere on the planet.

Ardavan Amir-Aslani is a lawyer specialized in international relations who allows Seeker to establish a connection between the ancient world of Hermes, Moses, Buddha, Jesus, and also Mohammed and the present world. He also helped Seeker reinforce his conviction that his own work can connect the two worlds the religious dominance of which shows in fact a search for harmony, justice, and collective happiness in connection with an eventual Creator or creators.

Seeker's wish is to avoid the catastrophic scenario of the multiplication and the aggravation of religious wars but also to reach a true and lasting peace through the application of the good ideas he and others express. Individuals, organizations of the civil society, governments, and the United

Nations could use those ideas to foster their goals of world peace and global wellness.

From his experience with the UN, he knows that the commissions on human rights, spirituality and religions, and health can do a lot for the world. He will never forget that one of his spiritual experiences happened the first day he entered the building of the most international of all organizations and went to its meditation room where after a short moment of concentration he felt a strong spiritual presence. It was frequent before that that the Holy Spirit manifests to him, but that day is among those during which his crown chakra was very stimulated with the descent of spiritual energy within him. His impression was that God had not abandoned the UN and was trying to help those who make decisions that are important to the world.

Seeker also knows that several governments are concerned with religious problems that they want to solve through their ministries of foreign affairs and homeland security. But a social welfare that judiciously integrates the spiritual needs of human populations should also work closely and mainly with the departments of education and culture, planning and development, and health.

In contrary to Ardavan Amir-Aslani, he does not think that the only hope dwells in the separation between the religious fact and the political one. Nothing says that the decision of the French in 1905 to have a national secular law separating the State and the Church and the privatization of religion in America constitute the most reasonable things there are to do even if one must admit that at a point of history religion has been a big problem.

Independently of the Church and the State, if it were to be proven that human nature contains a spiritual part and if proofs of spiritual phenomena and beings truly exist, then the best thing to do will not be to issue decrees and laws stating that a human being who is one and indivisible should separate his religious or spiritual affairs from those that put him in relation to the State.

It would be better to redefine or reformulate religion and spirituality which remain dominant despite everything; on more logical and more scientific grounds. In so doing, the world will come to realize that the law of separateness between the Church and the State does not need to be eternal. New facts and news analysis can bring the human society to reorganize itself making a better consideration of elements that have escaped its attention in the past.

To achieve the global goal of changing society and make it happier, it is fundamental to well understand the theological, philosophical, and psychological aspects of the notion of the divine. That is why God, gods, and defied humans have been studied in a first volume. Now a more anthropological development of the same concept of *change* is necessary centered on practical human life and not solely on theoretical philosophy and theology.

An anthropocentric work with the purpose of creating the best society cannot avoid central issues such as human nature, human origin, the philosophy of humanism, the philosophy of education, spiritual science, sexuality, reproduction, marriage, recreation, politics, economy, and the concepts of cooperation, harmony, equality, beauty, health, and justice. All these themes will be discussed in twelve chapters followed by a conclusion that will summarize what the book is about and invite the reader to another step toward the realization of the ideal of great happiness for all.

Part I

HUMAN NATURE AND ORIGIN

Chapter 1

The human nature according to 23 important thinkers

Any individual who longs for a happy society ought to answer the fundamental question: '*Who is responsible to build that ideal?*' The question is simple and may even be pointless since the answer is obvious. However, the purpose of instruction renders it necessary to be asked and answered.

The obvious answer is that human beings are those who have to build a happy society. Whether they should do it alone, as the human race, or whether other actors or agents should be associated is another question which is best to answer subsequently.

Since humans are considered the central elements in the building of that society, it is important to study their nature. *More the human beings know themselves; better will be their capability to build the kind of society in which everyone fully benefits from life.* This chapter presents the viewpoints of 23 important thinkers. Chapter 2 will display the ideas of three religious movements and chapter 3 will synthesize those of esotericism centered on two individuals and two schools. Lastly, chapter 4 will present Seeker's opinion.

Nineteen ancient thinkers on human nature

Roger Trigg, professor of philosophy, saves those who inquire on the subject of human nature a lot of time by brilliantly summarizing the thoughts of twelve great philosophical minds in his book *Ideas of Human Nature*. Immediately following is a brief summary of the ideas of eleven among them.

In Trigg, one can read that *Plato* [429 B.C.E.-347 B.C.E] assimilated the psyche with the soul and considered that *reason* should care for it and control emotions and desires [especially sexual desire]; not at the expense of the later but in harmony with them. The soul for Plato is immortal, but in this earthly life, it is disfigured through its association with the body. *Knowledge* is the virtue that can prevent evil since people always do what they know is right.

To *Aristotle* [384 B.C.E-322 B.C.E], instructor of Alexander the Great, *reason* is also at the center of human nature as a moral and intellectual faculty. It distinguishes a human from an animal and from a plant and it makes civilization possible. Reason is the sole capable of generating a happy life. Human beings must strive to live in accordance with the best thing in them which is divine.

In the Book I of the *Nichomachean Ethics*, Aristotle declares that human destiny is controlled by the *gods*. He also teaches that wisdom, contemplation, and virtues are essential though politics, beauty, familial and amicable relationships, material things, and pleasures should be taken into consideration as well.

Reason and *knowledge* again appear in the thoughts of *Thomas Aquinas* [1225-1274] as preeminent. Aquinas, in addition, believed in the accountability of human souls to *God* because those souls live their earthly lives freely. According to him, souls are helped by their natural inclination to virtue. *Aquinas also thought that a tendency for one of two contrary elements necessarily reduces any tendency towards the other making training important.* Nevertheless reason remained for him the fundamental nature of human beings.

From a behavioral angle, *Thomas Hobbes* [1588-1679] declared that humans are *selfish* beings who will to take advantage of others for their own gain and give no place to morality. Humans therefore *compete* against each other and seek glory and honor for themselves. Even charity and pity are self-centered for Hobbes.

John Locke's point of view is that *reason* is a transcendental faculty that belongs primarily to *God* who secondarily gives it to humans as their dominant trait. Locke [1632-1704], like Aquinas, believed that mankind is accountable to God who sometimes assists human reason with *revelations through his envoys.*

To *David Hume* [1711-1776] in contrary, reason is the slave of *passions*. It cannot change them and is itself an instinct which drives a person with fixed preferences from one phenomenon to another. Reason cannot modify *preferences* declares Hume.

He illustrates his point saying that when reason determines that all people should be treated with equal respect, in fact humans prefer the welfare of their families and friends to that of strangers. A man naturally loves his children better than his nephews he adds. Therefore, in Hume's mind, reason does not determine morality. The reasons which push Seeker to disagree with Hume will be given in chapter 4.

The next philosopher that Roger Trigg introduces is *Immanuel Kant* [1724-1804]. Kant explains his *moral categorical imperative* saying that humans do not do things because they are inclined to do them but because those things are right. Therefore *reason* is not a faculty limited to humans but a faculty that is *transcendental* even to *God*. To Kant, the reason for an action is more important than its result.

Charles Darwin [1809-1882], like Hume, thought that morality cannot be determined by reason without the intervention of *natural impulses and instincts*. Yet, he joins Aquinas in thinking that virtuous habits with time can become an inheritance though not transmitted genetically but acquired through *teaching*.

Hence, Darwin adds a *moral aspect to his biological* theory of *natural selection*. He also adds to this moral aspect of human nature, other elements, shared with animals and linked to genetic transmission such as self-preservation, sexual love, the love of a mother for her new born, and so on. To Darwin morality is the main difference between humans and animals.

To *Karl Marx* [1818-1883], the *human potential*, the need for *altruist social life*, and *individual freedom for self-realization through creativity* constitute the core of human nature. For him, even those who benefit from the capitalistic system are not truly free and their own human potential is not reached.

To *Friedrich Nietzsche* [1844-1900], the basis of human nature is the *will to power*. Each human being has to follow his/her own moral standards because there is no objective external source of morality. In his mind, religion is certainly not that source. *Corruption* is a consequence of the natural will to power.

This will to power is not limited to the domination over other humans and includes control over personal impulses as well. So, for Nietzsche, human nature does not have to do with 'what one is' but with 'what one wants to be' which is the *superman*. However, super humanity is not accessible to all, but to a very small number.

The center of human nature to *Sigmund Freud* [1856-1939], considered as the father of psychology or the father of psychoanalysis, is the *sexual desire which can be hidden in the unconsciousness in a different form than conscious sexual desires*. For him, human personality consists of three elements: the 'ego' [*reason and common sense*], the 'super ego' [seat of the *judging activity of the conscience*], and the 'id' [*unconscious* seat of *passions*].

The super-ego is the center of morality that seeks to guide the ego which is also under pressure from the id and the external world. To Freud, sexual desire yields the way only to the necessity of life preservation. If the life of a person is not in danger, his/her first priority is sex. So, Freud joins David Hume to think that reason plays a role in human life, but that passions always have the last word as the true rulers of human nature. Hence, man acts more unconsciously than consciously. Freud's ideas will be answered alongside those of David Hume.

Apart from the eleven thinkers from Roger Trigg's book; eight other scholars have expressed views on human nature that have been so influential that this chapter cannot bypass them.

Hence, according to *Arthur Schopenhauer* [1788-1860], reason or wisdom is not the fundamental element of human nature. To him, the dignity of man rests upon his *morality built by virtues which are attributes of the will and not of the intellect*. Schopenhauer however seems not to believe in the possibility of human perfection on the moral ground because even the noblest person will sometimes surprise his fellows by isolated traits of depravity.

Jean-Jacques Rousseau [1712-1778] believed[1] that two fundamental principles govern humans who are naturally good: *personal preservation* and well-being which is first in importance, and *compassion* to fellows. A human being is complete only when in relationship with others. A good human has many needs and does not compare him/herself often to others while a wicked person has also many needs but depends very much on opinion.

---

[1] Peter Loptson, *Theories of Human Nature* (Peterborough, Ont: Broadview Press, 2006), 104-06.

Alfred Adler [1870-1937] was a physician and psychotherapist highly regarded together with Sigmund Freud and Carl Jung. He equated the understanding of human nature with the understanding of the *psyche*. The psyche to him determines an adult's behavior. Its foundations are laid in the earliest days of childhood and do not depend on the hereditary factors.

Confucius's opinion about human nature was mainly that humans have the potential to access the *morality of Heaven* in order to become *sages* through the culture of *virtue*[2]. However, Confucius [551 B.C.E.-479 B.C.E.] also declared that human beings have the capacity to resist the Decree of Heaven. Their *nature* is the same at birth but differences appear with *practice*.

To *Augustine*[3] [354-430], *faith*, *reason*, and *free will* are complementary in the achievement of *truth*. He believed in contrary to Pelagius and like Paul that only the *grace of God* can save man from *original sin*.

René Descartes [1596-1650] defended the argument that a human being consists of a *soul and a body*, two interacting substances which can exist one without the other[4]. The soul or mind is the immaterial entity that thinks, feels, perceives, wills, and cannot be studied by the methods of physicality or physical science. It is immortal and represents what a person is after death.

According to *Benedict de Spinoza* [1632-1677], *mind and body* are *not two different substances*. The mind is the result of the functioning of the brain[5].

---

[2] Leslie F. Stevenson and David L. Haberman, *Ten Theories of Human Nature* (New York: Oxford University Press, 2004), 13.

[3] Ibid., 107-08.
[4] Ibid., 114.
[5] Stevenson and Haberman, *Ten Theories of Human Nature*, 115.

The ideas of *Jean Paul Sartre*[6] [1905-1980] are not far from those of Nietzsche because he affirmed that the destiny of a human being is solely in his/her own hands. But in contrary to Nietzsche who thought the fundamental nature of humans to be the will to power, Sartre believed they have no essence but only an existence and that there is no general truth about what they want to be. Sartre made freedom the basic element of human condition.

Human nature according to four contemporary thinkers

In his book *'Is There a Human Nature?'* Bhikhu Parekh [1935-...], a professor of political theory, offers a useful description of the concept of human nature. To him, human nature is a set of permanent properties that all human beings, and only they with perhaps some exceptions, share in common by virtue of being human.

These properties which are not socially or culturally derived but inherited from birth are the physical and psychological capacities, desires, dispositions, and tendencies to act in specific ways, and so on. Animals possess some of those properties. Society can change or regulate them, but it cannot eradicate them entirely.

Bhikhu Parekh also thinks that human nature is only a small part of what makes humans who they are. To him, it is now difficult to identify that nature because of the deformation it underwent under the influence of culture. Additionally, in his mind, the nature of a human being is not static but evolves with the appearance of new natures that he/she gives him/herself.

Bhikhu Parekh's insights did not lead him like to conclude like Seeker that culture, education, evolution, and change are elements of human nature and that culture and nature should not be opposed. In other words, it is

---

[6]Ibid., 182.

natural to humanity to change its nature through the cultures that itself creates.

If Professor Bhikhu Parekh considers animals at some point of his description, the philosopher *Peter M. S. Hacker* [1939-...], in *Human Nature: The Categorial Framework*, prefers to start his explanation with them. Animals are for him different from *inanimate* objects because they are *animate* substances and *living* things that ingest matter from their environment. He distinguishes animals from plants in the sense that the former have the senses of sight, hearing, smell, taste, and feeling; and are generally self-moving.

Hacker, like many other philosophers, is of the opinion that thoughts, emotions, will, and self-consciousness are rudimentary in animals but developed in humans who act because of some reasons and not by mere instinct. This is a reason why a human being is moral, legal, and socio-historical.

In contrary to humans, animals do not know good and evil and are not susceptible to feeling guilt, shame, and remorse. That is why only human beings are said to have a soul. Animals, additionally, do not speak. Still according to Peter Hacker, human beings have a mind which may be sharp, lively, or dull; and a body which may be healthy or ill.

In *Everyday Creativity and New Views of Human Nature* edited by Ruth Richards, the contemporary psychologist *Mark A. Runco* expresses his view point that creativity is an important part of human nature. In the same volume, *Riane Eisler*, a social scientist and an attorney, declares that the most urgent creative challenge is to build a sustainable future which does not have to be perfect or be a utopia.

Chapter 2

The human nature according to Hinduism, the Jehovah Witnesses, and the Unification Movement

THE nature of human beings is not a concept often systematically described in religious systems and spiritual schools. Nevertheless, by paying attention to their scriptures, one could come up with some general ideas. Three movements appear to reflect the variety of opinions expressed on human nature in the religious landscape. They are: *Hinduism* which stresses the connectedness of all life; the *Jehovah Witnesses* and the *Unificationists* who offer the opportunity to consult the Bible and other scriptures. These three organizations also give the opportunity to engage in religious and spiritual philosophy on the question.

Human nature in Hinduism

The Hindu text of the *Brihad Aranyaka Upanishad* gives a rare description of human nature declaring that because of the interconnectedness of all life, human are not different from the other beings[7]. The self or *atman* that is present in a being is the same that is present in the other beings.

In Hinduism, there is another self which is the ego, the body or *ahamkara*; however, the true self is the *atman*, the subject, object, and witness of consciousness; the all-pervasive consciousness. Some Hindu philosophers believe that the self that reincarnates or go to the world *of Brahma or Atman* after *moksha* [liberation] is different from the *atman*.

The point of view of the Jehovah Witnesses

Jehovah Witnesses believe that in ideal conditions, the process of regeneration of the human body would never stop and humans would eternally live[8]. They provide several biblical passages to support the idea of human beings living on earth eternally: Psalms 115: 16/ 139:14/ 37: 29/ Isaiah 48: 18/ 25: 8/ John 3:14-16/ 3: 36/ and Revelation 21: 3-4. To them, because God has planted eternity in the human heart [Ecclesiastes 3: 11], humans want to spend an everlasting life on earth for which they are made and which is made for them [Genesis 2: 8, 9, and 15].

To Jehovah witness, humans and animals are aware of nothing after they are dead[9] [Ecclesiastes 9: 5 and 10/ 3: 19-20/ and Psalms 146: 3-4]. Adam did not exist before his creation from the soil and at his death he returned to

---

[7]Stevenson and Haberman, *Ten Theories of Human Nature*, 31-4.
[8] Watch Tower Bible and Tract Society of Pennsylvania, *Vous Pouvez Vivre Eternellement sur une Terre qui Deviendra un Paradis* (Brooklyn, New York, U.S.A., 1989), 7-10.
[9]Ibid., 76-80.

that state of non-existence [Genesis 3: 19]. Since man and the animal alike are souls [Genesis 1: 20 and Numbers 31: 28]; logically, the soul of man dies with him.

The Bible contains no passage which stipulates that the human soul is imperishable. According to Ecclesiastes 12: 7, at the death of a person, the spirit which is the vital force leaves little by little the cells of the body which decays.

The human vital force, to the Jehovah Witnesses, does not literally leave the earth and cross space to go to God. The spirit returns to God means that from the moment of the death, whether the person will live again or not depends solely on God. If Lazarus who was a good man has been to heaven at his death, he would have said so once resurrected by Jesus.

The Scheol or the Hades or hell is the place where the dead go[10] [Acts 2: 31, Psalms 16:10, Genesis 37: 35, Job 14: 13]. It is not a place of torment since God could not have let Jesus go there and neither Jacob nor Job would have chosen to be there if such was the case. The Scheol is a place of inaction [Ecclesiastes 9: 10].

Hence, Scheol or Hades or hell is the common tomb of humanity and it is possible to get out of it [Jonah 2:2, Matthew 12: 40, Acts 2: 31-32, and Revelation 20: 13]. When Jesus told some religious leaders of his time that they will not escape the judgment of the Gehenna, he meant that they were unworthy of resurrection. The Lake of Fire [Revelation 20: 14] has the same meaning; it is the second death for which there is no resurrection.

If earth is the place for eternal life for the great majority of humans in the ideology of the Jehovah Witnesses, there is however a few good humans, 144 000 [Revelation 14: 1-3] who are destined to heaven in order to participate in the activities of Jesus Christ [Daniel 7:27, Luke 22:28-29, 2 Timothy

---

[10]Ibid., 82-7.

2:12, Revelation 5:9, /20: 6]¹¹. Before Jesus Christ no human has been in Heaven except himself who had come from Heaven [John 3: 13].

If Adam and Eve had remained faithful to God, resurrection would not have been necessary. Proofs that people hoped for resurrection and some have indeed resurrected figure in Hebrews 11: 17-19, Luke 20: 37-38/ 7: 11-17/ 8: 40-56, John 11: 17-26, 1 Kings 17, 2 Kings 4: 32-37/ 13: 20-21, Matthews 27: 62-66/ 28: 1-7, Acts 2; 32/ 9: 36-42[12].

Some unjust people such as the thief who was crucified on the right of Jesus will resurrect too [Acts 24: 15, Luke 23: 39-43]. However, when Jesus said to the thief that he will be in the paradise with him that day, he did not mean that the thief would actually go to the paradise, but that he [Jesus] will fulfill his spiritual needs from heaven from the day he is resurrected on earth.

Those who have willingly sinned having known the divine will would not resurrect [Matthew 12: 32, Hebrews 6: 4-6/ 10: 26-27]. Others will not die and will directly enter the new society under the sovereignty of God [John 11: 26, 2 Timothy 3: 1]. *It is not the body which resurrects for heavenly life* [1 Corinthians 15: 35-44]. Even in the cases of the resurrection of the body, new bodies are provided by God. The persons resurrect; not their ancient bodies, the elements of which could have been recycled by other living beings.

---

[11]Watch Tower, *Vous Pouvez Vivre Eternellement sur une Terre qui Deviendra un Paradis*, 120-24.
[12]Ibid., 166-74.

The Unification Movement on human nature

In the *Divine Principle*[13], one reads that the body of a human is created by God from physical elements while the spirit is created from the elements of the spiritual world. Hence, a human, as a microcosm, contains the essences of all things in the cosmos and can dominate both the physical and the spiritual world.

It is through humans that God governs [indirectly] the universe because the universe itself does not have an internal sensitivity toward God. They can communicate between the two worlds similarly to the way invisible waves in radios and televisions are transformed into perceptible images and sound.

The physical person is dual in nature and comprises the physical body and the physical mind, the role of which is to guide the body to survive and reproduce. Instinct is an aspect of an animal's physical mind. Likewise the spirit self is also twofold having a body and a mind. The eternal, substantial, and incorporeal spirit self which can only be apprehended through the spiritual senses and which can communicate directly with God is the subject partner of the physical self.

The spirit self develops thanks to two types of nourishment: the yang type or life elements [truth, love] which come from God and the yin type or vitality elements which originate from the physical body's good deeds. Because of this, the spirit can grow only when a person is alive on earth and attains perfection passing from the phase of form spirit to that of life spirit and then to the stage of divine spirit. The multiplication of human spirits takes place when physical selves multiply. Sins make a spirit evil and ugly and/or crippled.

---

[13]Sun Myung Moon, *Exposition of the Divine Principle* (New York: The Holy Spirit Association for the Unification of World Christianity, 1996), 46-51.

A divine spirit has the potential to precisely feel and perceive the spirit world the realities of which resonate through the body and manifest as physiological phenomena recognizable by the physical senses. After death, the divine spirit lives eternally in heaven. That is why the Kingdom of Heaven in heaven is established only after its equivalent on earth has been. Only those who have reached perfection on earth being totally immersed in the love of God can fully delight in the love of God as spirits after death.

Sinful spirits cannot fully breathe the love of God and find it extremely difficult to stand in his presence; so they voluntarily prefer to dwell in hell far from God.

The spirit mind and the physical mind are the internal nature and the external form of the mind of a human being which has a consciousness that continuously guides the individual toward what he/she thinks is good. Because of the Fall, human beings became ignorant of God and consequently of the absolute standard of goodness. Therefore what is considered good varies from a person to another and this fact is the origin of disagreements and conflicts even among those who recommend living a life based on the consciousness.

The part of the mind or consciousness that seeks goodness is the original mind opposed to the evil mind which is the part of the mind or consciousness that is ruled by Satan and continuously drive people toward evil.

The existence of evil and Satan as well as the importance of the physical self in the development of the spirit are the reasons why Jesus had to come on earth in the flesh to save sinful humanity. That is also why according to the 5th chapter of the *Divine Principle*, resurrection is centered on earth. This chapter also disagrees with the theory of reincarnation.

The second chapter of the same unificationist volume affirms that Satan gained control over Eve and pushed her to eat of the fruit of the Tree of the Knowledge of Good and Evil. Eating that fruit is to commit fornication. So, Satan as the archangel Lucifer and Eve had had a sexual relationship. When Eve in turn made Adam eat of the same fruit, when she had sex with Adam out of guilt, the evil elements received from Satan entered Adam too and became transferable to their descendants who are thus the children of Satan as Jesus mentioned in John 8: 44.

Satan's motivation dwelled in his jealousy toward Adam who was better loved by God and in the fact that Eve who was receiving the love of God too appeared beautiful in his eyes. Eve disobeyed God because the power of the unprincipled or false love between her and Satan was stronger than the power of the principle of growth.

God made the power of love the strongest power and the base of human happiness. God also governs humans through love; that is why people seek the love of God more than the principle or truth. That is also why despite the fact that Jesus raised his disciples with the truth, it was his love which saved them.

Chapter 3

Esotericism on human nature

ESOTERIC teachings are by nature not available to the general public. However, people like Manly P. Hall and Helena Blavatsky respectively a Freemason and a Theosophist, and organizations such as the Temple of the People and Rosicrucians of the AMORC have made available several documents from which a researcher could get ideas about their understandings of human nature.

Readers should however be aware that rosicrucian meanings for terms such as 'spirit', 'mind', 'nous', and so on could be different from dictionary definitions and therefore from the standard adopted by Seeker.

Manly Hall and Helena Blavatsky

To *Manly Hall* [1901-1990], the basic theory of human nature in esotericism is that a human is a microcosm representing the macrocosmic universe with equivalents of its laws, elements, and powers within him/herself[14]. Unificationists adopted this esoteric teaching as one of the fundamental aspects of their theology with however some limitations as it will be shown in chapter 4.

Hall states in the *Secret Teachings of all Ages* that all things exist psychically in humans who are naturally able to know them by exciting the powers and the images in themselves to the point of illumination. Man is fundamentally an immortal divine principle which lives several times in the prisons that its successive bodies constitute.

All the parts of a body have corresponding centers in the brain and these brain centers have equivalents in the heart. To Hall, the heart is the most spiritual and the most mysterious organ, the brain is the second center and the most important physical dignity, and the generative system is the third center and least physical dignity.

The heart symbolizes the source of life, the brain represents the rational link which unites life and form, and the generative system which is the most important physical organ symbolizes the source of the power by which physical organism are brought into existence.

Ancients, says Hall, were of the opinion that it is *righteousness associated with rationality which make a person spiritual rather than spirituality being the cause of righteousness and rationality*. They considered that the esoteric teachings related to the human nature should not be imparted to the unregenerate because once he/she totally understands how a human being functions; he/she can create phenomena without the ability to control them. Hence those ancient philosophers imposed long periods of probation to students in order to select only those worthy to become as the gods.

To Hall, *no faculty in the human equals the rational intellect and* he who did not comprehend the dignity of the reasoning power could not properly be

---

[14]Manly P. Manly, *The Secret Teachings of All Ages* (New York: Jeremy P. Tarcher/Penguin, 2003), 223-26 and 229-31.

said to live. Where reason reigns supreme, inconsistency cannot exist and wisdom lifts man to the condition of godhood.

Hall has not been silent on the issue of astrotheology for he clearly stated while explaining the mystery of the Apocalypse or Revelation that the twelve gates of the city of Jerusalem in the 21st chapter are the symbols of the twelve signs of the zodiac through which the celestial impulses descend into the inferior world.

Theosophy is a teaching that encompasses the esotericism of the West and that of the East particularly of India. Consequently, it is not uncommon to identify similarities between Theosophy and religions originating from India such as *Hinduism, Buddhism,* and *Jainism*. The use of words of Indian origin, the reference to Indian sacred texts, and the history of Theosophy itself illustrate this remark.

Helena Blavatsky [1831-1891], a founding member of the Theosophical Society, explained that in esotericism, the cause of good and evil in humans is in their nature: in their ignorance and passions[15]. To her, *a person of great intellect and too much knowledge may enslave the others or save them while somebody without self-consciousness and intellect is a brute in human form.*

---

[15]Helena Petrovna Blavatsky, *The Secret Doctrine: the Synthesis of Science, Religion, and Philosophy (Second Edition,* 1888) 162-63.

The Temple of the People on human nature

The Temple of the People is a theosophical movement which like all such movements adopted several of the teachings of Indian religions.

This school of spirituality distinguishes 7 principles of the universe and man which are: 1- Atma [Pure spirit and creator], 2- Buddhi [spiritual soul and vehicle of Atma], 3- Manas [Universal Mind or Higher Mind or The Thinker or Consciousness of identity], 4- kama or soul or higher astral which comprises kamamanas [manifestation of desires in the mentality or lower mind] and kamarupa [manifestation of desires in form], 5- prana [vital sparks or life principle present in the elements of fire, air, water, and earth which are the constructors and devourers of form], 6- lower astral body or etheric double [light body attached to gross or physical matter atom by atom and molecule by molecule], and 7- the physical body.

To the Temple of the People and certainly for many other esotericists, two realities exist in every human being: the Higher Self or Spiritual Sun or God comprising the three principles of Atma, Buddhi, and Manas and the lower self-made of the four remaining principles. Hence, human nature is not separated from the nature of God.

In the *20th lesson* of its first volume of teachings, the Temple of the People affirms that there are several forms of matter including the physical one. Those matters are electricity in various forms. There are a total of forty nine electrical forms divided into seven octaves according to these teachings. The highest aspect of mind [reason] is a higher order of energy comparing to the energy of the physical plane and is different from the highest forms of energy in plants and minerals.

The following lines will endeavor to offer more details about the theosophical views on human nature successively tackling the 6th, the 5th, and the 4th principles.

To the Temple of the People, the ether, the 6th principle, is the body or the envelope of the life principle or prana or 5th principle. The astral body or etheric double is also attached to the physical body, the 7th principle but so slightly that it can be projected *at some distance of it* by a highly developed will even in sleeping state or trance or through the use of stimulants and narcotics [*14th lesson*].

This lesson adds however that any unnatural method of access to the astral plane leaves the soul vulnerable to several threats on that plane. The pole of gravitation of the astral body can be reversed at will and a person can therefore freely move in the astral or etheric medium [*Lesson 97*]. The lower astral corresponds to the human soul of man [*Vol 2, The Manasic Plane or Sphere of Thought*]. Ether is the basic substance of the forms that are visible to the psychic senses in vision, trance, or sleep [*Lesson 226*].

Chakras and nadis are energetic centers pertaining to the astral body. There are also seven master chakras or tatwas or tatwic centers located in seven cavities of the brain which direct the functioning of the organs of the body while being in contact with the tatwic centers of the universe itself [*Lesson 212*].

The etheric double is also described as having the ability to take other people's appearances and deceive psychics. It is the medium of communication between the soul and the body and it is similar to the etheric waves set in motion between wireless telegraph stations. This esoteric comparison has also been adopted by Unificationists. Theosophists consider light, heat, and sound [waves-entities] as some of the subdivisions of ether [*Lesson 183*].

The Temple of the People is of the opinion that the etheric double sticks around the tomb of a deceased person until the physical body has disintegrated and returned to the elements. To it, the etheric body has a life of its own which is shortened in case of cremation and prolonged when the body of the dead is mummified.

Coming to the 5th principle or prana or great creative force, the inquirer also learns in *Lesson 20* that desire, will, and the highest aspect of mind [reason] are its constituents. Desire is made up of emotions; the highest of which is love. Desire is the ruling force of the universe and the energy of the power of Mesmerism.

Will is the motive power, the propelling energy that dwells in matter [not only physical matter] and is the basic principle of sound. Will is the energy of the power of sound.

The highest aspect of mind is the generating force, the energy of the power of light which molds desire and will. It is inferable that this description corresponds to intelligence or reason. Faith, will, and mentality are all forms of substance, says *Lesson 97*.

Lesson 112 gives further explanation about the 5th principle or prana or life force by introducing the vital or life *spark* as its distinct division which contains in essence the fundamental substance of every form of life that the evolutionary laws can bring into material manifestation. Hence, it seems that the spark in Theosophy is a unit of desire, will, and reason.

The life sparks are present in the physical cells and also contain the masculine and feminine forces as well as the power of becoming or the power of growth. The fiery sparks continue to exist from life to life and build up the astral body. *The blood stream is the conveyer of the life principle* [*Lesson 35*].

The sparks rest at the very center of atoms [*Lesson 183*] as little electric bodies the polarity of which is changeable by the will and the mind. The sparks, also called ferments, are according to the Temple of the People, the real missing links in the chain of evolution of modern science. The life principle is said to send impulses first to the master chakras or tatwas of the brain [*Volume 2, Lesson 29*].

Those impulses are forms of energy known as motion, sound, heat, light, electricity, cohesion, and electro-magnetic force or nerve force. Prana is the very substance of God [*Lesson, 238 and Vol 3, Silence*].

The 4th principle is the planc of the soul or higher astral where there are also angels and archangels who surround the throne of God in the heart of every human being. To explore the higher astral, the astral sight which is potentially present in everybody must be used. It is only to the vision of the third eye that the astral light is visible [*Lesson 104*]. This is the psychic sight or clairvoyance.

There is an intuitionally perceptive energy which operates in the atrophied pineal gland of man. A golden light surrounds the pineal gland and the pituitary body sometimes when an advanced disciple is in deep concentration [*Vol 2, Lesson 13*]. However, *the nature of that golden light, the cause of its appearance in those moments, and its effects on the rest of the brain have not been made public affirms the author of this lesson*. The golden light rapidly vibrates in rotary motion and is in the form of globes [*Vol 2, The Spiritual Creative Will*]. *These globes of golden light are the elements used to change various parts of the body according to the will of the individual.*

Soul, mind, and psyche are equivalent notions [*Vol 3, Psychic Forces*]. The soul, like the body, needs to be nourished regularly and with food in sufficient quantity. Every human being is the builder of his/her soul and immortality [*Vol 2, True Knowledge*].

The substance of the Universal Soul as well as that of the individual soul is inter-etheric or inter-atomic. It is a substance ruled by Higher Manas [3rd principle of Wisdom] and Buddhi [2nd principle or Spiritual Love]. It is easier for the matter on higher planes to obey the will and thoughts better than that on the physical plane because it is not so crystallized and is elastic [*Vol 3, Psychic Forces*]. As the vibratory rate of matter decreases, from the substance of the soul to ether and to physical matter, the power of Wisdom and Spiritual Love decreases as well.

The pillar of fire that guided ancient Israelites, the fire of the bush of Moses, the tongues of flames at the Pentecost in the New Testament, and so forth, are manifestations of the energy of the 4th plane in the physical plane [*Lesson 179*]. This spiritual fire does not consume gross matter and appears to the inner eye of the psychic as an intense white light.

Akasha, the spiritual will or absolute light is the firstdifferentiation of spiritual energy [*Vol 2, Power of Akasha*] and the substance of the soul plane or higher astral [the Devachanic plane, Heaven, and the Nirvanic plane]. Its vibration is so fast that the human senses cannot conceive or measure it. The lessening of the degree of vibration of Akasha is at the origin of the formation of the etheric states of substance [*Lesson 234*]. When the degree of vibration continues to diminish, the astral and the physical states of substance are born from the ether. The diminution of the vibratory rate of electric matter or energy corresponds to its condensation.

Akasha is the stored up power in the atom and the electron. It is the basic principle of electricity the manifestation of which is ether. Ether is the basic principle of air [*Lesson 97*].

Buddhi, the 2nd principle or Spiritual Love is the very light of the mind. *When the inherent light of the mind is very strong it does not allow evil images to modify it into their likeness.* Thoughts or lower manas are substance [*Vol 2, The Manasic plane or sphere of thought*] but do not create matter and form. Thoughts are recorded in the aura which serves as memory and is part of the Book of Life by which all will be judged according to their actions.

The atoms of the *aura* are in a state of vibration unimaginable to mortal humans [this is probably Akasha]. This substance is the essence of the mind. The aura should not be mistaken for the light of the lower astral. *The images of the lower astral are distortions of the images of the mind.*

The mind sphere corresponds to the divine soul or Ego while the human soul of man corresponds to the lower astral. A human being also has an animal soul made up of the opposite qualities stored in the human soul and must strive to raise the animal soul into the environment of the human soul [*Lesson 159*]. Transmutation is accomplished by the action of spiritual fire or Akasha or light. This resurrection of the soul is accomplished by the spiritual fire by means of pain and joy.

Heaven or Devachan is a real place for life where particular senses of sight, hearing, touch, and understanding operate. The kindest acts, the highest and purest Ideals and Desires of a person form the basis of his realizations in Heaven [*Vol 2, Reality*]. Sympathy, compassion, sacrifice and other qualities are also important [*Vol 2, Spiritual Treasures*]. There are as many heavens as there are individual souls.

When a normal human being passes away and his/her soul is totally released from the body; it ascends to heaven [*Vol 2, The plane of Devachan*]. An initiate can reach a point of development where the physical body is no longer needed. Such a person no longer needs to rest in Heaven [see the description of reincarnation in the next lines]. Through the powers of the will and concentration, such an individual, for a short time, can even create an illusory body visible on the physical plane when the need manifests.

That is what the resurrected Jesus did says this lesson. However the author the lesson *The Mystery of Resurrection* thinks that it was another phenomenon of recognition which took place in the case of Jesus. According to this author, the disciples of Jesus had had a vision or a trance and were able to identify Jesus.

To Him, Jesus did not adjust himself to be visible on the physical plane; rather, the disciples where raised in their capacities and could experience a higher plane of existence where Jesus existed "naturally" at that time. Samael Aun Weor expressed a third opinion similar to the Catholic view: that Jesus resurrected with his physical body which can live in the spiritual world thanks to a special knowledge he has [putting the body in the state of jinas]. To Theosophy, great people renounce earthly compensations to help others and at the same time win the power to enter the Nirvanic state where they would no longer need to incarnate in flesh.

Nirvana is the state of cosmic consciousness, the highest state reachable by the incarnating Ego, and it is temporarily accessible to the great hierophant and Sun Gods or Regents of the planets [*Vol 2, Soul Consciousness*].

The Temple of the People also declares as true the notion of reincarnation in a lesson devoted to it. What reincarnates, it says, is the reincarnating Ego [divine soul or higher mind], the Real Self, a consciousness different from *that* of the physical body [*which is the human soul or mental vehicle*]. This consciousness is the moving power behind the body and the mind which are not the Self. It is the first individualization of the principles of Atma, Buddhi, and Manas.

It is because the organ of the brain which serves as vehicle to memory is only partially developed in the average person that he/she is not conscious of the events of past incarnations. The seat of memory is in the soul and the soul is the vehicle of the Ego [*Vol 2, Reality*].

Generally, the lower mind is only conscious of the events of a single life; however, sometimes, the latent memories are revived when the individual lives similar circumstances. At death, the divine soul passes a period of natural rest in heaven after which it reincarnates according to karmic law or depending on the will of the soul when it is an advanced one.

To Theosophy, belief in reincarnation should not be accompanied by the fear of losing one's identity, because that identity is not well known yet. Besides, clothes as well as the molecules of the body itself are periodically renewed without a loss of identity.

The fear of separation from loved ones is not justified according to this lesson because people can feel those persons in the relationships of their new incarnation. However, *transmigration* [the incarnation of evil humans in animal bodies and the incarnation of animal souls in human bodies] is unfounded because in the Secret Doctrine, it is taught that the soul of man, the real individual, cannot reincarnate in an animal body since it is a spiritual being.

What happens to those who persist in evil from one incarnation to another is that the divine soul becomes 'lost' separating from the matter of its lower envelopes or bodies [not the physical one]. A future reincarnation is thus considerably delayed because once the higher bodies have disintegrated and returned to the elements, it takes a long time for the divine soul to build new ones and incarnate again.

The application of the karmic law is under the surveillance of the Keepers of the Cosmic Tablets or the Lords of Wisdom. When a race indulges in great spiritual evil like the Atlantean Race did, it is destroyed and removed from the surface of the earth as a race. Absolute Justice or the exactness of the findings of Karmic Law is beyond people's power of imagination, but its complete understanding will show the Beauty and the Perfection of Life.

The Temple of the People also establishes a correspondence between different planes of existence and various states of consciousness [*Vol 2, Addendum*]. Hence, the following pairs of *plane/state of consciousness* are established: physical/ waking, lower astral/waking dreaming, higher astral/dreaming, lower mental/sleeping, higher mental/psychic, buddhic plane of pure intuition/super psychic, and auric or synthetic or spiritual/pure spiritual.

Still according to this spiritual school, *jealousy which is the negative aspect of the force of zeal* and which exists more or less in humans as long as they live in matter, *is the basic principle of evil* [*Lesson 120*].

The brains of the majority of human beings are not able to withstand the fast vibrations of ether without a catastrophe [*Vol 2, Soul consciousness*].

The Temple of the People believes that the Supreme Creator of the universe has implanted in the human heart a spiritual seed, a fundamental desire for righteousness similar to "His" own [*Vol 2, Fundamental desire*]. *Freedom of the soul, eternal wisdom, divine power, and unutterable love appear when the words of God are released from the bonds and cloths made for them by some individuals* [*Vol 2, Freedom for the soul*].

Through physical and spiritual senses, a person experiences the physical and the spiritual worlds and these experiences lead him/her to *true knowledge or the light of wisdom which is the key in discriminating between good and evil* [*Vol 2, True Knowledge*]. A human is an image of God as a drop of water is that of the sea containing all its elements, forces, and potencies.

A person who knows him/herself shall truly know God [*Vol 2, The Geometry of the Soul*]. A human can climb to God only as he/she becomes God [*Vol 2, Faith and Devotion*]. The prevailing trait of human nature is the desire for power which can be for good purposes [*Vol 3, Psychic Forces*]. This affirmation seems Nietzschean.

Dreams, to Theosophists, constitute one possible aspect of reality which in certain cases actually manifest on the physical plane [*Vol 2, Dreams*]. A correspondence is to be found in the various reflections of an object given by a concave mirror. The reflection perceived depends on the angle of observation. Some humans reach a point where they know the point of observation that makes them able to dream true dreams; a point where they are no longer subject to illusion.

Consequently, prophets and psychics can make mistakes [*Vol 2, Prophecy*] and this means that there are inaccurate and accurate prophets and psychics. God is the most accurate prophet who makes predictions only when a great benefit is at stake.

An analysis of this theosophical school reveals that it distinguishes in reality a total of two planes of existence: the physical plane and the astral or etheric plane. However, the astral or ether comprises two sub-planes: the higher astral or higher etheric which corresponds to the soul's sub-plane and the lower astral or lower etheric which corresponds to the sub-plane of the etheric or astral body. The higher astral comprises Devachan [heaven] and Nirvana [where one becomes completely one with the Universal Soul or God]. The lower etheric or astral is the realm of the *forms of energy known as motion, sound, heat, light, electricity, cohesion, and the electro-magnetic force.*

Rosicrucianism on human nature

The Rosicrucians of the AMORC broadly teach about human nature in their *Rosicrucian Manual*[16]. The next paragraphs present some of their ideas.

---

[16]Lewis Ralph M and H. Spencer Lewis, *Rosicrucian Manual* (San Jose, Calif: Supreme Grand Lodge of AMORC, 1987), 86-87, 90,94,96, 110, 145-47, 150, 154, 156-160, 163-65, 172, 175, 186-87, 190-91, and 199-203.

First, Rosicrucians put an emphasis on the blood and state that it emerges from the two lungs vitalized or being magnetically positive. This blood is said to become negative after using its vitality.

They explain that special breathing techniques help gain an extra amount of positive energy for psychic experiments and for special healing works. For those purposes then, it is the vitalized or positive blood that flows in the arteries and capillaries from the heart which is used; not the devitalized blood which returns to that heart.

Both physical and psychic energy are contained in the arterial blood. Rosicrucians declare in their manual that they know the methods to increase arterial blood's vitality or to prevent it from decreasing so that the necessary psychic energy reaches diseased parts of a body and perform its healing work.

Second, the AMORC highlights the nervous system and the work of the autonomic nervous system and its connection with the psychic body of a human being. In its healing techniques, it focuses on the autonomic nervous system instead of giving priority to the injuries and pressures inflicted to the spinal nervous system as done in most modern treatments.

The spinal nervous system conveys gross energy that takes care of the physical actions and functions of the body while the autonomous system carries energy of a higher rate which is almost cosmic energy. Each spinal nerve has a nervous note which corresponds to a musical note. *Musical sound helps awaken he psychic energy of the autonomous system and causes it to fully perform its function.* Colors too offer that kind of support to the autonomous system.

According to the Rosicrucians of the AMORC, the mind via thought waves can reach the sympathetic connections of the autonomous system so that healing could be performed. Teachings on healing methods centered on the blood, the autonomic nervous system, and the psychic body are given at the sixth degree.

Rosicrucianism also gives information about the composition of matter. To it, Albert Einstein's equation $E = mc^2$ expresses a knowledge that is ancient.

Like Theosophists, Rosicrucians declare reincarnation to be true. They consider their view on reincarnation to be unique, non-sectarian, just, understandable, and revealing. This view states that the human soul possesses a memory and a consciousness which constitute the personality of the individual ego or individual character.

The personality passes through successive periods of incarnations, rests on the cosmic plane, and accumulates knowledge and wisdom. How many times a person incarnates is not known. The mystical doctrine that supports the theory of reincarnation is the process of perfection of the soul personality. Perfection is reached when the soul personality is equivalent to the soul force and the individual is one with the consciousness of the Cosmic.

While the *Rosicrucian Manuel* accepts and defends the theory of reincarnation, it rejects like the Temple of the People the theory of *transmigration* which stipulates that the souls of lower beings evolve and become souls of a higher class of beings. To Rosicrucians too, the regression and reincarnation in animal bodies never happens because humans are spiritual beings.

They also describe the phenomenon of cosmic initiation or illumination in which an invisible master often transfers knowledge to a disciple who is ready to receive it in sequences preceded by preparatory events. These teachings are given especially during the night or when the disciple is distant from worldly affairs.

As his/her consciousness broadens, the disciple awakens spiritually and his/her physical body even rejuvenates, heals, and become vigorous. He/she is then admitted into the invisible Great White Brotherhood and attends a physical lodge to help others without receiving any earthly teaching from masters, books, lectures, papers, or diagrams.

However, the Rosicrucian Order also declares it can help disciples achieved their goal by offering teachings that train the brain and augment the knowledge of the mind concerning the fundamental laws and principles which lead to the understanding of the higher laws. Students additionally pass tests that develop the psychic centers and the mastership and control of natural forces. Some of the psychic progresses are not apparent to the objective mind as the functioning of several physical organs is not noticed by that mind.

Some people, continues the *Rosicrucian Manual*, experience psychic phenomena without receiving any help from Rosicrucians because the abilities they gained in a previous incarnation manifest but without control or direction. *Nature* stops the psychic abilities for a while so that the students can learn the laws and principles necessary to control them.

However, a whole life time is not enough to learn all that is necessary. The manual also suggests a code of life [based on old and modern manuscripts] that a human being especially in the Western civilization should use.

In Rosicrucianism, only two planes of existence are acknowledged. One is the worldly or material plane. The second is the astral plane also called divine plane, or ethereal plane, or psychic plane, or cosmic plane, and so forth, where the human soul lives free from the limitations of the body and where his/her subconscious mind operates, sometimes independently from his/her objective mind.

The psychic plane is the plane where those who no longer have a physical body live and can be contacted. It is the plane where thoughts, hopes, plans, and requests are projected along with personalities and where inspiration, illumination, guidance, and direction come from. Humans on earth can access this plane at any time if their purposes are pure and noble.

The psychic body is defined in the *Rosicrucian Manual* as '*a kind of conscious field that corresponds to the physical body*'. Both bodies cooperate through the silver cord which links them.

Similarly to Hindus, Rosicrucians express the view that there is no such a thing as an individual soul. To them, there is only one Universal Soul which is the Soul of God or the living and vital consciousness of God. This Soul of God is present within each living being. The Soul in a human is God in him/her and it makes all humans parts of God as brothers and sisters under the fatherhood of God. The AMORC also admits the existence of the Spirit which like the Soul is a universal divine and all-pervading essence.

A first difference between the Spirit and the Soul is that it is not limited to living beings but exists in all the entities of nature including unconscious matter. A second difference is that the vibratory rate of the Spirit is lower. Third, because of its high rate of vibrations, the Soul manifest only psychically while the Spirit manifests first in the form of the electrons which compose an atom.

The mind of a human is immortal because it is a part of the Soul and personality which functions through the brain *or without the brain as proven by tests on animals*. The mind like the Soul subsists after a person passes away. It has two basic functioning parts: the objective mind and the subconscious.

The subconscious or the ego is the part of the mind that predominantly governs [as a consciousness] the activities of the psychic body such as its projection and other psychic works. It is directly connected with the Universal Mind. Memory is located in the subconscious mind and transcends incarnations.

The objective mind is the mind that acts through the physical body in a self-centered manner keeping the body in good conditions. It governs the five physical senses, voluntary actions, recollection, inductive reasoning, and complete reasoning. It works under the leadership of the subconscious.

Humans experience a borderline state when the objective mind and the subjective mind [imagination and memory] merge into the subconscious or ego. This state is experienced while going to sleep or awakening. It can be beneficially induced through concentration or suggestion [with cooperation of the self] and *in a non-productive manner* through drugs, injury, fever, fear, anxiety, or strain.

The AMORC defines Nous as the combination of the Vital Life Force and the Cosmic Consciousness moving from the source of all life [God]. Nous is an energy or force magnetically polarized [positive pole and negative pole]. That energy manifests as vibrations of various rates and speed giving birth to different visible and invisible forms. There are eighty octaves of vibrations from two vibrations per second up to trillions of vibrations per second. The first ten vibrations are those of feeling and sound.

Electronic vibrations, according the manual belong to the fourth dimension different from the fourth dimension of the theory of relativity. An explanation of this declaration as well as Seekers' ideas on time relativity and the concept of Nous will be given in the next chapter.

Chapter 4

Seeker's understanding of human nature

In an attempt to explain what the human nature is, it is appropriate to first define the concept focusing on the words 'human' and 'nature.' Second it is important to present the elements that constitute human nature.

Defining the term 'human' can appear simple a priori. However, once this task begins, a theologian, a philosopher, or a psychologist discovers that it is not an easy one. Indeed, it is difficult to find a definition that satisfies entirely. One definition can suit "scientists" but offend religious and spiritual people while another arouses opposite appreciations.

This difficulty to define a human being is grounded on the fact that "science," philosophy, religion, and spirituality have different ideas about the constituents or the characteristics of human nature. Many of the actors within each one of these areas of knowledge even disagree with one another on several subjects.

Consequently, a consensual definition will emerge when there is a consensus on the characteristics of human beings. Hence, this section will describe the elements that compose the human nature prior to proposing a definition.

The best synonymous term for 'nature' in this study is 'characteristics.' Therefore 'human nature,' here, is a longer and more explicit version for 'human.'

One definition of the term 'nature' renders it as a primitive state of existence untouched and uninfluenced by civilization. But since human beings are the authors of civilization and of artificial creations, this potential or activity is part of their nature or characteristics as well.

In addition, because of the variability of certain characteristics, exceptions too belong to the human nature. Hence, there are fundamental elements common to all humans and there are specificities that mark sub human groups, societies, and single individuals. Fundamental or basic attributes and non-fundamental ones are both physical and non-physical and also anatomical [structural] and behavioral [physiological].

Contributions of quantum physics, biology, medicine, and other disciplines to the understanding of human nature

It is obvious that human beings have a physical existence. Physical reality is the organization of *energy-matter* into various forms and elements that perform various functions. Energy and matter are the two fundamental aspects of physical reality.

A proof of this dwells in Albert Einstein's discovery that matter is convertible into energy and inversely, according to the equation $E = MC^2$. The Rosicrucians of the AMORC should be thanked for reminding seekers that this knowledge is ancient and Einstein should becongratulated one more time for making it public and in clear modern language.

When physical reality is energy, this energy can be obvious or unobvious. As mentioned by Wikipedia, *potential energy* is the energy due to the configuration of a physical entity and *kinetic energy* is the energy due to its motion. When a physical entity like a soccer ball is in movement, it has a *mechanical energy* which is the total of its potential and kinetic energy.

Energy can be *thermal, chemical, electrical, magnetic, sonic, luminous, and gravitational*. It can also be static ["immobile"] or radiant ["moving"]. It is expressed in *joules or kilocalories or kilowatt-hours*.

When physical reality is matter, as one can read in the *Encyclopedia Britannica*, it is characterized by its *inertia* which in turn is characterized by a *mass* and a *rotational inertia*.

Inertia is the state of matter when unaffected by an external force independently of whether it is moving or not.

Mass is the quantity of matter commonly expressed in kilograms [kg] in the International System of Units and in slugs in the U.S. customary system [1 slug = 32.2 pounds = 14.6056624kg/ 1 pound = 0.453592kg].

Rotational inertia is the unaltered rotation of a quantity [or mass] of matter around an axis expressed internationally in kilogram.centimeter square [$kg.cm^2$] and in slug-foot square in the U.S.

In a human being, both matter [which possesses mass] and energy are present. Particles called *electrons, protons*, and *neutrons* form his/her *atoms* which in turn form *molecules* simple and complex among which the remarkable DNA. Molecules form *cells*, which make up *tissues* which constitute various *organs and systems*. All the organs and systems make up the physical *body*.

Electrons on the one hand and quarks which make up protons and neutrons on the other hand have no internal structure. That is why they are called elementary particles. Each of these subatomic particles has a *mass*, an *electric charge or electric energy* that generates an *electric field* and also a *magnetic field*.

The *mass* of each particle is small: $9.10938215(45) \times 10^{-31}$ kg for the electron, $1.672621637(83) \times 10^{-27}$ kg for the proton, and $1.67492729(28) \times 10^{-27}$ kg for the neutron.

Mass is responsible of *gravitation* which is one of *one of the four fundamental forms of energy or force or interaction of nature*. Gravitation or cohesion causes the coalescence of matter and the stability of that coalesced matter. There are theories, yet unproved that the gravitational force has an elementary massless particle called graviton.

The bigger the mass is, the stronger the gravitational force is. So, a ball of soccer exerts a far bigger gravitational force than a proton. In turn, the moon produces a far bigger gravitational or cohesion force than the ball of soccer. That is how the moon is involved in the tidal effect; when the sea level rises and falls.

The *electric charge* is static electric energy that secondly characterizes, besides mass, some forms of matter [mass]. It is expressed in coulomb. One coulomb corresponds to 6.242×10^{18} e [with e = 1.602176487 (40) x 10^{-19} C being the charge of a proton and – e or -1.602176487 (40) x 10^{-19} C that of an electron; a neutron according to its name is not electrically charged, its charge is zero]. When electric energy is not static and is radiant with electrons moving, it is called an electric current or electricity.

The *electric field* surrounds the electric charge of a proton, an electron, or other charged particle and *exerts a force of attraction or repulsion on other electrically charged particles*. There is repulsion when two particles are either positively or negatively charged and there is attraction when one particle is positively charged while the other is negatively charged.

The notion of positive and negative here is just a convention according to Wikipedia. What is interesting is that the force in the field generated by a "positive" charge is centrifugal [from a center] while the force in the field generated by a "negative" charge is centripetal [toward a center].

The electric field generated by the electric charge has a force with a strength or magnitude expressed in newtons per coulomb or volts per meter or $kg \cdot m \cdot s^{-3} \cdot A^{-1}$. It also has an energy density.

There are three kinds of *magnetic fields* associated with electrically charged particles. The first is induced by moving electric charges, the second by the variation of electric fields in time, and the third by the rotation of a particle around its axis [the spin]. Inversely, a changing magnetic field generates an electric field. The magnetic field too is characterized by a direction and a strength or magnitude.

Hence, an electric charge always generates an electric field and a magnetic field. Said differently, the two fields or *forces,* which are interrelated, are the consequence of the electric charge. That is why they are associated under a unique name: the *electromagnetic force* or *electromagnetic interaction* or *Lorentz* force. When the electromagnetic force is not static, it is called electromagnetic *radiation.*

If matter's smallest unit is the quark with a mass which makes up protons and neutrons, the basic unit or elementary particle or quantum of the electromagnetic energy whether static or radiant is the *photon* which is without mass but has an electric charge inferior to 1×10^{-35} e, almost zero e. Hence, the photon is said to have no charge.

So, a proton in the nucleus of an atom has a mass and electric energy while the neutron also present in the nucleus only has a mass, the same as the proton. The electron which revolves around the nucleus, like the proton, has both a mass and an electric charge. Differently from the neutron then, the proton and the electron have each an electromagnetic field.

It was said two paragraphs above that the photon is the basic unit of electromagnetic force or energy whether static or radiant. As there are various kinds of quarks for elements with mass, there are also various kinds of photons which constitute different types of radiations.

All electromagnetic radiations, each with its kind of photon, constitute the *electromagnetic spectrum.* Visible light is the part of this spectrum visible to the naked eye. The other radiations which are not visible to the eye are on one side of the visible light: gamma rays, X-rays, and ultraviolet rays [which have shorter wave lengths and higher frequencies than the visible light]; and on the other side: infrared rays, the microwaves, and radio waves [which have longer wave lengths and lower frequencies].

A photon has no mass and no charge. Its energy is electromagnetic. Photons vary according to their quantity of electromagnetic energy and other parameters as well. For example, the photon of the blue light has a higher electromagnetic energy than that of the red light. Electromagnetic energy is expressed in electron volt convertible into joule the more general unit of energy according to the formula 1 Joule = 6.24 x 10^{18} electron volts.

Various photons of electromagnetic radiations [X-rays, UV, IR, visible light] intervene in some biochemical reactions and are used in medicine for diagnostic or curative purposes[17].

Electromagnetic force is also one of the four fundamental forces of nature being viewed in this section. A third force is the *strong nuclear force or energy*.

There are six types of quarks that can form protons and neutrons, but only two kinds, the most stable and most common [up and down], are present in protons and neutrons in a human body [two up quarks plus one down quark form the proton and the contrary for the neutrons]. The other kinds of quarks not present in the human body are charm, strange, top, and bottom.

Quarks are kept together in the protons or neutrons of an atomic nucleus thanks to the*third fundamental interaction force of nature* called *strong interaction or strong nuclear force*. Protons and neutrons too are bound together to form the nucleus of an atom by the same strong nuclear force called this time *residual strong force*. The strong force's elementary particle is postulated to be the gluons which are the exchange particles between quarks.

---

[17]Sprawls, Perry. *Physical Principles of Medical Imaging.* Rockville, Md: Aspen Publishers, 1987.

In addition there is a *weak nuclear force,* the *fourth fundamental force, responsible for the radioactive decay* of the subatomic particles and for the starting of hydrogen fusion in stars. The mediators of this force are thought to be the W and Z bosons. *The strong nuclear force and the weak nuclear force are the two other components of the four fundamental forces besides gravitation and electromagnetism.*

After describing, to some extent, these fundamental forces and the particles that compose a nucleus; it is now important to give a little explanation about the conditions of existence of electrons around the nucleus which make it possible to have an atom.

According to fundamental physics and chemistry and as summarized by Wikipedia, the atom is formed from the relationship established by the nucleus with proton(s) and neutron (s) on the one hand and electron(s) on the other hand. This happens when the negatively charged electrons are near enough the positive electromagnetic field of the nuclear proton(s) to be trapped in it.

So, it is the attraction between two opposite electromagnetic forces or particles which is at the origin of the formation of the atom. The mass of the nucleus is almost that of the atom [more than 99.9%] meaning that the electrons' weight in the atom is very small.

Electrons almost always *move* around the nucleus in zones called orbitals comparable to the layers of the atmosphere thus forming the electronic cloud. *Moving* electrons tend to be evenly distributed in that cloud. The number of layers or orbitals, the level of energy of each electron, the shape of the orbitals, and other features of the electronic cloud are determined by the quantum numbers n, l, ml, and ms.

The energy level of an electron changes when it absorbs or emits photons. Electrons are responsible of atoms' chemical properties and play an important role in their magnetism.

Some atoms are positively charged because of "missing" electron(s) and are called cations. They usually are metals. Other atoms are negatively charged because they have more electrons than protons. They are called anions and usually are non-metals. Cations and anions of various kinds attract each other and form different kinds of molecules. Again, *electromagnetic attraction is responsible for the formation of molecules.*

But there are other *intramolecular forces* that stabilize molecules such as covalent bonds. Ions conduct electricity when reduced in liquid form and when their non-solid form is put in solution. *Intermolecular forces* keep molecules linked to each other. Molecules form cells which form tissues, which give birth to organs. *Hence, all the entities, from protons and electrons to the body have electromagnetic potentials.*

Ferrimagnetism is the strongest form of magnetism involving atoms; those of iron in this case. It is the only type of mineral magnetism that produces a force strong enough to be felt in everyday situations.

When one remembers that the blood's main constituent is the molecule of hemoglobin containing a high amount of iron, its electromagnetic potential becomes clearer and justifies the emphasis placed by Rosicrucians on magnetized or vitalized blood for healing ends. Oxygen (O_2) has its own vitalizing strength independently from iron.

The electromagnetic power of the blood might also explain why the Bible says in Leviticus 17: 11 and 14 that the blood of an animal contains its life and why blood is used in many rituals for the benefit of the people of ancient Israel in the Old Testament. According to the way they are described, the healing methods known as Reiki and qigong certainly involve electromagnetic energy.

Theosophy describes prana as the cause of electromagnetism and the other etheric waves such as sound and light and gives the precision that this prana's units [the sparks] are conveyed to each cell via the blood stream. The teachings of Theosophists, Rosicrucians, Ancient Israel, Jesus, Reiki, and so on, complete each other to rationally explain certain types of miracles.

The fact that their methods require refinement does not mean that all their teachings are incorrect or harmful. It is the task of research to continue working on the harmony of spiritual teachings and physical manifestations.

Seeker knows from experience and as described in some forms of Reiki that a flow of energy can penetrate the body through the crown chakra at the top of the head. He can also confirm that Rosicrucians are right when they say that a focus on the arterial blood leads to the release of energy through the hands.

One can see here an explanation of the laying of hands by the first Christians so that others might receive the Holy Spirit [Acts 8: 17], and what kind of force left Jesus to heal the woman of Luke 8: 43-47.

This confirms the connection between the Holy Spirit, electromagnetism, the Chinese chi, and the Indian Shakti as Seeker has suspected in *Abode of Divinities*. Moses, Jesus' baptism, Acts 10: 44-45, Reiki, and Seeker's experiences also show that the Holy Spirit can be received without the laying of hands or any other physical contact. Acts 10 adds that a speech can serve as the trigger that enables people to receive the Holy Spirit.

Seekers of all places today and in the future should be encouraged to formulate new theories centered on proofs they have identified based on their research and experiences in all sciences and domains of life including medicine, theology, psychology, and philosophy.

The organs or systems that should be prioritized are the mind or psyche or soul, the brain and the remaining of the nervous system, and the blood flow and the heart. Then the other organs and systems beginning with the genital organs come. Manly Hall's order of priority as he expressed it in his *Secret Teachings of All Ages* is heart—brain—genital organs. Seeker's is soul— nervous *system*—cardiovascular *system*—genital organs.

Description of human nature predominantly using a philosophical, spiritual, and religious language

Spirit

Definition and proofs of the existence of a human spirit

In *Abode of Divinities*, it was shown that a human has a physical body which is the organization of physical substance under a particular form perceivable by the physical senses and a second body which is the organization of spiritual substance under the same form perceivable by the spiritual senses.

This definition was then adopted as the main definition of spirit while other meanings of spirit such as spirit as spiritual substance or a form of energy and spirit as soul have been considered secondary.

The proofs of the existence of the spiritual body were then said to be scriptural, logical, and experiential. It was mentioned that the scriptures of many religions and spiritual and philosophical schools acknowledge the existence of the second body and that based on the existence of holograms which do not have individual consciousness, it is possible that such a kind of body with individual consciousness actually exists.

The first experiential proof was that everybody can dream and sometimes perceive oneself acting, moving, speaking, hearing, seeing, touching, feeling, smelling, and tasting. In dreams, the activities of the physical body and the consciousness of the soul are considerably reduced while those of the spiritual body and the unconsciousness of the soul increase. Waking up after a dream, a person is able to remember what was experienced and can analyze it.

Hence, the conscious soul comes to understand better the spiritual world and the unconscious realm and becomes capable of making decisions that shape the form and content of future dreams. Then, consciousness gradually grows in a new environment different from the physical one. Astral projection is a way to be completely awakened in the subtle realm. From that point, a person can proceed to more investigations using the reason or intelligence of the conscious part of the soul.

The anime *Naruto Shippuden* often presents its characters moving in various environments such as the forest in the way people move in their dreams. Seeker too experiences that phenomenon. He often makes amazingly long and high jumps on top of trees and other places and sometimes he sees himself simply flying without wings however.

Watching *Naruto* and other animes and listening to spiritual shows such as those of Patrick Nguemadon on the Gabonese radio station Africa n°1 convinced Seeker that he is not the only one to have such experiences.

The second experiential proof of Seeker is the experience he had a morning waking from a dream and literality perceiving an energy body taking place or filling back his physical body. This experience is similar to other experiences reported in various books and in which, like Seeker, the spiritual bodies of people is attracted toward a white and brilliant hole.

However, while many narrated their experiences passing through that hole, Seeker in his dream refused to do the same thing fearing death and telling God about his desire to accomplish a few things on earth before to go to the other side of the hole. Then, the attraction force that was pulling him up toward the hole loosened and as he descended he woke up witnessing a subtle or energy body taking place back in his physical body in a parallel way.

But after consulting the experiences of others, Seeker knows that the next time he has such experience, he will decide to go to the other side of the white hole since many people have come back from that kind of trip.

The books that report this sort of experience are usually spiritual or religious books; but there are more and more experts in psychology and the medical field who are reporting and studying out of body experiences [OBEs] and near death experiences [NDEs].

A third experiential proof of the existence of the spiritual body dwells in the fact that Seeker several times has been able to observe in himself the manifestations of the 1st, 2nd, 4th, and 5th chakras as described in the writings of Buddhism, Hinduism, yoga etc...

He is convinced beyond any doubt that those energetic centers of the spiritual body respectively located at the top of the head, between and slightly above the two eyes, and in the at the heart region really exists because he can sense their presence just as he can sense the physical heart beat when he wants.

He is certain that the 2nd chakra or third eye is associated with the pineal gland and that a golden light truly can appear around that gland. But the golden light he observed was one that slowly glowed.

The fourth experience that Seeker can bring forth to support the reality of the spiritual body is what happened when his father was about to pass away.

A few days and hours before his passing, the father on his hospital bed started calling the names of several of his relatives who no longer lived on earth. At the same time he appeared less connected to people around him in the hospital room. He often looked at them as if they were transparent his attention focused on things no one else was seeing.

The experience was so vivid that Seeker could not help but remember the writings of Emanuel Swedenborg on the moment of death of a person marked by the fact that relatives appear to welcome the deceased in the spiritual world. There is also a popular belief in his village that babies smile without apparent cause because they can see spiritual beings. Seeker senses that if babies were able to talk like his father they could interestingly teach those older than them.

Most religions and spiritual or philosophical schools admit the existence of only two bodies and two planes of existence. Names given to the other body beyond the physical are: divine body, spiritual body, ethereal body, psychic body, spirit, cosmic body, subtle body, astral body, and so on. Seeker prefers to use 'spiritual body' or 'spirit'.

Nevertheless, the Theosophical description presented in chapter 3 can suggest the existence of three bodies or more including the physical, the lower etheric or lower astral or spirit, and the soul body or higher etheric or higher astral.

With this description, several important questions emerge. Does a human being has just one body that survives physical death and is maintained for life in heaven as most religions and spiritual schools think or are there two or more surviving bodies, one of which disintegrates sometime after the physical death in a form of second death as Theosophy says?

In case there is a lower astral body that disintegrates, does the soul have a body of its own made of higher or finer substance as one can infer from Theosophical teachings or should one consider that the soul is without substance and just made of reason, will, creativity, memory, consciousness etc…? Are reason, desire, will, memory, consciousness, unconsciousness, ideas, and so on, high forms of substance? Can anything unsubstantial exist?

These questions will be tackled in the next subsection.

Since the spiritual body is made of pure energy [which can be of various sorts], it is evident that there is a link between its study and quantum physics, biology, and medicine as shown in the previous section. Elemental particles in atoms, light and the other electromagnetic radiations, magnetic and electric fields, electric charges etc… are the links between those disciplines including spirituality.

These links have already been perceived and explored by Rosicrucians, Theosophists, and others who have made astonishing and trustworthy descriptions. For instance, Rosicrucians describe the realm of subatomic phenomena as the 4th dimension or the spiritual or energetic realm different from the 4th dimension of the theory of relativity.

What is wrong with the general and special theories of relativity and why time travel appears to be only pure fiction

The Rosicrucian 4th dimension is still a space dimension and is considered without height, length, and width because the subatomic level is so minuscule that it is hard to speak of height, length, and width.

On another side, the 4th dimension in the theory of relativity is not a space dimension but a time dimension. This concept was born from the observations and explanations of scientists such as Hendrik Lorentz and Albert Einstein that the state of a three dimensional being is perceived differently when it is influenced by high speed and gravitation. The change is said to be a time dilatation because clocks slow down under high speed or high gravitational influence.

The experience truly is about time relativity. Indeed a person perceiving or measuring time in those extreme conditions collects different data. But Seeker seriously doubts the concept of time dilatation.

To him, the experience is about human beings not being yet able to conveniently measure time with appropriate instruments that are not affected by extreme circumstances such as high velocity and gravitation.

As long as such reliable instruments are not invented, humans will have to use the same clocks to measure time and adjust them according to a correspondence table. Inferring that the time measured is different is not correct in Seeker's eyes.

In reality, time is even more relative than explained in the general and special theories of relativity because it is based on the relationship between the sun and the earth. A second measured by a clock is not a universal time standard value but a helio-geocentric standard. This was explained in *Abode of Divinities* to support Hugh Ross whose concept of time relativity is different from these two and involves God who is beyond space and time.

Once Einstein's theory is revised, Seeker thinks that physicists and science fiction writers would quickly take the idea of time travel on which so many movies have been based less seriously.

He has always wondered about the moral and logical implications of time travel on human relationships and history and found the idea more than odd. Now he can add that Einstein's theory of relativity remains a theory thus belonging to the area of the speculative philosophy of physical science rather than a scientific fact. Nevertheless, he wants to pursue his research and discuss with several physicists to confirm or not his position.

In his mind, a sort of time travel can be created when people who have lived in various époques reconstruct worlds they lived in based on their memory and let others experience that worlds. This can be done in two ways: through the technological knowledge of animes and movies or through spiritual power.

The growth of the spiritual body

Since the spiritual body is made up of energy or energies, it is capable of growth and can be healthy or sick. It can receive and give energy from below or from above. The fact that people are conscious of this body only after several years or decades on earth engaging in specific spiritual activities is a strong indicator that the spirit body too grows and gradually become powerful through particular nourishments to the extent that even the physical body begins to feel its presence.

Of course some people at a very young age might come to be conscious of their spirit body and even use it. Seeker thinks this is the work of some adults who have mastered some techniques of partial separation or projection of the spirit body and have helped some children do the same. For example the molecule called DMT is more and more known to be able to connect individuals to the spiritual realm.

Seeker does not have enough information on the physiology of the spiritual body to say if introducing children to the energy world is premature and somehow harmful or not. He only has negative suspicions that require confirmation.

What is certain is that the spirit world and the spirit body have a great power. The question is if it is beneficial for society when children and ill intended people use that power. That is why some spiritual schools delay initiation and why some teachers only talk about methods that are slower but harmless to the students and society. These methods empower the soul with wisdom and love so that it can control and direct spiritual phenomena for good purposes and not be overpowered by them.

The primary help in an attempt to mastering the spiritual world is given by the energy from above commonly known as the Holy Spirit of God and it can take various aspects as reported in Seeker's first book, *Abode of Divinities*. However energy from below too also participates in the individual's growth. It is obtained through rituals, initiation ceremonies, and sacrifices which can be good or evil.

Blood sacrifices of animals and Jesus versus education and good actions for spiritual growth: the place of the Holy Spirit and rituals in spirituality

The author of the book of Hebrews [9: 13 and 22] is correct saying that the sacrifices of the time of Moses had positive effects and were used to purify nearly everything. Explanations about the purifying or cleaning potential of animal blood will be offered in the next paragraphs.

But everybody can admit that it is better not to sin rather than to sin and be purified by the blood of animals. In addition, even when someone sins, shedding blood is not absolutely necessary because there still is the possibility to repent and change attitude. This is the reason why Isaiah 1: 10-13 says the God of the Old Testament has become sick of offerings.

Repentance and change is a way of purification certainly better than blood sacrifice. As medical professionals and psychologists know, some people's sicknesses come from addiction. Sometimes people just cannot do what is right even if they know it and keep repeating harmful habits until an external *force* helps them somehow to stop.

There was a situation of global addiction to evil in Genesis 6 which caused the flood. The flood was a radical measure. Animal offering is a less radical one certainly because the faults committed are less important and less generalized comparing to the time of Noah. Nevertheless, there is something odd with a system that stresses purification rituals against sins rather than preventing them.

If the shedding of animal blood is not the best way for reconciliation with God as the author of Hebrews admits [10: 5], shedding the blood of Jesus is even less acceptable. But it seems that this author while writing some parts of the book of Hebrews has completely lost sight of the Tree of Life and built a theology or more precisely a soteriology [salvation doctrine] solely on the animal sacrifice and the cross of Jesus.

But as Unificationists stress it, Jesus himself knew something was not right with him being crucified and he tried to avoid the cross at some important occasions. In the thesis that he wrote while graduating from seminary, Seeker has shown how Jesus hesitated until the last minutes being sometimes very determined to be crucified and other times wishing or behaving for an alternative solution.

The most dramatic part of the crucifixion story is that even in his last moments, Jesus could not see the benefits of his actions so far, asking God why He has abandoned him. The conclusion of the life of Jesus was that God abandoned him.

Many Christian denominations know about this abandonment of Jesus, but it is difficult for seekers to get a good explanation from them. Even the Unificationist explanation that God abandoned Jesus to give him the possibility to restore Adam's abandonment of God is not satisfactory for two main reasons.

The first reason dwells in the persistence of the error of Paul and others that the world needs one person in particular as Savior or Messiah. This error has been explained and corrected in *Abode of Divinities*. The second main reason, related to the first one, is some sort of infallibility of that Savior or Messiah.

However *anybody who reads the Gospels carefully can see that Jesus though amazing in several ways did make mistakes.* And the explanation of God "forsaking" Jesus dwells in those mistakes and more importantly in his limitations.

One thing that is evident in the Gospels is that God never asked Jesus to go on the cross. There are three critical moments during which God could have clearly informed Jesus about His-Her choice to go or not to go: Luke 9: 21-36, John 12: 27-35, and Luke 22: 39-44.

In the first passage drawn from Mark 8-9 with some additional information, Jesus is pretty confident that he should die on the cross though there was no direct word from God in that sense. In the second passage, Jesus' doubts begin to manifest. Indeed he starts by saying that his soul is deeply troubled to the extent of making him want to ask God to save him from the crucifixion. However he regains his composure by "remembering" that it is to be crucified that he came to this world.

In the third passage, Jesus clearly expressed his personal opinion that he should not follow the crucifixion path and seriously asked God to help him. At this step he personally does not care about any prophecy that predicted his death or about any benefit that his resurrection would bring. He has forgotten that he has called Peter 'Satan' for expressing the same idea [Matthew 16: 23]. An angel manifested to him, only to strengthen him, not to tell him what to do and there was no voice of God like at the Baptism and the transfiguration.

One can ask the question: where did Jesus get the idea of dying crucified from anyway? The answer dwells in his' own interpretation of the Old Testament, his understanding or philosophy or wisdom about God, and his analysis of the human spiritual and physical condition. However, his conclusions were not strong enough to give him absolute confidence. That is why he kept looking for a direct answer from God.

Even his disciples were mad at him because his crucifixion project came as a surprise to them. They were not recruited on that basis. They did not sign up for that. What they were told was that the Kingdom of God was near and that people should repent.

Jesus told Peter who was at first against the crucifixion that he was seeing things merely from a human point of view, not from God's [Matthew 16:23]. But as said, there is not a place in the Gospels where God expresses directly His-Her opinion. So in this passage, Jesus is telling Peter that his opinion is the one God would have.

Additionally, disciples could also have held like several other Jews the view that Jesus came as a liberator even if it had to be through military means like in the times of Kings David and Hezekiah. They must have felt betrayed by Jesus, especially Peter, but they were too engaged with Jesus to pull back and depended on his spiritual power.

So, the crucifixion was unlikely to be the will of God at first as Unificationists affirmed, but also not even as a last measure as they concede. Jesus was not crucified only because of the disbelief of Jews as they affirm[18], but also because of Jesus' own limitations. Since Jesus went voluntarily on the cross, Seeker did not hesitate to call this action a ritual suicide in his thesis from seminary.

What was Jesus hoping to achieve through his death on the cross? In Matthew 16, he says the crucifixion is necessary. But why? He gave two explanations: the need for Old Testament prophecies to be fulfilled and the

---

[18]Moon, *Divine Principle* 1996, P 117.

hope behind his resurrection. But the disciples never understood those explanations and even feared to tell him about their true situation [Luke 9: 45 and 18: 34].

When the time really came for him to choose the cross or not these two reasons no longer influenced him. The cause of this weakness is that in fact neither of these reasons is strong enough to justify the crucifixion.

Abode of Divinities demonstrated that most prophecies of the Old Testament were not about Jesus but other people and have been forcefully reinterpreted to suit him. This reinterpretation was started by Jesus himself or at least the Jesus portrayed in the Gospels. But that volume also showed that at least the prophecy of Daniel 9: 26 was most probably about Jesus. Since it contains elements about the sacrificial death, it must have played an important role in giving Jesus the conviction that he must die on the cross.

But there is one rule of prophecy that Jesus did not consider and this played against him. The essence of this rule is that as long as humans can exert free will, there is no definitive prophecy to shape their lives. A prophecy is a possible future revealed to or perceived by a seer according to past events and the inclinations of those it is about. But though it is often difficult, people can change their inclinations and actions thereby changing the prophesized future into a different one. This is one important meaning of the book of Jonah where the God of the Old Testament spared a kingdom which turned away from evil.

So, Jesus should have known that he was the last person able to impact his own future and that of the world based on his observations, analysis, understanding, choices, actions. So, God wanted Jesus to make a choice but Jesus thought the choice had to be God's. Finally, he considered that God had abandoned him.

Seeker is convinced that Jesus could have help humanity better by opening a school like Hermes Trismegistus and Pythagoras or initiate a social movement like Moses and by not letting someone like Paul elaborate an important part of the Christian theology. Though Paul was talented, sincere, and devoted he could not have expressed the opinions of Jesus like himself.

A fundamental difference between the stories of Moses, Hermes Trismegistus, and Jesus is that in the case of the first two, a powerful angel and God gave clear guidance to free a people and start a teaching while Jesus had the possibility to determine what to do. To Seeker, it appears that Jesus was given a greater responsibility: find the right path with the help of the Holy Spirit, follow it, and guide others.

Seeker also thinks that he is in no position to accuse Jesus of anything. In his opinion, Jesus did what he could in his situation and even achieved outstanding results in terms of healing. Seeker is not sure at all if he could have achieved a least what Jesus accomplished though the latter clearly stated that he could be surpassed.

What other humans should do is not to spend all the time complaining about the past or living solely according to the past but they should also contribute to the divine work with their best potentials during their respective earthly lives.

It looks like since the time of Jesus, God trusts more and more the human capability to use the power of the Holy Spirit to unite with Him-Her and create a better world. That is why all are needed; not only a person called Messiah. *All should be the messiahs, the pathfinders who can create the happiest society.* Nevertheless, humanity should also reestablish a spirituality in which people are in conscious relationship with the spirit world.

Seeker's understanding of the best sacrifice is not the literal shedding of blood. Good education [wisdom, physical and spiritual science] and good actions are the best way for a spiritual body to be influenced by what is below or the physical world. That is the reason of being of the 10 commandments and many other laws.

There is inflow and outflow of energy when the spiritual body is considered. Seeker thinks that good education and actions affect the soul qualitatively and that the soul in turn affects the spirit both qualitatively and quantitatively. When the soul is positively impacted it manages the substance of the spirit in a good, powerful, and beautiful way in the same manner a good soul knows what is good for the physical body.

Some physical activities [good nutrition and sport] are decided by the soul and result in a healthy, powerful, and beautiful body. In this process, thanks to the soul, physical matter and energy is well organized in the physical body.

The same relationship exists between the soul and the spiritual body. However, there are two major differences. First, the activities through which the soul impacts the spirit are less self-centered. Second, the spiritual body responds more quickly to the soul's will than the physical body as Theosophists and others explain.

The human soul is also influenced by the Divine Soul through the Holy Spirit which not only conveys spiritual substance or energy, but also the divine Word, Understanding, Wisdom, Will Power, Intelligence, and so forth as narrations in the Bible show.

The way the soul is nourished is different from the way the spirit body is. *Soul nourishment can be better understood as philosophy* [whether theology or general wisdom] *the Tree of Life* as explained in the section devoted to the soul and in chapter 10 in much more details.

Good rituals are ceremonies in which spiritual energy is generated and conveyed for spiritual enhancement. Good rituals can be designed by the wise soul to support the work of the Holy Spirit. But not all rituals are to be recommended. The crucifixion though it has some benefits is one example.

The question of the death and external appearance of the spiritual body

If the spiritual body can grow or become sick, it can die as well, some might say. This would support the theosophical statement that the lower astral body finally disintegrates and frees the soul. But still according to Theosophy, the soul has a second body called kama rupa different from the lower astral body. *This statement is a philosophical possibility which requires experiential validity.* Nevertheless, the kama rupa like the traditional spirit body described in other movements is not said to come to die.

The explanations given on child conception in the next section are in favor of a construction of the spirit that is parallel to that of the physical body and therefore constitute an argument that makes the disintegration of the energy body possible but not necessarily historical.

Since the soul of a grown person is very different from that of the seed-soul that incarnated [in terms particularly of consciousness], the return of this consciousness to unconsciousness [Nirvana] to merge with God is not philosophically sound and useful. It is not known if there is a way for a fully grown, beautiful, and lovely consciousness to be wasted in such a way.

What is certain is that though the physical world affects the spiritual one, all the laws in it are not applicable in the spirit world. For example, *a certain number of actions can kill the physical body, but not the spirit.* So, until humanity knows better about the laws of the subtle world, the immortality of the spirit is the soundest possibility.

The second death through the Lake of Fire mentioned in the book of Revelation has a symbolic meaning as explained in *Abode of divinities.*

People who created facial esthetic surgery and those who undergo it have proven that a decision made in the soul can change the external appearance of the body. Since the spirit as explained in the next section is built in parallel and connection with the physical body, it is affected by the changes applied to it.

However, the current state of knowledge does not allow saying the extent of spirit transformation. But because the person continues existing, the soul or mind can repair the damages of the spirit by itself or with the help of others. Hence, the external appearance can continuously change if wished. Wise souls certainly can reach a high degree of beauty of the spirit.

Soul, mind, nous, psyche, or ego: its nature, constituents, functions, qualities, and problems

Tabula Rasa? Archetypes and Prototypes?

According to Jonas Hans' rendition of the *Poimandres*, 'Nous' is the Universal Soul or Universal Mind while 'nous' without capital 'n' is the soul or mind of a human being. This is one level of the likeness between God and a human. This assertion is supported by Theosophists of the Temple of the People who have declared that the substance of the Universal Soul and that of the individual soul are of same nature.

In Theosophy, kama is the 4th principle and the plane of the individual soul. It comprises kama manas [manifestation of desires in the mentality or lower mind] and kama rupa [manifestation of desires in form]. It is from this definition of kama that the idea of a third body or soul body or higher astral body or higher etheric body emerges.

Kama manas is 'lower mind' or 'individual mind' in comparison to Manas [the 3rd principle] which is 'Higher Mind' or 'Universal Mind' or God. They correspond respectively to 'nous' and 'Nous.' So, the individual mind manifests because of the desires of the Universal Mind. It is a localized, minimized, *representative, or microcosmic* manifestation of the Universal Mind.

The Universal Mind desires or wishes the individual mind. One could say that the first fathers the second, but it is more appropriate to use 'generates' in its largest meaning or 'Creates'.

By equating kama manas with the lower or individual mind, Theosophy shows that Indian spiritual philosophy acknowledges the existence of thinking, willing, and loving parts in the human soul just as mentioned by the Merriam-Webster's definitions of the soul or the mind. This is the functional part.

By describing kama rupa as the manifestation of desires in form, Theosophy and Indian spiritual philosophy clearly introduce an important notion in soul philosophy: the form or structure of the soul. This notion of soul form is only implicit in the definition of the mind said to be a 'complex of elements' and the characterization of the soul as a vital principle [see dictionary]. It does not state whether this vital principle has a form or not.

Now the question that should be answered is whether 'form' in kama rupa is as abstract as 'a complex of elements' or as 'vital principle' or whether it means 'form like the physical body.' In an online article[19], G de Purucker, quoting famous Theosophists such as Helena Blavatsky and William Q Judge, affirms that Kama rupa is indeed a body; the higher astral body.

From everything above, it appears that the Theosophical kama rupa is none other than the spiritual body mentioned in the other religions, spiritual schools, and Seeker and that the Theosophical concept of soul includes boththeconcepts of soul and the spirit body of the others. Kama manas is what is known as soul. Hence, there is an agreement between all schools of thoughts concerning the fact that there is an energy body that carries consciousness and that is able to live in heaven after physical death.

Consequently, the theosophical lower astral body, a transitional and heavy spiritual body which is said to disintegrate sometime after the death of the physical body, remains to be identified by spiritual research as well as the evidence for the 5th principle called prana.

'Psyche' and 'ego' are equivalent terms to 'soul' and 'mind.' Plato and Descartes agree that soul and psyche designate the same reality and the Temple of the People agrees that mind and ego are other terms for the same reality.

---

[19] http://www.theosophy-nw.org/theosnw/death/de-gdp4.htm (accessed July 8th, 2011).

Manly Hall mentioned that all things exist psychically in humans who are naturally able to know them by exciting the powers and the images in themselves to the point of illumination.

Seeker does not think that the soul should be described that way. Hall appears to be diametrically opposed the idea of Tabula Rasa advocated by Ibn Sina, Thomas Aquinas, John Locke, and Sigmund Freud. Seeker also disagrees with that idea. So, he neither thinks that the soul contains all things nor is completely without content at birth as Immanuel Kant and Sang Hun Lee affirmed.

A human new born and an animal one appear to be governed solely by physical reflexes. But as both grow up, the human baby develops advanced reason, emotion, will, memory, and so forth while the animal mind remains almost the same. Human children grow up to become the managers of the world.

The potential to be an "advanced program" existed in the human new born from the start. The human mind is a sum of data or information that gradually becomes manifest and more complex. That several elements of the mind are unmanifest or unable to be perceived by thinkers does not mean their inexistence. At least the instinct is always manifest; so the tabula rasa theory is totally unfounded.

The human soul has the potential to appreciate reality progressively in a more sophisticated matter. There is a difference between being able to appreciate and know all things on the one hand and having all those things psychically within oneself on the other hand.

However, it is possible that Hall's declaration was symbolical or that he used the term 'psychically' instead of 'psychologically.' The first word is related to 'spirit' and the second to 'soul.' But even the use of the second term would not fully accurate because all ideas and concepts do not exist in the mind from the start. Many are progressively learnt and integrated in the mind. From the start, the mind has a *potential* that gradually manifests.

Hence, it is acceptable to say that the human soul contains archetypes as Carl Jung stated in *The Archetypes and the Collective Unconscious* or prototypes as Sang Hung Lee affirmed in *The Unification Though*. Both admitted thatnot all archetypes or prototypes exist in the mind from the beginning.

Alfred Adler equated the understanding of human nature with that of the psyche and Socrates and Plato were of the opinion that knowledge of human souls is capital in dealing with human beings. Adler's view point that the foundations of the psyche are laid in the earliest days of childhood and that they do not depend on the hereditary factors does not appear completely sound.

A child comes into life with the foundations of the psyche already existing in him/her. Hereditary factors and environmental factors [human and natural] impact the full expression of the original foundation of the soul.

Why the mind or soul is not a brain product and destroyed like it at death: origin of the soul, preformationism, epigenesis, soul judgment and justice

The mind or the soul is not a result of the activity of the brain as Benedict de Spinoza [and also Paul Edwards, David Hume, J.J.C. Smart, Colin Mc Grinn, and others][20] thought because of three important reasons.

First, thinking is not a chemical process. The DNA mechanism which works via proteins and neuromediators is too slow to account for it. Only the wave phenomenon which underlies TV images for example can explain ideas. Waves belong to both physical and spiritual science and they can exist with or without the brain.

---

[20] Paul Edwards, *Reincarnation: A Critical Examination* (Amherst, N.Y.: Prometheus Books, 2002), 279-80.

If the mind was simply the result of the brain, it will not require affection, love, understanding, teaching, and so forth.

The mind develops and functions not only because the physical senses enrich it via the brain but most importantly because it exists in relationship externally with other human minds and both internallyand externally with the Universal Mind. *What drives a human mind toward wisdom, goodness, and beauty is more God and humans that have the same characteristics than the physical world. Madness, evilness, and ugliness too are more the result of bad human and spiritual influences.*

Ideas and memories are naturally stocked in the mind because it is a "place" reserved for them. *The substance of that "place" is similar to the substance of ideas and memories; like when a small lake becomes bigger receiving water which is a similar substance or like when a child with a small physical body become bigger with an adult body after ingesting physical substance similar to that body for years.*

Memories [from consciousness and physical senses and from unconsciousness and spiritual and soul senses] are present but no dissection, chemical analysis, or scanning of the brain can help perceive them. Humanity cansomeday discover ways to access memories.

The mind or soul is a complex of substance[s] finer than the already subtle substance of the spirit body as affirmed in Theosophy with intellect having the highest vibration followed by love and will.

To better understand the mind, the methods used to investigate it should not be exactly the same used for the study of the brain. Physical scientists should investigate both the spirit body and the soul which are <u>*beyond*</u> the physical.

Second, a hardware is very physical or material in comparison to a software. It serves as a support through which the program of the software is executed. Similarly, the brain is dense physical matter through which the mind [very subtle] expresses itself.

A software can be removed from a hardware; similarly, a mind can leave a physical body. Like a software, the mind can also be upgraded or degraded. This explains how a person can become divine, good, mad, or evil. Thus, that the soul needs food and care as many religions, spiritual, philosophical, and psychological schools assert is understandable.

Hume's observation that the mind and the physical body are weak in infancy, become vigorous in middle age, and decay in old age is admissible though many old people keep a sharp mind until they die. But inferring from this fact that death is the dissolution of both the body and the mind is not correct because the two reasons given above show how the mind though it has a relationship with the physical world can develop and can exist without it. And mental energy of high vibration can exist in a low vibrational body [the physical] or in medium vibrational body [the spirit].

Since a pure energy body can survive the death of the physical body, consciousness, mind, or soul can continue to be carried by that energy body. When Professor Ian Stevenson said that memories can exist in the brain and elsewhere as reported by Paul Edwards himself, this is how his words can be explained.

If pure energy can exist outside the physical body, what can prevent it to be organized like the physical body and carry the mind?

Third, the concepts of *preformationism* and *epigenesis* at the opposite direction of death help shed more light on the question of the survival or not of the soul. A good article on this topic can be found in the *Stanford Encyclopedia of Philosophy*[21]. It presents epigenesis as the idea according to which a human being is formed from unformed material and preformationism as another idea which states that the person actually started in some preformed way.

---

[21]Stanford Encyclopedia of Philosophy.http://plato.stanford.edu/entries/epigenesis/ October 11, 2005 (accessed June 18th 2011)

Some philosophers and scientists supported epigenesis and others preformationism. Still others attempted to fuse both theories because there perceived some truth in each. Aristotle for example acknowledged that a person starts from unformed elements from both parents. However, he added that the development of the individual is done under the guidance of the soul which is present when the generative materials of both parents are combined.

Because the Aristotelian soul appears only at that moment, his view on how the human life starts has been classified as epigenesist and because he mentioned the soul as guiding factor, his concept has been called a vital epigenesis. His vital factor or the soul is different from Henri Bergson's élan vital which is defined as a mere creative impulse.

However, the soul described by Aristotle is different from Seeker's because he does not differentiate between soul and spirit body. Seeker agrees with his physical epigenesis or synthesis and with his vital epigenesis and calls it spiritual epigenesis.

Remark: Aristotle does not differentiate spirit and soul; divine humanism does.

Physical epigenesis: since the physical body is built only when the genetic materials of both parents are combined, one cannot talk about physical preformed human beings.

Mind: preformed or not?

Case study: Jeremiah 1: 5. In this verse, the God of the Old Testament [G.O.T.] says that he knew Jeremiah before forming him in the womb and consecrated and appointed him as prophet before he came out of the womb.

Two problems:

1st problem: This statement seems paradoxical. Indeed, how could one be known before being formed?

2nd problem: it is not said how much of Jeremiah was formed and how much of him was known. Did his mind or soul exist and was known as seed soul with characteristics that directed the formation of his body or the G.O.T just had an idea of who was need for a particular mission and formed him from scratch, meaning also "synthesis" of the soul?

Currently, divine humanism cannot say which possibility is real. It cannot yet say if mental preformationism plus physical epigenesis is reality or if there is complete epigenesis with ideological preformationism, meaning the "synthesis" of the mind and every other component of a human being based on an idea or archetype or prototype. Theological and spiritual research will help us know better.

Spirit body:

Based on scriptures, dreams, and spiritual experiences; there is a part of a person X which has the same image [looks like] the person X, but is not physical.

Since the spirit body looks like the physical body, one could say that it could not exist before the latter which takes shape according to the kind of DNA contained in the two parents' gametes. Therefore complete epigenesis plus ideological preformationism will be justified.

However, since we have not ruled out mental preformationism or the existence of seed soul, we should also consider the teachings such as those of the Temple of the People which say that the soul exist and make garments for itself: spiritual and physical bodies. Therefore mental and spiritual preformationism too cannot yet be eliminated as an explanation of reality and we should encourage sub-specialty research that can be called mental embryology and spiritual embryology.

Many scientists and spiritual seekers are already pointing to amazing information such as how various vibrations [sound, light, X rays, gamma rays, alpha waves, theta waves, love vibration, fear vibration etc...] affect matter including the DNA either positively or negatively[22]. In *Abode of Divinities*, it was also mentioned how electromagnetic vibrations from the hands have been photographed.

Hence, what could happen before birth [human soul from the Universal Soul] and after death [relatively developed soul] show that David Hume and Paul Edwards are not correct to think that the destruction of the brain implies the destruction of the mind or soul.

On the same basis, Professor J.J.C. Smart's affirmation that the mental states are identical with brain states cannot be accepted. It is also evident that the mind or soul does not depend solely on the functioning of the different areas of the brain as Colin Mc Grinn stated. The mind does not depend on the brain to exist. The brain is a temporary channel of expression of the mind or soul. *Beyond the brain, the mind or soul has a past and a future.*

The goal of showing that there was a program or soul or mind in development long before the brain is formed and begins to think is to prove by affirmation that the existence of the soul or mind is not a product of the brain. Hence, the soul or mind can exist as well after the destruction of the brain; no longer unconscious and immature, but conscious and mature.

An affirmative answer to the question of spirit and soul survival opens the door to another question: that of *spirit and soul judgment.*

There is an amazing phenomenon that people who deny the survival of the soul should carefully consider because it has the strong potential to make them revise their position.

---

[22] The DNA phantom effect. http://www.youtube.com/watch?v=1H7szhBgyVA (accessed June 19th, 2011).

While living on earth, it often happens that a human being goes through a certain experience and latter completely forgets about it. Then, a night, after some 20 years for example, the event is played backed in a dream state exactly as it happened. When the person wakes up, he/she truly remembers and is astonished positively or negatively according to the nature of the experience.

Whether the person accepts or denies it, the fact is that the record of the experience has always been with him/her. Scientists someday could succeed in locating the "wave-site" or "soul location" of memories and find a way to convert them into images and sound or download and upload them. It is quite possible if not almost certain that the waves which convey mental images and sounds are different from the waves responsible for physical image and sound transmission. When this is confirmed, how one type of wave is convertible into the other could also become clear.

A memory no longer depends on the five physical senses to exist. As said before, it is obvious that what are now seeing, hearing, smelling, feeling, and tasting are no longer the physical eyes, nose etc…Dreams also bring things never experienced in the physical world showing that there are experiences, a life, that take place in another realm independently from the physical world.

In fact many phenomena such as waves or radiations have remained unnoticed by physical science for a long time when it was undeveloped and without sophisticated instruments. At that time they were considered spiritual or invisible.

If it comes that memory waves become manifest thanks to some new technology, or if it happens that machines able to see spirits are invented, some could be tempted to classify spirits as physical entities. But in reality, spirits would still be spiritual beings. What would have changed is that ways to connect different realms would have been established and this has already started.

Therefore, some phenomena belong to the physical system and others to the non-physical system. Each type of phenomena can cross a sort of border and manifest in the realm of the other. *When elements from the noumenal or soul world manifest to a person living on earth for example in dreams or visions, this is called divine teaching. The opposite is called preparation for the afterlife.*

The physical can perceive the physical and connects to the soul to "comprehend" phenomena of the soul plane. Similarly, the soul perceives what happens on the soul plane and connects to the physical to comprehend its phenomena. Hence, *as a pure physical existence is possible, a pure mental existence is also possible. Such existence keeps memories which are the basis for "judgment."*

It is frequent to encounter people so scared of the word 'judgment' that they deny the possible existence of such a thing. Here is a less scary way of presenting it.

Let's take the same memory playback example given earlier. Suppose the memory is about an event which did not make the individual feel guilty at the time it happened. Then suppose the event was forgotten followed by new experiences during which the person became convinced that a particular action is bad. Lastly imagine that the lost memory comes back showing he/she has done something he/she is now against.

Whether a particular individual is aware of them or not, *there are universal standard laws according to which thoughts, speeches, and actions are good or bad. When the whole of memories is confronted to them on the soul and spiritual planes, this is judgment.* That is why religion and spirituality emphasize so much good intention, good speech, and good actions.

Sometimes, people do bad things just because they believe nobody is watching or because nobody can make them pay.

Imagine a human society that lived on earth 1000 years ago. Place cameras everywhere without telling people about their function. Would there be less crime? The answer is no. But as soon as people become aware of the function of the camera, crimes will significantly diminish in the areas of surveillance.

Now, take the society of this 21st century C.E. in which many believes that the camera is the only way of watching someone. The observation will still be that crimes will be more frequent in areas without cameras.

Then imagine that the population becomes aware of the existence of a mechanism that allows knowing what is going on everywhere including in bedrooms without camera. It is certain that there will be a big turmoil if a group a people declares itself being capable of making public what has been going on everywhere for the past five years.

As a famous saying states: "*If everybody knows what everybody else says about everybody, there will be no more greetings.*" Seeker is convinced that the consequences will not be limited to greetings especially when people have gone beyond bad words and intentions and have acted against one another. *Observation and record of events is one aspect of judgment and an element against secrecy.*

The second aspect of judgment is the existence of coercive just force that enforces order. Suppose cameras have been able to record several acts of injustice but there is no body innocent and strong enough to maintain order. The result would be a neglect of the cameras and the persistence of a *Jungle Law* system in which right is determined by might. The most dangerous situation is when the political, the judiciary, and the military become sanctuaries for crimes; not to mention the religious system.

In the religious and spiritual concept of judgment both "cameras" and "coercive just force" are present. An idea about how the "cameras" function has already been given with the memory example.

What to say about law enforcement on the soul and the spiritual planes?

Religious and spiritual scriptures are full of descriptions about world guardians or good angels who support the ideals of God.

Besides these scriptures, what can convince a person of the existence of a coercive just force [whether angels or not] on planes beyond the physical is that if such power was to be completely absent or weaker than the power of injustice or evil or madness, things that needs to be built will not be and those which have been built will be totally destroyed.

Moreover, in the physical world, as Socrates said, the soul's life is heavily impacted by that of the physical body. As long as that body finds satisfaction through pleasures of all kinds [even the self-destructive ones]; a bad person does not seem to care about goodness, justice, unselfishness, and so on.

But after separation between soul and physical body, the bad person now lives in a realm closer to the Universal Soul or God. Since that individual soul is unjust, evil, and destructive, it is opposed to God who is Good, Just, and Constructive.

To exist comfortably in the physical world, the physical body is nurtured by the physical world. Identically, a pleasant life on the soul plane requires nourishment from the Universal Soul. Since the individual bad soul had not educated itself to be in tune with the Universal Soul, the nourishment received is toxic. The desire to survive and live well then *forces* the soul to reeducate itself and there is no guarantee that the process is joyful or quick. *This is the other coercive aspect of judgment a part from the scriptural angels.*

Reason is a natural faculty of the soul which enables it to find and follow the good and just path. The Retaliation Law of Moses was given to help people who lack that reason to stay as far as possible from evil and injustice, anyway.

Since there are some people who have decided to live like beasts, a reconnection with reason must start from the flesh. Therefore, through equivalent pain inflicted to the physical body, the law of Moses intended to help people understand why it is not ok to harm others. This is also the goal of some Islamic laws.

Modern judiciary system is less strict than the law of Moses because it seems that the merit of age has brought advances in human capability to reason. Thus, besides preventing further harm, prison is destined to offer time for meditation, repentance, and change.

Seeker's personal opinion is that both the Retaliation Law and modern prison have strengths and weaknesses.

The Retaliation Law is a less expensive and certainly a more effective way to reduce premeditated crime. By intentionally causing physical harm, a criminal inflicts inhumane pain to a victim. A justice that does not consider this fact is limited. Equating for example the loss of a hand and the accompanying pain with years of prison does not look just. What would be is an exact retaliation plus prison. So, the advantage of prison is to support retaliation when the crime committed is not a voluntary homicide.

The problem with the retaliation law is that is seems to be as inhumane as criminals are. However, rejecting this law does not consider the victims enough not only for what they suffer but also because facts prove that prison is not dissuasive enough to prevent many criminals from perpetrating a first crime and to recidivate making further victims. *The way for humanity to avoid this temporarily necessary measure is to increase the level of theoretical and practical wisdom.*

Two examples, one from the military and the other from medicine, support the retaliation law. The possibility of a country possessing the nuclear weapon being attacked by another country is small because the attacking country is certain to undergo severe damage as well.

As a country with nuclear weapon does not bombard another with the same type of weapon because it has the guarantee not to get away and because it has the certainty of suffering a lot of pain as it inflicts, many criminals think twice before harming an innocent when they are assured to receive at least an equivalent pain. Organisms in general have the survival and self-preservation instinct.

Where is the nuclear dissuasion of an innocent person facing a criminal? It is a judiciary system that acknowledges retaliation. Why would this dissuasion be allowed at the national level and be denied to the individual?

Allowing each citizen to carry a gun can favor crime. A world in which some people are unreasonable enough to willingly harm others needs a *police, an army, and a judiciary system*. This means that these three sectors *are very precious and should be seriously protected from corruption. Only people with the greatest wisdom, morality, and compassion should be authorized and encouraged to join the police, the army, or the judiciary system.*

Wisdom should be broadly taught and practiced so that one day humanity lives without these three systems which exist only because of lack of theoretical and practical wisdom. So, wisdom teaching is even more important than the police, the army, and justice. People who serve in those fields certainly have better things to do than restrain destructive people. One aim of wisdom teaching is to bring them relief. The US and the Russian governments understand this well enough to want to reduce their stocks of nuclear weapons.

In the medical field, cancer is the severe alteration of a tissue which comes to provoke, when advanced, malfunction and atrocious pain in other tissues and the entire organism. In several cases, people's lives are saved because the tumor is removed though it is a living entity like other tissues. But it is better to use preventive medicine which is part of wisdom to avoid the development of cancer.

If the death of lethal tissues in the body is acceptable why would that of a murderer not be? What does the world gain by letting such a person live while an innocent life which could have been happy is destroyed? Additionally, there is no guarantee that no one else would be killed by that murderer. Assuredly, it is better for criminals to even not be born while the world eagerly awaits the birth of great souls.

When the number of wise people increases, the number of prisons and the use of the Retaliation Law will decrease. This is another goal of the philosophy of divine humanism.

People who meditate on dreams and books and listen to good words increase their knowledge and wisdom. They avoid learning things through harmful and painful mistakes or evil. By being good on earth, they learn how to dominate matter with the soul and see their desires fulfilled.

Matter in the physical world requires a lot of effort from the soul to obey it. Less effort is spent to move liquids comparing to solids and even lesser effort is needed to use the wind. *It is easier to breathe than to drink water.* Similarly, as Theosophy explains it, ether, which is subtler than air, responds even faster to the soul and akasha is even faster to respond.

When several religions and spiritual schools teach that desires in heaven are accomplished as soon as they are expressed, it is because of the ability of the good soul to influence the substance on the spiritual plane faster than breathing.

Reason, morality and virtues, laws, passions, love, goodness, evil, and freedom

The main constituent of the soul or mind is *reason* as shown in the chapter on the fatherhood and motherhood in *Abode of Divinities* and by thinkers such as Plato, Aristotle, Augustine, Aquinas, Locke, and Kant.

Seeker has chosen not to place *morality or virtues* before reason like Schopenhauer .The justification is that righteousness and morality come after reason has determined what people should be faithful to.

Reason, intelligence, creativity, truth, or wisdom is however useless without the moral will or moral force to follow. Being moral or virtuous based on ignorance or based on lies is either a waste of time or a danger depending on the situation.

In addition, the way reason can help the will and consequently morality is far superior to the way will can help reason. It is not too hard to will to reason. But when reason succeeds in uncovering amazing truths, the will can get so fired up that individuals and societies can accomplish great works for happiness.

At the light of these explanations, one can see that Hermes Trismegistus, the author of the John 1, and that of Proverbs 8 were right to call Reason or Word or Wisdom, the first born of God, giver of life, and so on. These explanations also demonstrate why Schopenhauer was not correct in stating that morality instead of reason or wisdom was the fundamental element of human nature. His theory, in addition cannot find any person who is perfectly moral.

Perfect morality is only possible when there is perfect truth or reason. If Schopenhauer had let reason reach its full potential, he would have discovered the *way* for his perfect moral person to come into existence.

Likewise, the position of Hume, Freud, and Darwin that passions and impulses are the rulers of the human psyche and that they are uncontrollable by reason is not admissible. Hume's example that people are more attached to and favor their relatives over strangers despite reason has a major flaw.

Indeed, what he does not seem to perceive is that the reason to treat relatives and strangers equally is not obvious while the reason to favor relatives is. Hume did not notice that people favor family and friends for some reasons and that all in all reason is at the base of his observations.

He should have known that when some reasons are stronger than others, except in the cases of madness or evilness, these superior reasons prevail. *It is possible to witness the emergence of a reason so strong that it will make people really practice equality.* This is one of the fundamental aims of this volume because *equality is a major determinant of the happiest society.*

Legal principles are instruments determined by reason [or the word] to help establish morality and virtues. This is the origin of all laws, from the Code of Hammurabi to the 10 commandments and to modern constitutions and secondary laws. Education, training, practice, prayer, meditation, religion, spirituality, psychology, philosophy, theology, and so forth are other important instruments of reason.

Love, delight, and pleasures are the ultimate goals of reason, morality, virtue, and all the disciplines just mentioned. *Reason sets life up and love enables its full enjoyment.*

Theosophy is correct in stating that reason shapes desire and will. P.M.S. Hacker formulated the same views saying that humans act because of some reason and not by mere instinct [passions] and thus are moral and legal beings able to knowing what is good and what is evil. Hence, they stay healthy or become sick either in the mind or the body, or both. The spirit too is involved in this health matter as the third element of the *human triadic nature*.

Goodness encompasses reason, laws, morality, and love. It has various degrees. The highest goodness possible is perfection. Aristotle was correct in associating goodness and *happiness*. The highest good presupposes the highest reason, laws, morality, and love. It is amazing that in the book of Genesis, each time the God of the Old Testament creates he says it is good or very good in the case of humans.

Evil is the opposite of goodness [wrong reason, unjust laws, immorality, and harmful love]. It also has various degrees. *Errors or mistakes* make up the boundary between goodness and evil. People who make mistakes are those who are responsible of damages unknowingly, because of undeveloped reason, or because they are ignorant of the law.

People who create damages being intelligent or knowing the law are those who are evil. The most evil are those who create the biggest damage with a big intelligence. Evil is a kind of '*cancer of the soul*.' That is the reason why an angel of great wisdom was called the Devil when he became corrupted [Ezekiel 28].

The narration of the Bible about the Devil synthesized by Seeker in conjunction with ancient myths particularly those of Mesopotamia and Babylon in *Abode of Divinities* shows that the theosophical affirmation that jealousy is the basic principle of evil is correct. But negative pride is deeper cause which can generate evil on its own or pass through the channel of jealousy. A deep understanding of the nature of humanity, the universe, and the Divine has the power to eliminate destructive pride and jealousy living only a sane desire for individual and collective improvement.

The religious notion of sin encompasses both mistakes and evil. Mistakes are minor sins and evils are major sins.

Freedom is the possibility to progress in goodness without obstacles. Any hindrance to reason, morality, love, laws, education, spirituality etc…, at the individual or social level, is a violation of freedom. Humans should be free to be smart, free to be virtuous, free to love, and free to learn.

Freedom can be extended to mistakes but not to evil because no evil person is free. Since evil people do not appreciate being victims of other evil people [with the exception of madness], this signifies that they are themselves prisoners of evil.

Because people cannot be free to be evil toward others according to the maxim '*Your freedom stops where that of the other begins*' and because being evil toward oneself is unconceivable or pure madness, there is no such a thing as freedom to be evil. True freedom is contained in the Golden Rule that can be found for example in the Old Testament [end of Leviticus 19: 18], the New Testament [Matthew 22: 39], and in many other scriptures.

The rest of the description of the soul will be presented in the next sections.

Reincarnation, resurrection, heaven, and hell

Reincarnation is a theory accepted and promoted by many spiritual schools such as the Temple of the People [of Theosophy], Rosicrucianism, Hinduism, and so forth. It includes the theory of resurrection. As long as resurrection is not complete they affirm the soul needs to reincarnate. Many scholars in religions and spirituality endorse that doctrine. Manly Hall is one of them.

Nevertheless, there are also many religions, spirituals schools, and individuals who reject reincarnation replacing it by a pure theory of resurrection which stipulates that the soul does not come back on earth but remains in the spiritual realm where it harvests the consequences of its earthly life. Several Christian denominations, Islam, and the Unification Movement hold this belief though the Unification Movement's theory of resurrection combines elements of both reincarnation and resurrection.

In Seeker's view, the doctrine of reincarnation has many shortcomings. It is true that it can appear non-sectarian, just, understandable, and revealing as Rosicrucians say. However, resurrection can be presented in an even more logical, understandable, just, and non-sectarianway.

Before shedding a new light on resurrection, it is important to bring forth the shortcomings of the reincarnation theory.

First, the *argument of the loss of memory of pass incarnations* has not yet been undoubtedly verified. Some consider the results of past-life therapies and hypnotic regression to be the experiential proof required.

Based on situations of memory alteration like in the Alzheimer disease, one can accept the possibility that memories can be altered or blocked. When past-life therapies are added, the argument of loss of memory is stronger. However, there is a significant difference between the Alzheimer and similar diseases on the one hand and reincarnation on the other.

In the first case, an overwhelming majority of humans agrees that there has been a loss of memory and can explain enough"the why and the how." In the case of reincarnation, only a few people agree and cannot satisfactorily justify their allegation. The greatest experiential proof so far given which is that of Jiddu Krishnamurti by Theosophy. But this example has been proven invalid.

Some theosophical leaders such as Annie Besant and Charles Leadbeater made public in the beginning of the 20th century that Krishnamurti was the reincarnation of a messianic figure, precisely Jesus. However, Rudolph Steiner, another theosophical leader of the time and others strongly disagreed. The situation led to a schism in Theosophy. Sometime later, Krishnamurti denied being such a reincarnated messiah.

If such advanced advocates of reincarnation as Besant, Leadbeater, and their supporters made that kind of mistake, who else can be trusted on the subject of reincarnation especially when several serious arguments, being presented, are against it?

Another wide spread way to present the loss of memory argument is the affirmation that *causing the loss of memory is an act of mercy and compassion from God which helps the reincarnated soul avoid being plagued with the memories of a preceding life while attempting to live a new one*[23]. Thus, for Steven Rosen, if the access to past lives' memories is not blocked, individuals will hardly develop relationship with new families and friends and learn necessary lessons.

This justification of the loss of memory is also not valid. If society is well organized, people can learn any lesson they need in one life. It makes more sense to accept human improvement through the establishment of a better society [theory a] rather than through the process of reincarnation [theory b]. Theory a is more logical and realistic while theory b is nebulous.

In one life a person can establish a great number of relationships. That is the case for of pop stars who relate to family, close friends, and millions of fans. The difficulties many famous artists face is not due to the necessity to lose the memories of some of their relationships. Their problem is that they do not know how to create relationships that will all be in harmony and how to completely suppress any harm that can come from those relationships. In addition, a human being does not necessarily need thousands of relationships to live well and be fine. A few good relationships can do very well.

Also, there are cases of adoption in which the adopted child has a memory of previous parents without becoming a problem to society. Furthermore, people can be taught a way of conceiving life that will make all the worries of the advocates of reincarnation vanish.

---

[23] Steven Rosen, *The Reincarnation Controversy: Uncovering the Truth in the World Religions* (Badger, CA: Torchlight Pub, 1997), 13.

Indeed, a new philosophy can appear and strengthen human minds with a truth, wisdom, and love so powerful that it will make it easy to handle relationships. Reincarnation should not be a response to a deficit of philosophy or creativity.

Moreover, all incarnations are not supposed to necessarily give bad results. There can be situations in which people have not achieved perfection but have lived a positive life with a lot of good lessons learned. Why should the memory of such people too be blocked? Such memories would be an asset for a new life rather than a liability. In these cases memory losses will not be acts of mercy but unwise or capricious acts that deprive people from qualities and skills beneficial to the entire human kind and the universe in the end.

For all the preceding reasons, memory loss cannot be used as argument to support reincarnation.

A *second argument* against reincarnation dwells in the *double analogy and scriptural argument* that Seeker has also elaborated based on existing information and meditation.

The first is the oil-water analogy which is similar to the ship-goat analogy used in the book of Enoch, by the ancient prophets of Israel, by Jesus, and by Christians. It is also similar to the wheat-weed parable of Jesus [Matthew 13: 24- 30]. Other versions could be entitled: sheep-wolves, sheep-fierce beasts, lamb-dragon, child-dragon, and so on.

When a certain pressure is used to introduce drops of oil and water into a recipient from the bottom, the drops of water constitute a layer on top of which there is another layer made of the drops of oil. As time passes, and the water layer becomes thicker, each new drop of oil would have to travel a longer distance to reach the oil layer.

Similarly, the goats, wolves, weed, beasts, and dragon pose a certain problem to the sheep, wheat, lamb, and child. But after a period of time, they are separated. The oil-water analogy explains why the sea and waves sometimes plays a negative role in the Bible like in the Psalms and in the story of Jonah and why oil is used for divine anointing. This is also an explanation for the calming of the raging sea [Mark4: 35-40] and of Jesus walking on water [Mark 6: 47-48] as many teach.

The same way, after a certain period of life on earth, good spirits and bad spirits separate and live in two different spheres in the spirit world: heaven and hell. Seeker thinks some descriptions of heaven and hell are symbolic while others are literal and that philosophy, meditation, and experience would help precise those descriptions.

The second analogy against reincarnation is a detailed version of the first. It is the particles' weight analogy which corresponds to Jesus' parable of the farmer scattering seeds [Matthew 13: 1-9].

When particles of various weights are put into water; the heaviest go to the bottom and the lighter to the top. But the number of layers is not limited to two. In fact there are several layers. The layers on top symbolize heaven and those of the bottom represent hell. The Qur'an teaches about seven heavens [41: 12] and Paul testified about the existence at least of 3 heavens [2Corinthians 12: 2].

In the parable of Jesus, the various kinds of ground on which the seeds of the farmer fall [footpath, shallow soil with underlying rock, thorns, and fertile soil] correspond to the multiple layers of particles. Additionally, some soils are more fertile than others.

Supporters of reincarnation could say that the double analogy supports resurrection but does not contradict reincarnation. That is why one should add the biblical scripture of 1Peter 3: 18-20. This passage shows that ancient sinners of the time of Noah have not reincarnated but awaited the Word of God which would transmute or resurrect them at a higher level.

There is a *third argument* against reincarnation. According to this view, *a seed that has become a plant cannot be sown again*. A former seed returns to the soil only through the many new seeds the plant produces.

This introduces the concept of heredity which explains why some passages of the Bible speak of the life of *ancestors impacting that of descendants* and why African traditional religions, the Native American Religion,

Shintoism, Buddhism, and the Unification Movement among others think that *descendants' way of life can impact ancestors'*.

This is also the basis for adoption, teachership, discipleship, and the veneration of old masters in eastern and African religions and that of saints and prophets in Judaism, the Catholic Church, and Islam.

However, the same Bible also teaches in Ezekiel 18: 2-4 that at a time, the God of the Old Testament did not hold descendants accountable for the sins of their parents.

Seeker does not think that the population argument and the identity argument should be used against reincarnation. Indeed, the number of souls is enormous and souls incarnate one after another. Therefore even without reincarnations, a world population growth can occur. *Population growth or reduction is rather a consequence of the philosophies and policies of the human society.*

Human reason can elaborate a philosophy of life that can keep the number of individuals who live on earth at the same time in a limit that is reasonable. The 21st century C.E. for example is a time in which such a philosophy is crucially needed.

The identity argument is neither against nor for reincarnation because even without that reincarnation, external appearance and the nature of the corresponding soul can change making it extremely difficult to recognize the person.

Nevertheless, there is a *fourth argument* against reincarnation that will be given after a review of different theories of resurrection. *Its purpose is to show that resurrection is even more moral and just than reincarnation.*

It is important to notice that the advocates of reincarnation do not reject resurrection, but consider it as part of reincarnation as well as its final goal. For example, to the Temple of People, an earthly life is used for the transmutation or resurrection of the soul toward its highest state or divinity.

Because of all the arguments given against reincarnation, only a pure theory of resurrection or transmutation or alchemy stands. Since *there is not enough reason to justify reincarnation at this time of human history, it remains just a hypothesis which is more likely to be proven wrong than confirmed.* But seekers should always keep an open mind and seriously consider any new explanation or experience mentioning reincarnation.

People and religions that defend resurrection do not always agree on the details. What resurrects is often an element of division. Paul in 1 Corinthians 15: 42-54 expresses the opinion that physical bodies resurrect, not to be physical as they were, but transformed into spiritual bodies. However to Islam, physical bodies resurrect as such [Qur'an 41: 39 and 79: 10-14].

In the 14th and 20th chapters of *Vous Pouvez Vivre Eternellement [You can Live Forever]*, Jehovah Witnesses assert that a small part of humanity, the 144 000, will rule with Jesus from heaven and will have spiritual bodies. Among the rest, those who have lived a good life will receive new physical bodies identical to former ones while those who have been evil will not resurrect at all based on John 17: 12, Matthew 23: 33, Matthew 12: 32, Hebrews : 4-6, and Hebrews 10: 26-27.

Unificationists in the 5th chapter of the first part of their *Divine Principle* and in other documents explain that resurrection occurs when a person still lives in the body and that it cannot be completed without the presence of the Messiah who is the antidote of the original sin brought in the world by Adam as Paul explained.

Consequently, the first coming of Jesus was the opportunity for the people of his time to fully resurrect while people who have lived before him, good or evil, would return to earth from their respective spheres of residence in the spirit world and also resurrect by helping those with physical body fulfill their missions. But it is easier for people who have been good to receive opportunities of cooperation with those living on earth.

Unificationists add that since Jesus has been misunderstood, he had not been able to grant humanity all the benefits needed and had to return. Hence, his first work though it opened the way for a higher level of resurrection should be upgraded at his second coming.

To the Unification Movement, the physical body is necessary for resurrection because it helps build or grow the spiritual body by sending vital elements to it through good actions on earth. This view is similar to the esoteric notion of transmutation.

However, this Unificationist emphasis on the physical body is only relative since in the latter development of the movement appeared teachings stating that workshops are conducted in the spirit world to raise people's spiritual levels.

In Paul's theology, the problem is that spiritual bodies are not the result of the transformation of physical ones. Probably the transfiguration of Jesus misled him. In addition Paul has not been able to figure out which part of himself has visited heaven during his earthly life [2 Corinthians 12: 2-4]. Augustine is a giant of Christianity alongside Paul, but he disagrees with Paul on this subject in *The City of God*[24].

From all the information given about the spirit and the soul, Jehovah Witnesses, Muslims, and all those who have admitted the resurrection of the body can see that in fact it is the spirit that resurrects and also the soul. The body may resurrect from a few minutes to a few days after death especially when some chemical substances are used to help revive the dead. The resurrection of the body can also be spoken of in a symbolic way for example to speak of rejuvenation.

When the Islamic view is analyzed, it appears hard to believe, as many philosophers have noticed that it will be hard for ancient bodies to come back to life especially when one knows that elements that were part of a body could pass to other bodies and even to animals and plants over millennia. In

---

[24]Augustine, and Marcus Dods, *The City of God, (Translated <And Edited> by Marcus Dods*. 1949), p 326.

addition, modern science has shown that elements of the body are renewed every seven years.

Jehovah witnesses have perceived this problem that the belief in the resurrection of the body raises. Therefore, they affirm in their theology that resurrected people will receive new physical bodies by the power of God. The difficulty here is that this view *"forces"* God to perform a world scale miraculous resurrection of billions of bodies.

Bringing up a miracle that never happened and depends solely on God to support anidea while reasonable and natural explanation is available cannot be a valid stand. Most of the description of the soul and the spirit offered in this volume have not been considered or have been misunderstood by the Jehovah Witnesses. If that information is well analyzed, they could eventually revise their position.

Here is a focused analysis that addresses the major arguments put forward by the Jehovah Witnesses to justify a belief in the resurrection of the physical body. In this analysis, arguments based on 'if' or 'in ideal conditions' or 'miracles' will not be considered because any philosophical or theological system can use these expressions to defend any position.

Therefore, the following explanation will stick to what is real, what is reasonable, and to how the scripture can be associated to reality and logic to support a view point. The next paragraphs will analyze and comment on the biblical passages brought forth by the Jehovah Witnesses.

Those passages are organized around themes such as: *'Proofs that humans are supposed to live eternally on earth', 'Is there an afterlife for humans and animals?', 'Examples of resurrection of the body', 'Scheol, Hades, Gehenna, Lake of fire, and Hell', 'The 144 000', 'The resurrection of the just and the unjust', and 'The case of evil people'.*

Additional reasons not to believe in an eternal life on earth

1- It cannot be said that earth has been created to meet all human needs because that would make heaven or the rest of the universe useless. Believing that the other stars and planetary systems of the universe are just to be observed from earth is not appropriate because the human knowledge can grow and come to find these entities more useful.

2- Psalms 115: 16

This verse does not mean that a particular human being will eternally live on earth. The verse is about the human species. It will be a truth as long as there are humans on earth, not necessarily, when humans do not die. The succession of generations is confirmed by Job 14: 1-2 which states that the life of any individual born from a woman is short [temporary].

3- Psalms 139: 14

Being a wonderful creature is not synonymous of eternal life on earth

4- Isaiah 45: 18 and Psalms 37: 29

As long as there are people who are just on earth; this verse is fulfilled, not necessarily when a particular just person like Mr. Y or Mrs. X never dies.

About the biblical examples of resurrection

All the persons resurrected in the Bible have been freshly dead [few days maximum]. They were not dead since millennia, decomposed, and massively resurrected by the invisible God. If medicine and spirituality are seriously investigated retrospectively as well as prospectively, Jesus' operations called miracles could be performed.

Verses confirming the existence of the spirit and that of the spirit world
Zechariah 12: 1: God forms a spirit within each human

1 Peter 3: 18: existence of a world of spirits where Jesus went and preached.

Luke 9: 30 and Deuteronomy 34: 5: Moses who was dead continued to exist as a spirit. He was not his body that went to the grave and decomposed.

Ecclesiastes 9: 5 and 10, Ecclesiastes 3: 19-20, and Psalms 146: 3-4 seem to indicate that there are no thoughts and plans after death and that there is no difference between humans and animals. When one reads comparatively Ecclesiastes 9: 10 and Ecclesiastes 3: 20, it appears that the attention of the author is on the grave and dust.

Apparently, the author of the Ecclesiastes was not aware that Moses continued to exist after his death and would appear to Jesus. Moreover, the entire book of Ecclesiastes looks like the work of a discouraged and depressed person whose wisdom is dulled by a life of pleasure. He seems to better appreciate the gratification of the physical senses. How can divine wisdom remain in such a person?

The question of the animal soul will be tackled in the next pages.

The supporters of the idea that there is no memory after death should remember that the Jesus of the Bible never taught such a thing. In fact he actually taught that the future of humanity after the physical death is in the spiritual realm.

When asked a question on resurrection in Luke 20: 27-40, Jesus' final response was that the God of Abraham, Isaac, and Jacob was not a God of the dead but of the living meaning that the three patriarchs were living beings at that very moment. If they were still living but could not be seen on earth, the only other place they would be is heaven or the spirit world. Jesus knew this and the idea finds confirmation when Moses who has physically died showed he was still living in another form by appearing from heaven with Elijah whose death was portrayed as a journey to heaven.

Centered on Abraham, Isaac, and Jacob, Jesus was also teaching that common humans [such as a woman and his seven husbands of the same brotherhood] also resurrect or continue living in the spirit world after physical death going as far as to make a comparison with angels.

Moreover, Jesus clearly taught what happens after the physical death when he talked about the rich man and Lazarus in Luke 16: 30. He gave the precision that Abraham lives in a good spiritual place where other good people go and that bad people go to a place of suffering that they cannot leave. The parabolic aspect of the story dwells in this suffering and moving part which was explained earlier as the consequence of the structure and function of the metaphysical or spiritual world in relation to goodness and badness.

This passage also clearly shows that people called 'dead' can still think, talk, act, and can even visit the physical world in contrary to the declarations of the authors of Ecclesiastes 9: 5 and 10, Ecclesiastes 3: 19-20, and Psalms 146: 3-4. So *the dead are not dead* as BiragoDiop said.

The reader should to be reminded that biblical contributors or authors are different people who tried each to embody Divine Wisdom and that some did a better job than others. Here, Jesus proves to be more reasonable and accurate than the author of Ecclesiastes.

Scheol, Hades, Gehenna, Lake of fire, and Hell

The names by which certain realities are called can vary from a person to another and from a philosophy or a religion to another. What is important here is that tombs exist as Jehovah Witnesses affirm; that Hell exists as explained in the double analogy and scriptural argument previously presented; and that the Lake of fire is a purifier, not a destroyer as explained in *Abode of Divinities*.

As stated by The Temple of the People and as shown by the Bible, there is a Divine Holy Fire also called Holly Spirit which does not consume but purifies.

Nevertheless, it ought to be said that in several biblical versions, the word *Hades* appears in Luke 16: 23 in the story of the rich man and Lazarus as the general place of the dead not necessarily hell. The versions that put hell in the place of *Hades* have performed a misinterpretation. When the context is well understood and when one follows logic, it appears that the place of the dead is the place where all kinds of dead [good and bad] go; but once there, good and bad people live in different places as the existence of prisons for truly criminal people illustrates.

So in Jesus' mind, *Hades* is not a place of inaction and absence of memory and thought.

The 144 000

Manly Hall explains in *The Secret teachings of All Ages* that this number is a code, a symbol of mankind represented by the number 9. Addition of its elements shows that 144 000 is 9. As Hall mentioned, the author of the book of Revelation was certainly familiar with esoteric and cryptic language. The prophet Daniel too was such a person [Daniel 12: 9]. Both authors communicated with angels according to scripture.

The resurrection of the just, the unjust, or evil people has already been explained by the double analogy and scriptural argument against reincarnation. The purification by the Lake of fire reinforces the preaching of Jesus to evil spirits of the past.

Before moving to the Unificationist understanding of resurrection, it is important to say more about the number 144.000. This number is composed of 144 and three zeros [000]. Since the addition of the elements of 144 is 9 and since 9 represents a human being for various reasons that will be given in the next paragraphs, 144000 means 1000 humans or 10.000 humans …..or all humanity. So, the number of people who will be saved is the entire humankind.

The number 144 is the second after 120 to have the greatest number of dividers in the order of appearance of numbers. And this second place is only because its divider 12 is repeated allowing a total of 15 dividers against 16 for 120. Indeed, the dividers of 144 are 1, 2, 3, 4, 6, 8, 9, 12, 16, 18, 24,

36, 48, 72, and 144 and those of 120 are 1, 2, 3, 4, 5, 6, 8, 10, 12, 15, 20, 25, 30, 40, 60, and 120.

One must wait the double of 120 [240] to find the first number with clearly more dividers. Attention is brought on the dividers of 144 for several reasons.

The first reason is that the important number of the dividers allows the broadest variety of structures and functionalities or experiences on a small scale. The second reason is the quality of these dividers. Attention must be drawn in order on 12, 9, 3, 24, 36, 72, and 144 itself.

Since $144 = 12^2$, 12 can be considered as one of its fundamental dividers or units. Indeed 144 "looks" internally and externally centered on 12 in a perfect manner.

Internally, the number 12 corresponds to a square or a house or a city or a universe with a perimeter of 12, an area of 9 and a side 3. A connection with the symbolic celestial city of Jerusalem spoken of in the book of Revelation [21: 1-26 and 22: 1-5] is thus established. The city is a representation of its population or humanity; so is the number of that population, 144 000. A house also symbolizes a human just like Jesus and Paul said a temple does.

The biblical passage just mentioned shows that the city of Jerusalem that comes from heaven is the symbol of a new heaven and a new earth; a new world which is good and where all will be happy satisfying their needs and be among the living with their names in the Book of Life. Hence, life is connected not only to a person, but also to the house, the city, the world, and the universe.

The perimeter 12 represents the 12 gates [3 on each side] that surround the area 9. This is the first indication that 12 is external and 9 is internal. The city of the book of Revelation has 12 gates. This indication is related to space.

The second indication that 9 is internal and 12 is external is related to time. A human being spends in general 9 months within the maternal womb and then takes one of the 12 gates of the year [a month] to be born in the outer world.

Third, the 9-shaped spermatozoon is internal comparing to the ovule. The central nervous system also has that shape as does the fetus in the womb, a person in the environment, a human in the universe, the microcosm in the macrocosm.

The numbers 12 and 9 represent the external and the internal parts of a functional structure or unit. It is almost certain that more information on how a human being is internally connected to 9 and externally to 12 will be furnished by research. For example Samael Aun Weor's report that the physical body has 12 gates is worth investigating.

This analysis also offers the opportunity to connect with the others uses of 12 in the Bible particularly with the 12 tribes of ancient Israel. Since 'Israel' means 'victorious', it goes beyond the historical people of Israel and encompasses the entire world or the whole of humanity bringing one back to the true meaning of the city of Jerusalem in the Book of Revelation and the 144.000 as explained above. There is also a connection with the 12 signs of the zodiac as taught in astrotheology.

The number 3 is a structural and functional unit of 12 and 9. These three numbers are interconnected in a fundamental way. Indeed, $12 = 9 + 3 = 3 + 3+3+ 3/ 1 + 2 = 3$, and $9 = 3 \times 3 = 3 + 3+3$.

The number 12 introduces the number 24 as another important divider of 144. There are 24 hours in a day of 1 day and 1 night [2x12; notice the time connection]. In the equatorial zone and at equinoxes in the inter-tropical zone [notice the space connection], the day lasts 12 hours as well as the night.

With 144, also manifest 36 and 72. Both numbers are internal because they are connected to 9by [3 + 6] and [7 + 2] and also by $36 = 9 \times 4$ and $72 = 9 \times 8$. They are also external: $36 =12 \times 3$ et $72 = 12 \times 6$.

The internal part of a circle [space] or its area is connected to both numbers presenting 10 parts of 36 degrees or 36 parts of 10 degrees and 72 parts of 5 degrees or 5 parts of 72 degrees.

The numbers 36 and 72 are internally connected to space but also to time.

Indeed 1 hour is dividable into 3600 seconds with a connection to the degrees of a circle thus establishing a space/time connection or circle/hour connection or 1 degree for 10 seconds. And 72 is connected to 2 hours or 7200 seconds.

Also a day of 24 hours is made up of 36 times 2400 seconds, 72 times 1200 seconds, and 144 times 600 seconds. A day or a night of 12 hours corresponds to 720 minutes and a day of 24 hours is 1440 minutes.

If the connection between 144 and humanity is obvious in the book of Revelation in the Bible, it is less obvious in the book of Genesis. Indeed Genesis informs that the God of the Old Testament created humanity on the 6th day and 6 times 24 hours gives 144.

Externally, $144 = 12^2$ opens the path to analyze $12^3 = 1728$, $12^4 = 20736$, $12^5 = 248832$, $12^6 = 2.985.984$, $12^7 = 35.831.808$, $12^8 = 429.981.696$, $12^9 = 5.159.780.532$ etc…If geometry shows that 12 is external and 9 internal, from 144, the numbers in the form 12^x …show they are inner expressions of 9 directly through the addition of their elements while being the outer expressions of 12.

It is interesting to look more closely at 12^9 because it is under the form of the external empowered by the internal. That many people on earth are making fast spiritual progress in an era during which human population has reached the $12^9 = 5.159.780.532$ seems not to be a coincidence.

Resuming with the analysis of the different versions of resurrection, the Unificationist one this time, one must say that it seems to be correct except for the part on the return of spirits which requires confirmation and except the Messiah part. A detailed understanding of the term Messiah with the analysis of several biblical passages has been offered in *Abode of Divinities*.

In brief, historically, 'messiah' meant an anointed person, king, prophet, or priest who was in position to save or help.

In contemporary society as well, anybody can save and be a messiah having received the spirit or reason or wisdom or knowledge from God. It is possible that Unificationists have been misled by Christians who in turn were misled by Paul. A study of Paul's theology reveals deep inconsistencies and misunderstandings about Jesus. The way some of the aspects of the work and sayings of Jesus have been reported in the Gospels can also mislead.

Seeker's thesis when he was graduating from seminary was on those inconsistencies, misunderstandings, and misleading passages of Paul and the New Testament. A small number of his findings appeared in *Abode of Divinities* for clarity purposes. Others, not all, are being displayed in the present volume as the need arises.

Now, how can one prove [*fourth argument*] that the theory of resurrection is at least as just and moral as the theory of reincarnation? The basis for reincarnation is that people are given additional opportunities to improve themselves and reach perfection. This gives ascendancy to reincarnation over the formulation of resurrection which stipulates that levels of spirituality reached on earth are fixed for eternity and that some people will eternally burn in hell while others will rejoice forever in heaven.

However, in the Bible, 1 Peter 3: 18-20 demonstrates that it is possible for evil spirits to improve their nature and condition. Emanuel Swedenborg also mentioned cases of divine intervention in hell.

If the situation of the dead can improve as suggested by 1 Peter 3: 18-21; resurrection is at least as just and moral as reincarnation is. Resurrection is even a better theory because people immediately answer for their actions and in a conscious way. Conversely, in the reincarnation theory, people are not even sure when they are paying for something that they could have done in a very distant past. This smells irresponsibility and is certainly not the best way to learn a lesson.

Internal nature of animals, plants, mineral, and of the particles of quantum physics; meaning of pantheism

In the writings of the major thinkers summarized briefly in the first chapter, it is clear that to Professor Bikhu Parekh, animals have some properties in common with humans. Those common properties for Peter Hacker and several other thinkers are rudimentary thoughts, emotions, will, and Self-consciousness. These are characteristics of the animal soul. Therefore Seeker's opinion is that animals have rudimentary souls or minds.

The hardware software analogy confirms that the animal soul or animal mind is less sophisticated a software comparing to the human soul or mind. Peter Hacker rightly pointed out that the fundamental differences between the human soul and the animal soul is that the advanced human notions of reason and self-consciousness confers to human beings the ability of the knowledge of good and evil and also gives them moral and legal status to which animals cannot pretend.

Hermes Trismegistus[25] in contrary to the Theosophists of Temple of the People and the Rosicrucians of the AMORC supported the theory of transmigration according to which depending on the conditions, animal souls can reincarnate in human bodies and inversely.

Divine Humanism so far has disagreed with reincarnation. It neither accepts transmigration as a valid theory. However, its disagreement is not based on the fact that humans are spiritual beings as affirmed in Rosicrucian and theosophical thought.

---

[25] Clement Salaman and Hermes, *The Way of Hermes: Translations of The Corpus Hermeticum and the Definitions of Hermes Trismegistus to Asclepius* (Rochester, VT: Inner Traditions, 2000), p 47.

Seeker thinks that the idea of animals having spirits and souls is philosophically accurate as the next lines will show. He does not accept the theory of transmigration because he has disagreed at a supra level with reincarnation. He finds transmigration even less defendable and thinks that pantheism should not be described in such manner.

It is obvious that animals have souls. But do they also have spirits? Are the animal soul and spirit immortal like the human's?

Animals have physical bodies. They also have rudimentary souls or minds with which the souls or minds of human beings interact. If humans have spiritual bodies that live in the spirit world after the shedding of the physical body, it is not incongruous to think that animals too have spiritual bodies which interact with human spirits in the spirit world. Consequently the argument for the existence of the animal spirit is both logical [with sense] and teleological [with purpose].

Seeker thinks that an animal has a spiritual body which also serves as hardware for the soul or mind as its physical body does. The major argument that remains missing to totally validate his opinion is the experiential or the empirical one: a direct spiritual observation of the animal spirit knowing that several spiritual schools such as that of the Native Americans claim to have observed it. Spiritual research should help make that observation a reality to all.

Before this happens, one can add more philosophical and theological proofs. The fundamental difference between the human and the animal is not that the first is spiritual being and the second is not. That difference dwells in the transformative power of the soul or mind of a human being which is far superior to that of the animal.

Thanks to their souls or minds, humans significantly influence their physical bodies and the physical world. The same way they are able to transmute or resurrect through an increase of power of the soul or mind which helps them reach the level of divine beings. The consequence for the human spiritual body is that it develops harmoniously, beautifully, and powerfully. That is the reason behind the teaching that spiritually advanced human beings have glorious, luminous, and impressive spiritual bodies as demonstrated by Jesus when he transfigured.

Like animals, plants and minerals have more and more primitive physical bodies, spiritual bodies, and souls or minds. The soul is the program, the software which deeply impacts the development of the two kinds of body. The programs or souls according to which plants develop also comes from God. This applies to minerals too.

Seeker's idea of pantheism is that all beings have bodies or hardware [physical and spiritual] which interact with one another; and souls or minds or programs or softwares which also interact with one another. The soul of a being belonging to a realm can affect the souls, spirits, and bodies of beings of the same or a different realm.

Similarly, bodies too impact the souls. Seeker's pantheistic idea is a universal, ontological [existential], and teleological [purposeful] community of beings of various realms [human, animal, vegetal, mineral, quantum, angelic, Divine] in God. The term 'Divine' here refers to God the Superconsciousness or Supraconsciousness [see Samael Aun Weor] or the Universal Mind or Universal Soul. The phrase '*in God*' means '*in the larger definition of God*' which includes the Mind or Soul, other beings, Energies, and Matter.

The question of twins

The question of twins can appear difficult; however it is a simple one. Several categories of twins exist philosophically. Twins are physical bodies and/or spiritual bodies and/or souls that look alike. They can manifest during the same period and place or belong to different times and places.

For example a person born in ancient Greece can have the external appearance of an American and two people from different parents in different countries can have similar mind sets. Also two twins born from the same parents have different souls as evidenced in their tastes and choices. In some cases, these souls too have a lot in common.

Heredity, culture, and human nature

Heredity and culture both determine and are determined by human beings. Both are parts of their nature. Culture is a form of heredity and heredity is a form of culture. So, in the broadest sense madness, evil, and diseases are natural. In other words, they are part of the possible expressions of human nature. The fundamental question is what nature human beings want to express? *Not everything doable is worth doing.*

When reason is put to contribution, it determines that humans want to express their nature in a way that leads to harmony and happiness. This excludes madness, evil, and diseases. Consequently human nature is *fundamentally* reason or truth, love, goodness, health, and happiness.

Culture and heredity are long or short range more or less controllable systems or instruments which fashion and are fashioned by human nature; in the fundamental sense as well as in the broad way.

Astrology, prophecy, predestination, destiny, determinism, non-determinism, and the unnecessary character of pain

Predestination, destiny, prophecy, and astrology are concepts that are used by various scriptures, religions, spiritual schools, and philosophies to describe the fact that some existing factors [laws, events, and beings] impacts the lives of humanity on earth.

For example Clement Salaman in *The Way of Hermes* reports that to Hermes Trismegistus and his disciples, *astrology is based on the concept that stars are guided by spiritual or energy beings of the category of angels who influence the nature [soul education and body constitution] of humans on earth according to their birth times.*

These birth times correspond to period of influence or position or visibility of particular stars. In addition the place of birth also has an astrological importance because it intervenes in determining the ascendant sign. *Daniel 10: 20-21 in the Bible clearly shows that some angels are assigned to particular regions.* Astrology is logical and several astrological predictions and descriptions have been proven correct. This is evidence that astrology is not an empty theory.

However, Hermes himself acknowledged that humans are ruled by the stars or guided by angels only when their individual minds are not powerful enough to do so in a world in which many elements are useful but can harm if misunderstood and/or misused.

God, Angels, animals, plants, minerals and also particles of quantum physics temporarily serve as the guides of mankind from which it learns lessons. This is *functional determinism or functional predeterminism* in its broadest meaning. *Structural predeterminism* is explained by the concept of ideological or soul preformationism.

Having known how angels, animals, and the other classes of beings function and influence, a person must become free from those influences particularly from the angelic influence and be guided uniquely by God [with infinite knowledge] to freely and personally make life choices. This is *restricted or intrinsic determinism* which introduces the notion of *non-determinism* and the high exercise of free will.

If angels assigned to different places can fight one another, as described in the passage of the book of Daniel mentioned above, human beings must not replicate those fights on earth under the influence of the spirits. Humans must know what is good for them and avoid fights, wars, and the violation of others' right. As Paul affirms in Ephesians 3: 10 and as the story of Adam in the Qur'an shows, humans can and should teach angels.

Some beings can stop determining a person's future at a moment or another. However, they can remain in association with the person for the purpose of life enjoyment or love which has various aspects [see chapter 7]. So, freeing oneself from negative angelic influence is not a conflict with angelic spirits. It is a way of helping them solve their own problems.

A human with such a powerful mind can impact the lives of others with a lot of benefits, time saving, and pain reduction. Pain is not necessary for people to learn lessons as Sylvia Browne seems to suggest saying that when times are good, people do not learn much[26].

The only pain necessary is the pain during physical effort like in sport or the pain through study. However, even those pains can be avoided if humans develop their minds, philosophies, theologies, morals, and sciences. People suffer not because it is necessary but because the actual stage of development of mankind is still deficient.

When a human society has the accounts of the lives, deeds, and sayings of advanced human beings available, the power of astrology and pain diminishes. The situation is even better when living examples of powerful and good minds exist in the midst of society.

Definition of a human being

Based on the ideas developed so far, it can be said that a human being is an entity made of a soul, a spiritual body or spirit, and a physical body which have each their structures and functions as briefly presented.

---

[26] Sylvia Browne and Lindsay Harrison, *Phenomenon: Everything You Need to Know About the Paranormal* (New York: Dutton, 2005), 60-3.

The soul is the most important of these three elements which can all be influenced by or determine culture, heredity, astrology, laws, and various beings. Other names for the soul are mind, psyche, and ego. The soul's most important resource is reason. Reason determines laws, morality, dignity, love; as well as individual and social harmony and happiness. The human soul, spirit, and physical body can be masculine or feminine.

Chapter 5

On the origin of humanity

ONE of the saddest things on the surface of the earth is the fact that human beings in general do not know where they come from. Religious and spiritual communities accept that humans are a creation of God while secular communities reject this idea and think that humanity is the product of a random evolutionary process. Still others, not knowing who to believe, simply choose to live their lives without troubling themselves with this question.

No matter what position people take, the sad observation is that no one has been able to produce a proof of the origin of humans other than theology or philosophy or speculation. Though physical science claims to know the answer, its archeological discoveries which affirm that humanity is a species that descends from monkeys are inconclusive. These discoveries also make it difficult to accept that the first man was created during the night before Sunday October 23, 4004 B.C.E. as Archbishop James Ussher [1581-1656] declared.

In front of such confusion, the best attitude is first to assess the arguments of both religious and secular philosophers and then to foster research physically and spiritually.

Basically the strongest argument of creationists so far is the design argument which stipulates that a world with synergistic laws, structures, and functions could not have been the result of randomness but a creation that emerged because of the intelligence, the will, and the love of an Original Being called God. This argument constitutes at the same time, the Tendon of Achilles, the weak point, of the theory of evolution which states that the appearance of humanity on earth is pure coincidence.

Inversely, the strongest argument of evolutionists is that humanity could not have been created just in one day by God. This argument is strengthened by archeological discoveries and by the fact that even when a picture of the world is taken at an instant t, some beings appear superior and more advanced than others. The weak point of the religious and spiritual argument is that in contrary to secular philosophy, it has no material evidence to present and has various and conflicting versions.

As time passes, voices emerge trying to reconcile the two kinds of arguments. The Intelligent Design Creationism (IDC) is one of the movements which have proceeded to this integration. It states that God has created all beings using an evolutionary process.

In the book, *Abode of divinities*, Seeker has presented a series of arguments which support the idea that God is the origin of humanity. The God he talked about is not the nebulous God whose nature changes from a religious philosophy to another, but a logical and experiential God whose trail also appears here and there in scriptures. To him, the polemic about the question of the origin of humans cannot decrease significantly if the nature of God is not clear.

The strongest logical argument of Seeker apart from The Intelligence behind the organized world is a counter proposal to the idea of secular philosophy that the material universe is God at best and that there is no God as described in religious and spiritual scriptures. According to this counter argument, the Universal Body is the origin of the physical body of a human and the Universal Soul or Universal Mind is the origin of the human soul or mind.

One cannot accept the existence of mind in matter organized as a being called human and deny the existence of a Mind in the entire Universe. Denying God is equivalent to denying one's own mind or soul. However the proof of the existence of the Universal Mind needs to be produced. Since the Universal Mind is a mind, which is not the sum of all human minds as some affirm, it cannot be analyzed or dealt with as a mere thing in the laboratories or offices of physical science.

Respect and love are essential parts of human interactions because they have minds. That is why the religious approach is different. Despite the problems of the religious and spiritual schools, their attitude toward God is more reasonable and is more able to lead to the discovery or a better knowledge of the Universal Mind.

The third strongest logical argument for God comes from the art of research. In *Abode of Divinities*, Seeker has explained how arguments, experiences, or observations have led a scientist such as Wilhelm C. Röentgen to discover X-rays at the end of the 19th century. He has argued that the discovery of the X-rays only at the dawn of the 20th century does not mean that X-rays did not exist since millennia.

Similarly, he thinks God will come to be known more and more precisely especially when humanity has precious tools and methodologies for investigation represented by the body of religious and spiritual scriptures whether they have been made public or not.

Seeker's strongest scriptural argument is that the idea of the Universal Mind is not new and that religious and spiritual people such as Hermes Trismegistus, Moses, Jesus, and the author of the New Testament verse of 1 Timothy 6: 16 had laid the foundations for a consensus on God since ancient times.

From the experiential point of view, Seeker has been able to experience the Holy Spirit of God and other spiritual phenomena which are not the product of delusion, but authentic experiences. These things that Seeker has personally perceived and lived are not described in any document of physical science but rather in religious texts such as those of Hinduism, Buddhism, and Yoga. In contrary to Hinduism, Buddhism rejects the idea of God, but both religions admit the existence of supernatural or spiritual beings.

To Seeker, if spiritual experiences described in religious text are being confirmed in his own life, there is no reason he would prefer the evolution theory over religious philosophy. There is no reason he would doubt that there is a God especially when he remembers all the arguments he has developed. To him, the spiritual teaching that God reveals him/herself gradually is correct.

He thinks that he is on the path that will give him all evidences needed about God. So, his decision is to pursue spiritual and physical research and the application of spiritual and physical science. He is convinced that the day will come when humanity would be able to have a more direct relationship with God, mind to Mind and heart to Heart.

Some like himself are already in contact with the Spirit or Energy of God or Holy Spirit; a presence that he can feel everyday even in his physical body and which does many of the things religion and spirituality say it does. Seeker thinks that his experiences are similar to Newton's observation of the falling objects which drove him to formulate the law of gravity.

So, the argument from experience reinforces the logical argument from research. *That both Wilhelm Röentgen and Isaac Newton were spiritual researchers who admitted the existence of God has not been emphasized enough.*

Whether there are intermediary extraterrestrial intelligent beings or angels from whom and/or by whom humanity is created as the Babylonian creation myth and scholars such as Erich Von Daniken suggest is a question that archeology, history, astronomy, spiritual science, and research can help answer.

The existence of extraterrestrial intelligent beings such as the Annunaki who are said for example by Zecharia Sitchin to have come from the planet Nibiru is not in contradiction with the existence of angels nor with that of a Supreme Creator God, the Universal Mind. However, the case requires a thorough investigation which could prove the Sumerian stories deciphered by Sitchin right or wrong.

What is certain is that all beings including humans are creations of the All Pervading God whose Energy is the Holy Spirit. Logically and scripturally it is acceptable that angels [including the God of the Old Testament], electrons, atoms, planets, molecules, plants, and animals are necessary for the existence and survival of humans. So, one could be sure that the *"how"* of the creation of mankind includes the anterior creation of those beings.

It is when the process of creation is further explained that contradicting ideas start to appear. This is when the argument for the existence of pre-adamic humans comes up. It is easy to accept that the biblical Cain could have married one of his sisters and that his building of a city could have taken several decades or centuries thereby avoiding to agree with the existence of any pre-adamic human being.

The most serious problem that 'Adam and Eve being the first human ancestors' faces in the Bible itself come from Genesis 4: 14-15 where Cain told the God of the Old Testament about his fear to be killed by *'anybody'* while no human apart from Adam, Eve, and Cain was supposed to be on earth at that time.

Two different hypotheses can explain that passage. One is in favor of the account that Adam was the first human and the second is not.

To stick with the adamic view, one can argue that the 'anybody' that Cain talked about was an angel whether fallen or not.

Indeed contacts with angels were more frequent in the old biblical times. Angels impacted humans physically in the story of Lot in which they displayed a strength able to pull Lot back in his house when he was about to be molested by some people in Sodom [Genesis 19: 10]. An angel broke Jacobs' hip [Genesis 32: 25]; a destroyer of the God of the Old Testament killed all the first born of Egypt [Exodus 12: 23], and the angel of that God killed 185000 people of the Assyrian army who was fighting King Hezekiah in one night [2Kings 19: 35]. So if Cain feared to be killed by an angel, his fear would be scripturally and logically grounded.

The pre-adamic view would prevail only if the 'anybody' he mentioned was actually any other human being that the Bible does not introduce. However archeology allows some to find such people. The problem with this is the use of non-biblical argument to give a different meaning to a biblical story which is not illogical in its own context.

However, since no human living today was there when Adam was created and since the probability that Cain could be talking about other humans is not 0%, the best attitude is to consider that Cain was most probably talking about angels and to remain open to any revelation that can mention pre-adamic humans. This means giving the credit of coherence to the Bible in this matter while pursuing research especially the spiritual one to confirm or not that there was no human before Adam or at the same time he was created.

Part II

DIVINE HUMANISM FOR THE ESTABLISHMENT OF THE HAPPIEST SOCIETY

Chapter 6

Secular Humanism

 long time ago, human beings have understood the necessity of a philosophy on which to base their individual and social lives. Originally, that philosophy was a set of laws most of the time of religious nature. The Code of Hammurabi, the laws of ancient Egypt, those of ancient India, those of ancient China, and the Ten Commandments and secondary laws of ancient Israel are some of the oldest laws or philosophies known. Most of these philosophies in their highest aspects were encoded in symbolic languages accessible to a few initiates.

As time passed, Greek thinkers rose to the climax of human thought going beyond symbolism and offering life guiding rules that were more accessible to the common person. Prominent among those thinkers were Pythagoras, Socrates, Aristotle, and Plato. These new philosophers traveled a lot, studied various disciplines of physical and spiritual science, and gathered experiences for long years from their country and from abroad. Their ideas went beyond religious symbolism and mythology and challenged these traditional ways of thinking.

From that period, the world would witness the emergence of various philosophies especially in Asia and Europe. However, no matter how insightful the philosophies were, humanity always continued to search for better ones in order to solve problems such war and diseases; and assure a brighter life. Religious philosophy and religious humanism continued their development until the rise of secular humanism around the 14th century C.E.

Secular humanism like religious or spiritual humanism also seeks human happiness. However, the core of this new way to care about human kind and the world shifted from God and gods to values determined solely by human reason, more precisely by the reasons of some remarkable thinkers.

Before the introduction to Seeker's Divine Humanism in the next chapter, it is important to take a look at the definition, the history, and some of the major actors and ideas of secular humanism.

Definition of secular humanism

One of the most precise definitions of humanism is given by the *Encyclopedia Britannica* as followed: '*An attitude of mind attaching prime importance to human beings and human values, often regarded as the central theme of Renaissance civilization.*' This definition confirms that humanism is a system of ideas elaborated by human reason starting from around the 14th century C.E. though the term 'humanism' was coined only in early 19th century according to Jeaneane Fowler[27].

As mentioned by the *Encyclopedia Americana*, in humanism, the highest authority for the management of human affairs is human reason and not an external authority. Hence, it is clear that humanism was a philosophy developed in reaction to religious or spiritual philosophy and their divinities. That is why it is also called secular humanism.

Humanistic values are secularity, liberty, tolerance, method, and education.

According to both encyclopedias, the humanist philosophy of the Renaissance began with Petrarch in Italy and spread to all Western Europe. August Comte [1798-1857] made a remarkable contribution to secular humanism and established a non-theistic religion with a liturgy, sacraments, priests, and so forth.

---

[27]Jeaneane D. Fowler, *Humanism: Beliefs and Practices* (Brighton [England]: Sussex Academic Press, 1999), 12.

Beliefs and practices of secular humanism according to Jeaneane Fowler

Jeaneane Fowler's book offers great details concerning humanistic philosophy. According to her report, secular humanism rejects the notion of life after death, treats immortality as a myth, and considers a person who puts all his/her expectations into the afterlife as only living a half of a life[28].

Humanism wants to develop the considerable collective and individual innate abilities of humans to enrich the life of each person, family, society, and the world[29]. It wants a positive society in which people act, react, interact, and transact with care, sensitivity, informed knowledge, moderation, and constructive skill.

Concerning human nature, the view of secular humanism is monistic [body] instead of dualistic [mind-body] or triadic [mind-spirit-body]. Mind and body are the result generated by the interaction between genetic inheritances on the one hand and the physical and social environment on the other. To the secular humanist, the soul or mind does not exist because "*It is not something separate from what goes on in the brain and is wholly dependable on the senses.*"

Fowler asserts that when the senses of sight, taste, smell, touch, and hearing are removed, a person can no longer think. Thinking to her is a function of the brain and there is nothing beyond the natural body.

Ego is the most fundamental constituent of human nature according to humanism. It is neither to be denied nor to be considered the subject of divine will. The humanistic *ego* is the part of the psyche which is responsible

---

[28]Fowler, *Humanism: Beliefs and Practices*, 37-8.
[29]Ibid., 43.

of the reactions of an individual. Consequently, egoism is ok while self-denial and self-humility are not.

Ego is the motor of progress. Living without ego is impossible. Human beings do not have but *are* passions and those who chose not to *be* their passions become different from themselves. To Fowler, genes determine emotions.

Other values of humanism according to her are self-direction, self-worth, self-dignity, self-respect, self-assertion, and self-control combined with the philosophy of *'do to others as you would have them do to you.'* This does not mean that a person has to be under the authority of God, an institution, the government, tradition, and so forth. People should cooperate with each other to set legal and social rules.

Fowler's opinion concerning spirituality is that it should not be denied but interpreted in a secular way. Spirituality to her is close to Robert Ashby's definition which describes the concept as *'moments of being composed of emotion, imagination, and memory which somehow take people beyond everyday awareness.'* However, the phrase *'peak experiences'* of the psychologist Abraham Maslow, she says, defines better what spirituality is.

Peak experiences are elements of natural [not supernatural] life and should not be monopolized by religious people, adds Fowler. Religion then becomes a state of mind achievable in almost any activity of life.

To secular humanists, there is no God, no heaven, no life beyond death, no angels, and no miracles. Human happiness depends on people's action, not on the "grace" of some being that intervenes in their lives. There is no unanimous concept of God and the order of the universe does not necessarily mean that there is an organizer. Additionally, the so called order in the universe has not been demonstrated. Furthermore, there are many anomalies, illogicalities, and partial historic truths in the Bible and the Qur'an for example.

Humanists believe a woman has the right to proceed to an abortion if for any reason she does not desire her child or when circumstances are not favorable. They also advocate the right for people to use contraception, to be gay or lesbian, and to request euthanasia.

In the matter of the equality of sexes, Fowler declares that men and women are not equal but complementary. To her, their genes, their psychological histories, their possibilities for work, and their interpretations of life experiences are different but this should not justify discrimination against women. She believes like Polly Toynbee that what matters is not what *nature has given* men and women but what they choose to do about it.

Fowler disagrees with the way in which the myth of creation in the book of Genesis portrays Eve as inferior to Adam even before she ate the apple reaching for knowledge. Fowler does not appreciate the punishment of Eve which was pain during childbirth and submission to Adam.

Equality to Fowler and humanists resides in common good which includes people of various skills, abilities, natures, and personalities. This implies discrimination which is admissible when negatively directed toward criminals or when positively oriented toward excluded social categories such as the *Dalits* in India.

The secular humanist's social vision is a world in which good life is available for all. Good life in this case means freedom, democracy, peace, sound health, satisfying work, education, prosperity, creativity, fulfillment, cultural enjoyment, and sufficient recreation.

Secular humanists believe in the concept of *utilitarianism* according to which every person should participate in the well-being of the community without jeopardizing his/her own satisfaction: the greatest happiness for the greatest number now and in the times to come. The individual gives to society and society gives to the individual. To Fowler, humanism does not promote egoistic materialism for a minority.

Secular humanists also believe that human beings can change their nature following the assertion that one is born with brain but acquires mind. Fowler affirms that all human beings have the tendency to be successful in life when they have a minimum of material goods and when subtle or evident oppression is absent.

Resuming with the notion of good life, Fowler borrows Bertrand Russell's idea that life is inspired by love and guided by knowledge. Love implies integrity, sincerity, good will, kindness, compassion, trust, justice, peace, tolerance, fairness and so forth. The concept of good life is not utopian to the extent to believe in the perfection of human beings. Every character though full of potential possible evolutions has its limitations. The good life concept cannot be reduced to hedonism because of its altruism.

Secular humanism offers neither certitudes nor precise guidance to each person. Rather it encourages people to seek their own ways remembering that the truth of being human lies in its nuances. Its ethics is based on rationalism and reason.

The power of secular humanism as explained by Paul Kurtz

Another eminent advocate of secular humanism is the Professor Emeritus of Philosophy Paul Kurtz. Kurtz is considered by many as the father of secular humanism. Consequently, his ideas should not be neglected in an attempt to understand secular humanism.

In *Embracing the Power of Humanism*, Kurtz asks and answers the fundamental question of the meaning of life in absence of a belief in God, in case of the denial of the immortality of soul, and in a situation of non-recognition of a purpose immanent in nature[30].

---

[30] Paul Kurtz, *Embracing the Power of Humanism* (Lanham, Md: Rowman& Littlefield Publishers, 2000), 17-23.

Kurtz cannot see a consistency in the position of the religious believer who accepts the dependence of humanity on an all-powerful God and the existence of evil at the same time. He cannot admit that humans be the slaves of God whom they praise and implore for their every day's food and to gain immortality. He thinks that there is no real freedom if humans cannot disobey God without punishment. Why should God condemn a person for satisfying the natural penchants that he himself designed as elements of human nature? He asks.

Paul Kurtz neither accepts the punishment of innocent children with cancer for the sins of their parents. To him, the responsibility of humanity to find a cure for cancer means that God is in fact limited in power and is a finite being that is accordingly unworthy of worship.

Kurtz rejects the theist's fear of barbarism and exploitation of man by man in the absence of God on the ground that there is no logical connection between the fatherhood of God and the brotherhood of men and on the observation that the Church has supported the establishment of unequal societies in the past with classes and privileges for some.

He continues his illustration with the numerous wars and massacres perpetrated by theists of various religions and adds, like Fowler, the fact that concerns for the afterlife do not enable to fully live the earthly life. Kurtz then cites the names of thinkers such as Spinoza, Kant, and Sartre who developed a great sense of morality without being religious.

Trying to answer another fundamental question, whether life is worth living or not, Kurtz declares that humanists do not make universal claims like theists and that what is obvious to them is that the majority of humanity under normal conditions finds life valuable[31]. Since there is no eternal life, protection against injury and death is essential.

---

[31] Kurtz, *Embracing the Power of Humanism*, 23.

Kurtz acknowledges the importance of family and friendship[32]. He stresses the need for intimacy with at least one other person inside or outside marriage. He also affirms that parents should attempt to do their best for their children while giving them the freedom to choose whoever they want to become according to their unique personalities. Parental investment in a child should become limited if he/she is mean, careless, or good-for-nothing.

Concerning friendship, Paul Kurtz thinks that people are limited in the number of true friends they can have. To him, friends do not build barriers but eliminate them.

Friendship he says implies amicability, conviviality, congeniality, cordiality, harmony, concern for the other, caring, honesty, sincerity, trust, faithfulness, equality, and love in spite of fault. A friend to Kurtz can be of the same or the opposite sex.

---

[32]Kurtz, *Embracing the Power of Humanism*, 113-120.

Chapter 7

Divine Humanism

Religious and spiritual humanisms

LIKE secular humanism, *religious* humanism places human beings at the center of its attention. The difference resides in the values that sustain this care. While secular humanism is founded solely on non-religious reasons and love, religious humanism is based principally on religious values such as God and/ or gods, faith, rituals, and so on; and secondarily on "human" reason.

Indeed, most religious traditions and doctrines are often unquestionable and are to be followed while the believer can use his/her reason for secondary matters; most of the time to put the tradition in application, to introduce it to other people thereby contributing to its glory. From time to time a theologian or two emerge and use "reason" to question core dogmas.

When they come to strongly disagree with some of them, this opens the way for the emergence of other movements. When the new movement still relies a lot on dogma and assumptions and not enough on evidences, the new movement is called a new religion which in turn is challenged by a new generation of theologians.

Counting the situations of religious humanism in action is almost an impossible task because the examples are numerous. The history of Christianity alone is full of various movements organized around specific human needs even from the time of the first Christian community [Acts 2: 45].

The world is well aware of the many contributions of people like Jesus, Mother Theresa, and so forth. It is also well known that the forefathers who laid the foundations of the American nation were religious and that the health care system of the country was initiated by religious organizations.

Despite the truthfulness of some of the objections of secular humanism to religion, religious people have also contributed a lot to the well-being of mankind. One can argue that this is understandable because religion has dominated human history for a very long period. This would be a receivable argument especially when one knows that most important scientists, philosophers, and rulers before and even after the Renaissance have had a religion of some sort.

Secular humanism should try to find out why *religious reason* has prevailed over *secular reason* for so long before the renaissance and why also today a great majority of humankind remains religious disagreeing with secularism. But, secular humanism can offer two serious replies.

A first counter argument dwells in the theory of evolution which considers the secular mind as a developed mind comparing to the religious mind which accepts "strange" and unverified concepts. A second counter argument for secular humanism is the fact that in Europe, the "Old Continent;" religious people no longer represent the majority of the population. Most European countries though they acknowledge and respect religion, rather base their policies on secular reason which is the fundamental value of secular humanism.

Nevertheless, these two counter arguments are not absolute because the theory of evolution is not correct as Seeker has shown in *Abode of Divinities*.

Additionally, secular reason is not really an improvement of the religious reason because religious reason is rather an immature and biased version of *spiritual reason* which is better than secularism.

Paul, though he can be corrected for the inaccuracy of many of his affirmations should nevertheless be credited for finding out that there is a kind or reason which operates in spiritual people [1 Corinthians 2: 6-7, and 13-15].

In the first two verses of the scriptural passage just cited, he distinguishes the mature believer from the immature one. To him, mature believers understand and possess wisdom or reason; not the ordinary human reason but a human reason improved with the knowledge of spiritual reality and God. Seeker, like others, calls this second kind of believers, '*knowers*'.

Spiritual reason is a reason that interprets spiritual reality better than religious reason. Religious reason has less spiritual experiences the comprehension of which is also limited. So in terms of comparison, secular humanism uses reason better than religious humanism while the latter has the advantage not to neglect God and the spiritual. Spiritual reason is superior to both religious and secular reasons. Consequently, *spiritual* humanism is better than either religious or secular humanism.

This gives the opportunity to explain more about spiritual humanism. Spiritual humanism is marked by less dogma and a higher reason than religious humanism. Its origins can be traced back to Hermes Trismegistus and the Mysteries of ancient Egypt *and certainly beyond*. Indeed the Hermetic text of the *Poimandres* is one of the rare texts which present God in a very logical way.

Esoteric schools of spirituality such as Yoga, Rosicrucianism, Freemasonry, Theosophy, and so forth have all been influenced by this advanced spiritual reason. However, Seeker has identified a way to improve secular, religious, and spiritual humanisms which he calls *divine humanism*.

Comparison of the three traditional kinds of humanism

Types of humanism Features	Spiritual	Religious	Secular
Values and loves humans	Yes	Yes	Yes
Based on personal experiences of the manifestation of the spirit world	Yes	Often No	No
Acknowledges God	Yes	Yes	No
Admits the existence of life after death	Yes	Yes	No
Values reason	Yes	Often No	Yes
Values faith	Somehow	Yes	Somehow
Values dogma	A little	Often	No
Values scriptures	Moderately	Highly, often a particular one	A little
Highest authority	God	God	Reason
Understanding and tolerance of others	Often Yes	Somehow	Somehow
Knowledge of human nature	Advanced	limited	More or less advanced
Values material science	Yes	Somehow	Yes
Values spiritual science	Yes	Somehow	Not yet
Great importance of masters and messiahs	Often	Yes	A little
Values teaching	Yes	Yes	Yes
Can be and has been corrupted	Yes	Yes	Yes
Considers women	Yes	Yes	Yes

ascomplementary to men			
Individual freedom	Somehow advanced	limited	Too much
Values monogamous marriage	often	often	Somehow
Values lineage	Yes	Sometimes too much	Yes
Values friendship	Yes	Yes	Yes

Secular humanism compared to divine humanism

In a world in which it is hard to prove the reality of the existence of divinities [God and gods], the afterlife, and the supernatural; secular humanism does well to give a lot of attention to human beings. However this should not be a static movement that eternally rejects God and the supernatural and explains spirituality in a secular way.

The philosophy of secular humanism is so full of wisdom that it is better not to spend most of this subsection acknowledging such and such aspect. *By emphasizing here two of the elements he disagrees with, Seeker hopes that the reader would be able to categorize the rest of secular philosophy as remarkable and praiseworthy.* Other points of disagreement will emerge in the next chapters.

The first point of disagreement between Seeker's divine humanism and secular humanism is on the existence of God. His reasons figure in detail in *Abode of Divinities* and in a very condensed manner in the 4th and 5th chapters of the present volume.

His explanations hopefully have answered the objection that there is no unanimous concept of God. Identifying a concept of God acceptable to all was the main objective of *Abode of Divinities*. Unlike secular humanists, he does not accept that it is "nature" which gives things to humans for the simple reason that nature has no will and no personality.

If a will were identified in nature, it would be is what is called the Will of God. A scientist aware that physics acknowledges cases of appearance of particles in a "vacuum" according Heisenberg's uncertainty principle can see there a reason not to be quick in denying the existence of God who is said to be present everywhere unperceived by the material world and sometimes even by the spiritual or energy world.

The second point of disagreement is the question of the supernatural and life after death; in other words the immortality of the soul. Seeker has shown in the first three chapters how several ancient thinkers, religions, and esoteric movements admit those concepts as characteristic of reality.

In *Abode of Divinities* and the chapters 4 and 5, he also explained how realities previously known as supernatural have come to be called natural because of scientific advancement. He also showed how several facts still remain unexplained by physical science while they have been well described in religious and spiritual literature.

Seeker thinks that humans should not fall into linguistic traps but transcends the barrier that words can represent. What matters the most is what is *real, not its qualification as natural or supernatural.*

Divine humanism is a real holistic philosophy which recognizes spiritual phenomena and material ones for what they are and which does not force a monist understanding of life though, from a certain perspective, there is a connection between the various kinds of reality which enables monism.

However, a pure monistic philosophy is an oversimplification that would reap human beings of the possibilities to deeply investigate and understand spiritual reality. How the mind or the soul is something distinct from the brain and how it does not depend solely on the physical senses has been explained in Chapter 4.

The attempts of Robert Ashby and Abraham Maslow to secularize the term 'spirituality' are nice tries; however they have not truly succeeded.

Indeed, one could wonder what the *'beyond everyday awareness'* and *'peak experiences'* respectively of Ashby and Maslow mean.

Religion and spirituality can reply to secularity that everyday awareness is about physical reality while beyond it and peak experiences are about spiritual reality.

Moreover, the origin of the word 'spirituality' should have incited secular humanists to be more prudent in their attempt to secularize it. It comes from 'spirit' which Seeker has explained as the energy-world and energy-bodies. Therefore the true meaning of spirituality is *'conscious life and understanding of the nature and function of the energy-bodies and the energy world.'* A glimpse of that life and understanding is given by dreams but spiritual schools offer more.

Spirituality is the development of the awareness of the energy-world as physicality is the awareness of the material world. The soul or psyche or mind operates on both levels according to the development or maturation of each individual. In the first part of this work and in *Abode of Divinities*, abundant reasons for the existence of the energy-world and bodies or spiritual world and bodies were given.

Consequently Ashby and Maslow's renditions of the concept of spirituality are incomplete. Maybe with Seeker's explanations secular humanists can come to understand the meaning of spirituality for religious and spiritual people and abandon it secularization especially when research in the field is promising.

Seeker's view point on abortion, equality, sexes and genders, homosexuality, marriage, family, friendship, euthanasia, good life, politics, culture, education, peace, justice, health, worship, and so forth will appear in the next chapters.

What is divine humanism?

Divine humanism is a philosophy that acknowledges the existence of the cosmos made of the physical and the spiritual worlds created not by chance, "nature", or "evolution", but by God the All Pervading; and which encourages *humans* to become *divine* as fast as possible using their *reason* and *love* to care about *harmony* and *happiness* inthe entire cosmos.

In this definition, reason is to be understood as an attribute of the human mind, psyche, or soul which helps analyze and explain phenomena as they are experienced at the same time when it develops itself and creates phenomena of its own.

Experiences are perceived not only through the physical senses, but also through the spiritual senses. That there are senses beyond the physical ones is evidenced for example by the fact that none of the senses linked to materiality is involved in the perception of what happens in dreams and it is undeniable that dream-events are *perceived* and can be stored in consciousness and memory like physical events.

In divine humanism, humans use their reasons to agree that there are phenomena that have not yet been discovered or explained and that intermediary discoveries and explanations will lead to the finding and understanding of a more global picture of existence. *Therefore this philosophy encourages research.* Humanity needs to better understand God and spirituality and research would help in that endeavor.

In the first statement of this subsection, the love mentioned is one guided by reason and it presents various aspects according to the partner considered, whether a thing, a plant, an animal, an eventual supernatural being, a human, or God.

Divine humanism is a policy of human beings [trying to better understand the divine] for the universe. Therefore it is centered on humanity. Since it acknowledges God, this means that the center of its center is God.

Harmony means the proper relationship among all beings guided by reason and knowledge. For example if at a moment m1 a human behaves in a way b1 according to his/her highest reason and love based on available information, and if there is a better behavior b2 at a moment m2 [m2= m1+ time] based on new information; behavior b2 should replace behavior b1.

Consequently, there is an important place for creativity and progress in divine humanism which therefore is a self-renewing, self-upgrading, ever dynamic, and ever young philosophy. In this way, humans will gradually become divine beings manifesting new powers significantly superior to their previous ones.

A human is therefore the being not yet empowered philosophically and supernaturally and a *divine human* is a human with the new energetic powers managed by high reason, love, and truth or knowledge or wisdom. Divine humanism is not complete without an advanced morality or the broad and deep acquirement of virtues. Hence the divine human is more than a god who is generally super strong but lacks the additional intelligence, desire, and will to become completely virtuous or righteous.

So, the divine human is closer to God than the gods are. Here is another common element to God and humans which confirm that they are created in the likeness of God. Evil people like in Genesis 6 are not moral or virtuous or righteous, so their likeness to God is significantly impaired.

The divine human is much more than Nietzsche' superhuman who craves for domination. He/she uses personal greatness for cooperation and social happiness; not for unnecessary competition and domination. So the superhuman of Nietzsche needs to learn a lot from Rousseau's compassionate human to come close to the divine human.

The divine human is different from the human god of Jainism in the sense that he/she has a set of logical and scriptural proofs that allows him/her to affirm the existence of the Supreme Universal Mind and or the Essential All Pervading God. The divine human can also be a Jain god or superhuman seriously researching the Supreme Being unable to be satisfied with the idea that powerful beings such as human gods came out of nowhere or do not have a cause or origin.

One needs to return on everything said to prove the existence of God to check again if it makes sense or not. So, the seeker should not mind reading several times the book *Abode of Divinities* as well as the first part of the present work. The topic of God is so fundamental that tiredness or discouragement should stay far away from its Study. It is advisable to consider the whole argumentation and not just parts. The God being discussed is said to be the Universal Mind, so one cannot comprehend Him-Her without the individual mind, wisdom, reason, logic, philosophy, or theology.

Now a few words should be written about the superhuman of Samael Aun Weor [1917-1977]. Aun Weor is famous for creating the Universal Christian Gnostic Movement and for writing several books based on a teaching called 'Gnosis' or 'knowledge'. He has been one of the most prominent modern successors of ancient Gnostics.

From a quick assessment he made of him, Seeker consider Aun Weor as a important Gnostic teacher whose teaching is among the most elaborated of Gnosticism. Seeker places Aun Weor's ideas in three categories: those which require scientific confirmation, those he agrees with, and those he disagrees with.

Aun Weor's superhuman is a man *born again* thanks to sexual magic or Arcanum AZF or Perfect Matrimony taught by Jesus in John 3: 1-21[33]. The word 'magic' here and in serious works is often synonymous of 'spiritual science.' Consequently it should not make the reader feel uncomfortable.

According to Aun Weor, Perfect Matrimony is a science in which the masculine semen is not spilled during sexual intercourse allowing the conservation of the tremendous sexual energy generated to be used to

---

[33]SamaelAunWeor, *The Perfect Matrimony* (Australia: The Gnostic Movement, 1998).

quickly accomplish the desires expressed in prayer and to develop to the angelic state.

In his writings, Aun Weor states that people of the now "lost" continent of Lemuria living in the Garden of Eden avoided sexual orgasm and ejaculation and knew how to create a child with only one spermatozoon living the masculine body to fecundate one ovum.

Nature obeyed humanity at that time and women gave birth without pain, he adds. The command to be fruitful in Genesis 1: 28 in Aun Weor's mind means to transmute and sublimate the sexual energy in order to grow spiritually.

To this 20th century Gnostic thinker, the original sin of the first parents was the crime of spilling the semen; an act which orients human development toward a demonic state instead of an angelic one. Hence, Aun Weor was convinced that this is the origin of angels and demons. To him, this is how the biblical sons of God and sons of men are created.

Though he declares that love is the best religion available to the human race, Aun Weor also affirms that the superhuman is not a product of evolution but that of a tremendous revolution of consciousness.

He also expresses the idea that *the awakening of internal faculties should parallel a cultural, intellectual,* and spiritual development because for example *a clairvoyant needs logical thought, a powerful sense of analysis, and exact concepts to avoid causing divorce, assassination, adultery, theft, etc…*

What assessment can Seeker make of Aun Weor's ideas?

It is true that to see the Kingdom of God one needs to be born again as both Jesus in John 3: 3 and Aun Weor say. Since Nicodemus did not comprehend what this means, Jesus found necessary to add that the second birth is not from the maternal womb but *of* water and spirit. When a person familiar with the Bible comes across this precision given by Jesus; a remembrance of the story of the creation of the universe in Genesis 1 can occur.

According to Genesis 1: 1-2: '*In the beginning God created the heavens and the earth. The earth was formless and empty, and darkness covered the deep waters. And the Spirit of God was hovering over the waters.*' Both the spirit and the water mentioned by Jesus appear in this passage. It is possible to explain Genesis 1: 1-2 in at least two ways.

The first is 'Spirit or energy' that hovers over the 'waters or H2O in gaseous and liquid form.' The second explanation is that the spirit is the Mind of God that interacts with the waters which are primordial energy. The first explanation is more terrestrial while the second is more spiritual. Since it is the most spiritual meaning that is the most important in spiritual scriptures, one can come to better comprehend the words of Jesus in John 3.

In this passage, Jesus is telling Nicodemus that the second birth is from mind and energy; in other words from wisdom or truth and the building of a healthy spiritual or energetic body.

This is exactly what Aun Weor teaches in the *Perfect Matrimony*. The proof is his emphasis on both the revolution of consciousness or logical thinking and the need of energy.

But the problem with his teaching is that it exceedingly develops the topic of sexuality to the extent to be labeled the *Perfect Matrimony*. Aun Weor went as far as to affirm that the sexual sense is faster than thought waves. He considered the logical mind as a stumbling block for sexual sense and declared that love is the best religion available to human kind.

However, reason is the prime element in any process of creation including the second birth of a human. Reason or logic belongs to the mind or soul and it hovers over [interact with] energy for the new creation, the new human to manifest [see also Romans 12:2].

Energy no matter its quality only comes in second position. The mind thinks about how to use energy to create. Hence, all processes of energy production including the Perfect Matrimony are subordinate to wisdom or philosophy. How can one impact positively the physical body or the spiritual one if decisions have not been made in the soul?

Not only did Aun Weor underestimate the mind, he also overestimated sexual energy. Sexual energy, in reality is not all the energy that is. Equating the Holy Spirit with sexual energy displays some limitation in the knowledge and experience of the Holy Spirit as well a limitation in the anatomy and function of the spiritual body.

From scriptural descriptions, the Holy Spirit appears as a "totipotent" energy that can differentiate in any other kind of energy and perform specific functions. It looks like Aun Weor did not experience the pentecostal Holy Spirit that enters the human body through the top of the head and that he forgot or did not consider seriously the scriptural passages which mention this phenomenon.

So, there is tremendous energy out there not generated by the sexual act but freely available from God. Sexual energy is in reality one type of energy among those produced below or on earth. At this moment of human history, Seeker is not sure if sexual energy is of the same nature as the Holy Spirit because he does not yet have any scientific means to proceed to that verification in a laboratory.

What he is certain of is that there is a powerful divine energy which proves that God is alive and that everything is not limited to the sexual energy that a human couple can produce. In addition, the Holy Spirit is known to be able to cure, energize, enable prophecy, make wise, etc...

That is why Jesus summarized 'spirit and water' by 'Holy Spirit' showing Nicodemus that both the spirit of God or divine wisdom and energy can be gained through the Holy Spirit. The Holy Spirit is a "Teacher that conveys Word, Science, Logos, or Wisdom and a Comforter that cures, appeases, energizes, and loves."

Another declaration that Aun Weor made and which requires scientific investigation is that sexual energy is the best kind of energy a human couple can generate. Seeker is not that sure and even disagrees experientially.

Wisdom and Love are the two poles that grant eternal life and make a human a real image of God. Wisdom is pole + while Love is pole —. The

Holy Spirit of God feeds humans with various sorts of nutrients including Wisdom and Love from above. Humans who are designed as the image of God can also generate wisdom and love among many other things.

Human love is not limited to the sexual energy of the 7th chakras. There is a different love energy produced in other spheres such as the 4th chakra or heart chakra. Though the Greek language distinguishes four types of love: agape [unconditional love], éros [often equated with sexual desire], philía [love of friendship], and storgē [affection]; Seeker thinks that agape is an advanced stage of philía and storgē because unconditional love includes friendship and affection.

However, these Greek terms do not describe well love in the philosophy of divine humanism though they help understand it.

First, love is classifiable in two general categories: *good love and bad love*. The first is associated with divine wisdom and the second with corrupted or demonic wisdom. Details will be presented in chapter 10.

Second, good love is not whole from birth and is characterized by the growth process. So, there are *several levels of maturity of good love*.

Third, good love grows in two fundamental areas: the soul on the one hand and the bodies [physical and spiritual] on the other hand. So there are *soullove and bodily love*. The ways the soul and the bodies appreciate and feel love are different. Soul love corresponds to agape while bodily love includes but is not limited to éros as it will be explained.

Fourth, there is an interaction and mutual enrichment between the soul love and the bodily love. The soul love is elaborated guided by wisdom and is expressed through the bodies. This expression induces a reaction in the environment of the bodies whether humans, animals, nature etc…The reaction is thus transmitted to the soul which appreciates it or likes it.

Sometimes a soul does not express its love toward an element but rather registers expressed love from it and reacts. So, there is an *interaction and mutual enrichment between the soul love and the bodily love which manifests in terms of stimulating and stimulated love*.

Fifth, the kind of love just mentioned depends on the natures of the beings engaged in interaction, mutual enrichment, and reciprocal stimulation. There are proper ways to interact with, enrich, stimulate, and be stimulated by a cat, children, parents, friends, the spouse, and so on. Love takes each of these *environment-conditioned aspects* which are different one from another in the soul and the bodies.

Hence, *the soul and the body love differently in front of a human, an animal, plants, stones, children, parents, brothers, sisters, the spouse, friends, people of the same sex, people of opposite sex, unknown people, etc...* The soul directs the body not to behave toward a friend the same way it would behave toward a wife. This is a way in which people are born from spirit and water.

Coming back to the third aspect of love [soul love and bodily love], one must say that of all kinds of love relationships mentioned in the fifth aspect, only conjugal love should stimulate the sexual energetic center or 7th chakra of the spiritual body in direct and normal communication with the physical genital sphere. This is achieved through right theoretical and practical education.

Concerning the 4th chakra or heart chakra or heart energetic center, it can be tremendously stimulated based on any of the fifth aspects of love described. The rays that come out of the sacred heart of Jesus are real. Therefore it is important to deeply love all kinds of beings. Since most people have kept a good liking of the opposite sex while the other kinds of love have been impaired, falling in love today is a quick way to awaken and develop the heart energetic center.

There is a special manifestation of love channeled by the 1st or crown chakra. This love is the relationship between a human and the Cause of the Universe or God. God stimulates and is stimulated. The vehicle of expression of God's love is the Holy Spirit which can also make wiser. This is another way to be born of spirit and water; the highest way.

So, *the third aspect of love in its bodily dimension is about the awakening and development of **all** the energetic centers particularly that of the top of the head in relationship with God, the heart energetic center in relationship with all kinds of beings and the involvement of the sexual energetic center in relationship with the spouse [1st, 4th, and 7th chakras].*

The awakening and development of these three energetic centers has consequences on the soul as well as on the physical body. Seeker knows from experience that the sensations one gets from the functioning of these three energetic centers are energy related, but not exactly the same.

Samael Aun Weor seems also not to have experienced the sacred heard as well as the manifestations of the crown chakra; at least at a certain level. If he had had, he would have discovered that these two centers are astonishingly interesting, not in terms of voltage like for sexual energy but in terms joy and pleasure also called bliss.

The sexual energetic center is noisy compared to the other two which are cooler. Seeker thinks there are more wonders of the soul, spiritual body, and physical body that he will experience someday. Even at his current level, he meditates in awe about an experience which would involve the *simultaneous high functioning* of the 1st, 4th, and 7th chakras. He thinks that the best moment this can happen is when two spouses meet sexually without neglecting to let the other centers powerfully function.

According to the *Song of Songs* of the Bible, éros or sexual love should not be awakened until the time is right. The reason is proper to the well-being of the sexual act itself but also for universal communion. If the other energetic centers such as the 2nd, 3rd, 5th, and 6th chakras were also associated the communion or joy or bliss would be even more complete.

To end this analysis of Aun Weor's Perfect Matrimony, his declaration that it is a sin to spill the semen must be considered. It is possible that there is a body of knowledge which describes how sexual energy can be used for magical purposes. But at least six reasons go against several ideas he develops in *The Perfect Matrimony*.

First, animals spill the semen and this is not considered a sin. Some animals live very long though they spill the semen. Second, a physical body that plays at storing too much energy can be damaged. Third, according to the book of Ezekiel, a demon is born from the corruption of wisdom primarily. Fourth, the Holy Spirit can help people reach whatever goal they have without the need of sexual magic.

Fifth, the power of electromagnetism channeled by the blood can heal and rejuvenate too. Sixth, orgasmic pleasure is not a bad thing. It is a good thing obtained through semen spilling. The moment of orgasm is marked by such a joy and communion with the cosmos that some have suggested using it to formulate wishes or pray. Research should compare this method to the one advocated by Aun Weor.

Though his Perfect Matrimony needs serious revision, Samael Aun Weor has said several things about adultery and the sexual education of girls worth applying.

Based on the series of information available to him, Seeker uses his reason to establish the philosophy of divine humanism at the moment $m = 2012$ C.E. It is consequently clear that some of his ideas might be eternal truths already acknowledged in the past and the present while others are past ideas upgraded, and still others new ones.

It is important for God to use specific prophets and teachers from time to time to instruct human beings about the wonders of the cosmos via the wonders He-She accomplishes through those prophets and teachers. Through those signs, the masses of humanity can have a glimpse of the divine reality and work for their own deification.

These signs are like scientific evidences, manifestations, and thoughts which draw general agreement instead individual assumptions and conflicts. *This era is particularly important because God is using many as signs.* Communication means are very developed allowing every citizen of the world to be informed and make progress. *God truly wants to use this époque to speed up cosmic healing.*

Seeker is one of the signs God is using for that purpose. The details about his way to always look for and create a better existence for all will figure the next chapters. One important thing about the *divine humanism* is that it *wants all signs to get together as fast as possible for a more efficient work. Divine humanism at its current stage will be amended by others philosophers*.

The framework or blueprint of divine humanism gives the assurance that happiness for all is possible. Hence, humans will ultimately reach a point of philosophical maturity that would become the foundation for the maturity of love and its enjoyment.

Chapter 8

Education for the happiest society: generalities

Definition of education

EDUCATION, in a broad and positive sense is the process through which both the manifest and potential nature of a person are influenced by environmental factors, organized or not, so that he/she continuously acquires knowledge, skills, virtues, beauty, health, strength, love, and so forth.

So, there is a negative education in which the elements gained are contrary to those that positive education offers. Part of positive education is about the awareness of negative education, its consequences, and how to avoid them.

Environmental factors that influence education

The environmental factors in question are human society, nature, and the divine world especially God. Their influence begins even before the conception of a child. For example a spermatozoon or ovum in the body of the father or in that of the mother can be protected from a harmful genetic mutation that would have led after conception to a diseased and suffering child.

Based on human nature, education can be divided into three branches: the education *of* the physical body, the education *of* the spirit body, and the education *of* the soul. When the influential factors are considered, education also has three aspects: education *about* nature, education *about* humanity, and education *about* the supernatural and God.

Formal and informal education

The degree of organization of the influential factors enables a distinction between formal or institutionalized or official education and informal education. For the happiest society to emerge, formalized education has to continuously become broader based on its previous achievements and the contributions of informal education.

In other words people should bring to public attention the knowledge they have privately gathered to establish a social validity for them thereby improving the existing formal education. Such a process is efficient in helping future learners save time and bring public knowledge, virtues, love, etc…, to higher stages.

When knowledge is formal, it really saves an incredible amount of time because informal learning is sometimes uselessly painful and slow. Millions of people have died and continue to die without having access to vital information that could have made their lives happier or less painful and longer. This is a big waste.

When knowledge is public, it helps human beings concentrate on priorities and what is essential. Many times individuals spend time trying to figure out what others have already discovered while they could have devoted their precious time to other situations or phenomena so that humanity as a whole and every person in particular win in the end.

When education is focused on the desired outcome, one distinguishes several categories that parallel the outcomes. Hence there is biology, geology, botany, zoology, medicine, history, geography, philosophy, theology, spirituality, psychology, astronomy, chemistry, and so forth.

Education as a gradual process

Education being a process means that the individual gathers knowledge, skills, intelligence, love, beauty, etc…, progressively. The things a person needs to know are so many. That is why education feeds the person with information and practices of higher complexities after prerequisites have been assimilated.

This means that the complexity of an educational process should correspond to the level of maturity of a person and needs not to be a rigid procedure that cannot adapt to particular gifted or ungifted people. Education should at the same moment be standard [based on information on the general development of humans] and flexible enough to respond to particular needs thereby showing consideration for the concept of *multiple intelligences* which acknowledges different talents to various people at given moments.

Everything that people need to know or be is not taught in one day. Most people understand this fact when the education about physical things is considered. But when it comes to spirituality, people often tend to be impatient and want to know everything at once. This demonstrates how hungry and thirsty they are to know about the divine and spiritual matters which indeed are essential.

However, despite the eagerness to access all the information related to the soul and the spirit, there should not be confusion between speed and brusqueness. Time is required for the assimilation of the theory and practice in spiritual education too. *The problem with spiritual science is that it is absent from secular education, is either diluted or deformed in religion, and often hidden in spiritual schools.*

Problems of hidden education

Spiritual schools and spiritualists such as Manly Hall affirm that spiritual knowledge has to remain hidden because most people are immature and cannot use it for good purposes. Jesus said the same thing when he asked not to give what is holy to unholy people and not to throw pearls to "pigs" [Matthew 7:6].

Seeker acknowledges the truthfulness of these observations and recommendations. However, he thinks that more effort needs to be devoted to making the common people more mature and holy so that they too become worthy to receive amazing teachings. Hence, hidden knowledge will become public in a unified educational body.

This strategy has a double advantage. Not only does it helps considerably improve the lives of billions of humans, it also helps get rid of the disadvantages linked to the hiding of knowledge.

There are five main problems with hidden education. The first is that sometimes, knowledge is so protected that it finally disappears and is lost. Reports exist about spiritually advanced human beings who could not find worthy successors to whom they can safely entrust their knowledge which "dies" with them.

The second problem with hidden knowledge after the risk of losing precious information is the implementation of dangerous and harmful experiments. Most of physical education is public. People are often aware of dangerous situations when those situations are created. So there are laws, regulations, and penalties that try to protect the entire society. However, when education is hidden, no one is aware of what is going on and dangerous phenomena can easily grow and create important damages.

A third trouble is that since education is hidden and is needed at the same time, some commend themselves to infiltrate organizations who are supposed to be watching over the secrets. This generates espionage and spies. However, *no one appreciates to be spied upon even the spies themselves.*

A fourth problem with hidden education is that it is not very appealing to human nature. Humans like to walk on known and safe grounds in daylight and tend to avoid mysteries which could conceal potential dangers. Manly Hall praised ancient mysteries a lot and Helena Blavatsky was exceptionally harsh toward Christianity though with some good reasons.

However, Christianity had replaced mysteries in many cities of the ancient world not only because of the help of powerful rulers such as Emperor Constantine of the Roman Empire. There were things in the Christian message that seduced people and made them abandon the mysteries. One reason is the desire to no longer hide.

Many *new* Christians must have liked Jesus' message in Luke 8: 17 and Matthew 10: 26: *'For all that is secret will eventually be brought into the open, and everything that is concealed will be brought to the light and made known to all.'* This declaration of Jesus was an echo of Job's saying in Job 12: 22: *'He uncovers mysteries hidden in darkness.'* The same message was in the mouth of the prophet Jeremiah [31: 33-34] and was dear to the author of the book of Hebrews [8: 10-12].

Some spiritual schools and spiritualists understand the disadvantages of hidden education. *Seeker suspects that this is one of the motives behind the book of Dan Brown, The Lost Symbol. In the book Freemasonry, one of the most important schools of spiritually is positively depicted with the acknowledgment of the necessity that all knowledge becomes available to all.*

Therefore people must prepare to handle great knowledge by assimilating as much prerequisite as possible in theory as well as in practice. This adds to the accuracy and the justification of a philosophy such as divine humanism.

The fifth problem is that there is a category of people which hides things because it believes there will not be enough "food" for all. This way of seeing life is not correct. There is an abundance of matter and human reason if freedom is strong enough to find ways for all to be happy.

There is a selfishness that characterizes the animal world *[law of jungle]* where a panther would fight a fox to get a rabbit. But humans should prove they are above the animal level able to live in harmony. This is another way in which divine humanism will educate people.

Titles and curricula vitae

There was a time during his studies when Seeker could not understand why some people who have studied a lot in official institutions become so proud of themselves that they represent obstacle to others. At the same time, he had the privilege to meet a worldly celebrated scientist who behave very simply and enabled people to access him. This let a durable positive impression on Seeker who could see someone apply a philosophy of life dear to him.

Titles and curricula vitae are useful in informing others about the expertise a person has in various fields of life. That is the only function they should perform. They should never be used in a condescending, patronizing, disdainful, pompous, or arrogant manner. On the other hand people who have not gotten the chance to study much should free their psyches and minds from any sort of inferiority complex. They should nevertheless acknowledge the hard work of those who have studied and look harder for opportunities to learn.

Seeker understands too well the value of a human being. That is why he does not try to establish social relationships mainly based on titles and curricula vitae and he does not like when someone feels inferior because he/she has not studied much. Educational deficiencies in individual lives should be acknowledges and corrected as soon as possible. This is another mission of divine humanism.

Language and education

Since an important attribute of humans beings is speech, language or rather languages exist and mediate communications among them. Education too employs this vehicle to achieve its goals. However, since there are thousands of languages in the world which correspond to places with specific knowledge and since it is best that each human benefits from the knowledge of the others; there must be a central language to serve as the repository of universal knowledge while secondary languages maintain their existence until the language problem is definitely solved.

This should be seen from the angle of utilitarianism rather than that of imperialism. Since the English language is more or less already fulfilling that role, it is better to strengthen its position. Humanity could work at the same time on a more universal language in terms of richness and coverage of the different sounds, phenomena, knowledge, and beings that exist. The limited impact of the *Esperanto* fluently spoken only by two millions peoples according to Wikipedia should not discourage the attempt to having a universal language.

Chapter 9

Spiritual science, Philosophy, and Theology

Generalities

Spirituality or energeticity?

In Chapter 7, spirituality was defined as the development of the awareness of the energy-world by humans. With the development of physics, physicality has come to be described as encompassing both the phenomena related to matter and energy as seen in chapter 4. The frontier between spirituality and physicality seems to disappear due to the understanding of energy.

However, physicality describes only part of the energetic reality and remains ignorant of several facts presented and explained in some spiritual schools and religions. The manifestation of the Holy Spirit or Holy Fire and chakras are two important examples. Consequently, spirituality still has its exclusive domain. When the science of energy develops sufficiently to cover all topics discussed in spirituality, either term will supersede the other.

A consensus that adopts both terms should use the words 'energy' and 'energeticity' in quantum physics on the one hand and 'spirit' and 'spirituality' in spiritual science on the other hand. That consensus should always remember that there is a direct connection between sprit and energy. This will help people better perceive the connections among the different categories of beings and not lose sight of the rich spiritual heritage of human kind.

Comparison of spirituality, religion, and spiritual science

History and archeology show that spirituality and religion are old. In a scripture such as the Bible, spirituality appears to be older, more universal, and more inclusive than religion.

Indeed, this scripture and also the Qur'an describe human spirituality beginning with the interaction of the first man Adam with supernatural beings called God and angels. No worship, atonement, or other elements of religion such as the clergy were described.

Religious elements entered the scene only after the disobedience of Eve and Adam in Genesis 3 that has come to be known as the original sin. The first religious element to appear was *expiation* in the form of "punishment" inflicted to Adam, Eve, and also the serpent. Second, was *atonement* when the God of the Old Testament sought to reconcile himself with humans through the acceptance of the sacrifice of Abel and his efforts to make Cain also correct his mistake and avoid creating a worse situation.

Scriptures show that it has been very difficult for humans to have a simple and direct relationship with the divine and the supernatural as Adam before his disobedience. Nevertheless, they mention Enoch, Noah, Melchizedek, Abraham, Moses, Balaam, the prophets of ancient Israel, Jesus, and Mohammad as people who have establish good and remarkable relationships with God.

These people were often spiritual and religious at the same time as have been several others in ancient Egypt, India, Persia, Africa, and so forth. Most of the time, their religious side was further developed when they had to raise the level of spirituality of the masses of humanity.

Hence religion became an attempt to enhance spirituality and global existence and consequently was less concrete and less powerful than spirituality. Most followers of the great founders of religion relied on the experiences and understandings of their leaders rather than interacting with the divine and the supernatural in their own spirit as recommended by Jesus [John 5: 24].

Some followers understood that the great founders were just examples to help them develop their potentials. Others made significant progresses but twisted some of the ideas of their guides while still others have come to simply think as impossible and irrelevant any personal attempt to handle spirituality.

But the fact remains that many founders wanted each human being to blossom spirituality according to his/her personal gifts leaving a position of subordination to them.

 Remarkable among them is Hermes Trismegistus who sought to use the mind of God in himself to call forward the mind of God in people so they might be saved. Hermes left ways to open doorways between the material and the spiritual, and means to handle spiritual realities. Remarkable is Moses who wanted everyone to have the Holy Spirit in abundance and who announced without sign of jealousy that a prophet like him will be born in the future. Remarkable is Jesus who taught that it is possible that some people accomplish greater things than he [John 14: 12]. Other names would certainly emerge if a broader research is done in the field of the history of spirituality and religion.

Spiritual science already existed in the form of the spirituality that humanity has known so far. However, that science can be significantly improved thanks to historical spirituality itself, but also thanks to methodical elements borrowed from physical science and the support of new spiritual scientists. It is therefore necessary to redefine what spiritual science is in this morning of the 21st century.

Spiritual science defined in a few words

Spiritual science is the methodic observation, description, analysis, understanding, use, investigation, and development of phenomena related to the spirit world and the spirit body. It is the education '*of*' the spirit body, '*of*' the soul, and '*of*' the physical body '*about*' the spirit body and the spirit world.

As such, spiritual science is different from theology.

Spiritual science, theology, philosophy, and psychology differentiated

Theology is the systematic study of the divine including a study of God, the gods, and the spirit world. As secular philosophy transcends physical science, theology transcends both spiritual and material sciences. This transcendence is reflective. The transcendence is also ontological since God, the Universal Mind exists beyond the energy of the Holy Spirit, beyond matter, and beyond all beings.

Depending on the part of human nature that is educated and depending on what is studied, one can distinguish several categories of education: the education *of* the physical body, that *of* the spirit body, and that *of* the soul on the one hand and the education *about* nature, humanity, the supernatural, and God on the other hand.

The aims of the education of the soul about everything are knowledge, virtues, and pleasures or happiness while those of the teachings of and about the spirit [which parallels the education of and about the physical body] are: health, beauty, skills, strength, and also pleasures or happiness.

Theology is fundamentally a soul-level discipline. Theological teachings can sometimes appear in spiritual science especially when gods are studied.

Philosophy and psychology, like theology, are education 'of' the soul and 'about' everything. The three of them seek to develop human reason or intelligence or wisdom; to safely orient human desires, passions, and loves; to strengthen human will; and to stimulate creativity. They have three goals: impart the truth or knowledge *including theoretical morality,* allow the acquirement of virtues or *practical morality,* and enable the true enjoyment of life through love and pleasures *or fruitful morality*.

This is the fundamental explanation of the teaching of Jesus that truth sets free [John 8: 32] and the justification of the statement of Toni Morrison made in 1986 and written on a wall at the Schwarzman building of the New York Public Library: *'Access to knowledge is the superb, the supreme act of truly great civilizations.'* Morrison is famous for winning the Nobel Prize in literature in 1993 as well as other high prizes such as the Pulitzer Prize.

Spiritual science is mainly about the spirit or energies [explained and unexplained]. Like physical science, it should include the "biology" of the spirit or its structure and functions. But also spiritual medicine, physics [quantum physics?], chemistry [alchemy?], zoology, botany, geology, aesthetics, sport, music, dance, loves, gastronomy, etc….

Spiritual science as known in ancient and modern spirituality and religion has a lot of improvement to make. Though notions of spirit anatomy and physiology exist in the teachings of ancient Egypt, Hinduism, Buddhism, and Yoga; human ignorance in the matter of spiritual science is still abysmal. Hence, research in this field is important. Dreams should be of great assistance.

Teachings of spiritual science

A discussion on the "voice" of God

During the spring of 2010, Seeker who was graduating from seminary visited a group of his classmates in the Bronx, New York. It was an evening; so after a little chat they sat around a table for dinner. Naturally their discussion which was about theological issues continued.

At a moment, one of the seminarian mentioned that he engaged in religion and spirituality because he heard the *call of God*. Several years before that day, Seeker would not have had anything to say about such a declaration. In fact it was one he could have easily made or have probably made in his past.

Seeker was nearing his graduation and had taken the time to think about an important number of spiritual topics including that of the *call of God*. Additionally he had had more experiences dealing with his teachers of theology, clergymen, lay people, atheists, skeptics, secular humanists, and so forth.

So, he decided to test his colleague and maybe gain something from a discussion about the call of God. He asked his classmate how he could be sure that it was God who called him. The answer of the colleague was that he heard God's voice *in his heart*. Then Seeker asked him how he could be sure that it was *God's voice* and not his own. As one could guess the discussion had much chance to end without definitive answers that reason could admit.

That may be why some consider religion as a belief system in which reason has no place. But Seeker was convinced that reason was the fundamental aspect of God and that it cannot be excluded from the interactions between Him-Her and humans. He was of the opinion that spiritual scientists should beware not to fall in love with their own ideas and reason and avoid falling into the trap of negative pride which closes the sense of judgment.

Seeker knew that beyond the "voice" of God the question of who God is was even more fundamental. Fortunately, he was already working on *Abode of Divinities*, so he also knew he would need that book [devoted to precisions about the existence and nature of divinities] to answer the question of the call, prayer, spiritual music, and also the question of worship.

The question of the call is important to discuss because it puts on the table human relationships with God and spiritual entities. When God calls a person, how does He-She proceed? Does God has a voice like humans or does He-She communicates telepathically? Seeker cannot say if he has ever heard the voice of God in the form of physical sound, though in a sense the voice of a created being is the voice of God. But this is not the topic here.

God is the Universal Mind who communicates with a human for example in visions and dreams. When this happens, the person is often able to hear not a physical sound but a spiritual one. Since the Holy Spirit is Divine Energy, it can have forms that convey spiritual sound. Soul sound from the Universal Mind to the individual Mind is also a possibility. Well educated or advanced human souls are more able to perceive the Speech or Word from the Universal Soul.

So, Seeker can now safely conclude that the response of his classmate was partially correct. Indeed God speaks through the heart but also and mainly through the mind as Hebrews 8: 10 confirms.

A way in which one can be almost certain to be doing the will of God is to consider all matters from the angle of the general interest that includes the particular one. Good people receive a lot from God. So, they frequently express the view point of God. Angels such as the God of the Old Testament, animals, plants, and things too can indirectly convey the "words" of God carved in their very nature. In the case of angels, the call can be audible to the spirit and even to the physical ear as several passages of scriptures show.

Prayer

Definition and goals of prayer

Prayer is basically a communication between a human and God or a declaration, wish, or command from an advanced divine human. Through prayer, people remember who they are and decide who they want to be. The communication with God can be unidirectional or rudimentary because humanity is still striving to determine at the basic level the identity of the partner that God represents.

The presence of God is often perceived through the Holy Spirit. Nevertheless this presence in Seeker's experiences is still not direct enough at list not as lived by Hermes Trismegistus and Jesus. He does not know any living human who can claim such direct relationship with God and who can pass at the same time basic tests of reason, honesty, and goodness. He hopes this will change as he meets more people.

Nevertheless, he favorably considers the reports about the experiences of Hermes Trismegistus, Jesus, and many prophets because they pass the basic tests. So he thinks that humanity should earnestly look for the kinds of relationships they had with God and even more.

Thanksgiving, praise, and glorification should be the first goal of a prayer to God and the second goal should be to ask or wish for a more direct relationship with God. Saying thank you to someone who has given things is important both for the person who has given, and for the person who has received. So, humans should thank God for their precious lives and everything they are able to enjoy.

The second goal of prayer should include a call for the manifestation and the understanding of the Holy Spirit and its gifts; and a better sanctification of the soul, the spirit body and the physical body in order to be able to perceive the Speech or Word of God in the spirit world, nature, and directly from Soul to soul. Once such a prayer is made to God, one just needs to continue studying, meditating, planning, and acting for cosmic happiness.

Once God manifests more directly, a person can perceive what else He-She wants and adjust his/her relationship with Him-Her. At that moment, one could better thank, praise, and glorify God based on experience and the words pronounced would have a profound meaning.

Though God is worthy to be thanked, praised, and glorified at any time, when people raise their personal level of divinity, they can come to acknowledge the possibility of abusive glorification of God out of lack of information and for personal psychological satisfaction. For that kind of psychological support, it is better to engage in fruitful relationships with other humans.

Glorifying God all the time without a concrete relationship does not seem reasonable or mature enough and it also has sometimes the secondary effect to portray God as a tyrant and egoistic being especially in non-theistic eyes.

Sometimes, some people come to refuse to be thanked because they know that the receiver is already thankful especially in the way he/she treats others. So, God can ask a particular human who has proved his/her own divine worth not to thank or glorify Him-Her. Such a person can even be praised by God Him/Herself as reported in the Bible about Jesus [at his baptism and transfiguration].

A more direct relationship with God includes a work for the growth and the manifestation of one's own sprit and the manifestation of supernatural beings such as angels present in religious and spiritual writings. Asking God for the intervention of angels or any kind of supernatural beings is best after meeting and knowing those beings from experience.

A person of divine character can directly ask angels for their intervention because he/she knowing God and the Universe can handle direct relationships with them [This is where vigilant social or group Kabbalah and magic in their positive harmless and non-violent aspect can help]. People must pay attention and study a lot not to reject a good spirit and avoid cooperating with a disguised evil spirit as Paul said.

The reason why a person must pray to God directly despite Him-Her knowing His-her responsibility is that through prayer, the individual is expressing and demonstrating his/her desire and readiness to advance on the divine path. This readiness includes repentance since the developing human being is capable of mistakes.

True repentance manifests in the self-sanctification of the deviant person through an exemplary life. But repentance should be rare and concern faults made out of ignorance. Situations of dependence should be appropriately diagnosed and dealt with in specific ways. At that moment God can answer with the minimum guaranty that His-Her new gifts will not be wasted, though the individual can still change his/her mind. So, prayer to God is also toward oneself.

Praying that God intervenes in other people's lives is not necessary at first because of the principle of freedom. The person who prays to God uses his/her freedom in this particular manner and the person who does not pray to God also uses personal freedom, but in a different manner.

Spiritual scientists should call God to intervene in other people's lives only when they are not equipped to deal with the degree of evilness of those people. Therefore by praying to God in this case, they are expressing their own weakness and limitation to protect their own freedom from evil. This is the fourth goal a prayer to God can have.

But before asking for the intervention of God, people should try to solve problems by themselves. Prayer in this situation mobilizes the energy of the spiritual world including the electromagnetic one to directly help people in need. The need could be a better health, goodness, food, clothes, etc... The prayer can be in the presence or the absence of the receiver depending on the circumstances.

When a person wills to receive a prayer, the impact of the prayer is stronger for three reasons. First, the receiver places himself/herself in a favorable posture to receive. This is equivalent to Jesus' declaration to the individuals he healed that their faith has saved them. The second advantage of direct prayer manifests when the receiver can hear the good words pronounced.

The receiver feels the care of the praying person. He/she gets a better knowledge of the world and improves his/her own intelligence and volition in order to make things better at the individual and cosmic levels.

The third advantage is a direct transfer of energy, not only the energy of words, but spiritual substance as testified by Rosicrucians, the practitioners of Reiki, and many other healers.

Prayer in the absence of a negative person could be made because that person is not in the mood to hear the words of reason, coolness, love etc…. With such a person, a direct prayer would be a provocation. The best attitude would be to let time show that person the good intention and attitude of the spiritual scientist. Then direct talk to wisely solve issues can be initiated and direct prayer given if necessary and if requested.

In case the problem of the negative individual cannot be dealt with in this manner, this implies evilness or madness. There is "passive" evilness and "active" evilness. In the first case, the evil person holds evil intentions and/or speak evil words but does not take action in the physical or spiritual worlds believing that he/she does no harm.

In reality, this evilness is not that passive because it can set up harmful energies at the levels of the soul and the spirit that can negatively affect the feelings, the will, the intelligence, the creativity, and the development of people who do not have countermeasures.

The most powerful countermeasure at the soul level is innocence or the mental attitude that does not plot the downfall or harm of people. One must never allow jealousy to take control of the soul. One should appreciate strength, beauty, health, money, and so on without conceiving plans to steal them or destroy them. Desiring such things for one self is good but the way to obtain them is to work alone or with people who have won them by working hard and honestly.

In case a strong or healthy or beautiful or wealthy person does not want to help others become like him/her, spiritual scientists should be patient knowing that all these things are part of their legacy from God. So they should use divine wisdom to get what they want. *The more people gather, the faster their desire will be achieved.*

Prayer in the form of positive attitude or innocence is sufficient to prevent the kind of harm caused by passive evilness or evil eye. In the case of "active" evilness, the human judiciary system can help. If people use them well and improve them, a lot of trouble can be avoided both for people who have difficulties not to try to harm others and their targets.

In the case of active evilness, prayers can be sent to God to help solve the problem. Again, such prayer lets God knows the limitation of the good spiritual scientist so He-She can take extraordinary measures to restrain evil by sending good angels for example. This is how the flood can be explained.

Means to help people avoid becoming evil or stop being evil no matter the degree of evilness or madness exists or can be elaborated. If a soul could degenerate to a great extent, efforts of another soul in the opposite direction can also find solutions upgrading medicine to that level. *Divine wisdom is mind medicine.*

Finally prayer should be addressed toward spaces, periods of time, events, animals, plants, and things, because good words positively affect them and help get rid of harmful energies that might have been stored in them or which can appear in order to negatively influence them.

This is how one can understand the blessing of things, houses, and places and also the existence of some spiritually dangerous places and holy places. Prayer should aim for the sanctification and the holiness of the entire universe beginning with earth.

Some benefits of prayer

Prayer sharpens the soul and helps it stay away from ignorance, confusion, madness, and evilness.

It keeps the spirit body and the physical body healthy, strong, and beautiful. It maintains a correct energetic building and function and spiritual awakening [chakras, parapsychological powers of telekinesis, healing, etc…]. Seeker has noticed that prayer literally keeps the energy-being [spirit body] focused and *tuned*. It also keeps the soul concentrated.

Prayer plays an important role in the restoration of the "health" of objects and living beings [Hence prayer has a preventive and a curative role].

Elements that support prayer including magic, alchemy, fasting and prayer frequency

Divinely advanced people understand better how to design their prayers and how those prayers accomplish their purposes. They have a better knowledge of the elements that support prayer.

Those elements are *positive magic, alchemy, fire, candles, frankincense, fasting, numerology*, and so forth. They can be used if they help concentration or if research proves their impact in other ways.

Magic and alchemy

Physical science is a kind of knowledge that helps transform physical reality thanks to the powers of the soul and the body. Magic helps transform both the physical and the spiritual worlds through the powers of the soul, the spirit body and the physical body.

There can be dangerous physical scientists who use dangerous methods. The same way, there can be dangerous magicians. The potential danger of magic is greater than that of physical science because it involves the spirit world and spiritual beings not well known.

This is where divine wisdom centered on goodness should come in. It is this philosophy which tells ethical commissions how to set limitations to scientists. As there is a philosophy of science, there should be a *philosophy of magic* which uses high reason and goodness to help spiritual scientists not to engage in dangerous or evil activities.

There should be *magical ethical commissions* to make sure that criminals do not use magic or spiritual science to harm others and there should be a *spiritual police, army, and judiciary system made of the wisest and good people*.

The core of the philosophy of spiritual science is the *opposition of goodness to evilness*. This is what determines how and why physical and spiritual materials are used.

Refusing to engage in spiritual science or magic is as unwise as rejecting the benefits of physical science. The challenge is to avoid destructive methods and beings and look for constructive methods and beings.

Many who reject spiritual science or magic justify their position based on the fact the God of the Old Testament forbids it in the Old Testament in passages such as Deuteronomy 18: 9-12. But a little meditation shows that what is rejected is evil and not spiritual science.

The God of the Old Testament forbade associating with demons for evil but at the same time, he sent other angels to teach Moses and Tobit a spiritual science that is used for good. The work of Jesus in the New Testament is also based on positive spiritual science. God also sent angels to teach the prophets Daniel and other prophets.

So, it is ok to look for spiritual science and be taught by some spiritual beings especially in public. Aspiring spiritual scientists should first strengthen their soul with divine wisdom based on goodness. Thus armed they can endeavor to test spirits as said in 1 John 4: 1 examining everything and keeping what is good as Paul asks in 1 Thessalonians 5: 19-21.

Spiritual scientists should however remember that demons can disguise as angels of light [2 Corinthians 10: 14]. They should be vigilant at all times while associating with a spirit whether human or not. *Disguised evil spirits at a moment or another would ask to violate the Divine Law especially when they think a person trusts and relies on them more than anyone else. That is when they begin slowly trying to shift a person from the good way.*

Seeker has five pieces of advice about how to deal with evil spirits who might be in disguise: 1- avoid any harm to any one through the relationship with a spirit, 2- always pray to God about that spirit and remain vigilant, 3- build communities of good people and avoid isolation in exclusive relationships with spirits, 4- discuss anything a spirit says in that community of good people, 5- never call any kind of spirit but without that community, pray God to send angels if necessary, wait that the spirit initiates the relationship, or wait the level of divine human.

Fasting

Fasting reduces the attention given to the physical body and increases that given to the spirit and the mind. By reducing the competition from the physical body, an individual lets the mind and the spirit express themselves better and can deliver more powerful prayers.

When the power increases the need to fast decreases because the person is now functioning at a high level and needs less incentive to "charge." Fasting should be a mean used in the education on prayer. Instructions about fasting are supported by several biblical passages.

In his fasting experiences, Seeker also observed the reduction of the manifestations of his stomach while the 5th chakra or the energy center of the solar plexus on the spirit body radiates actual power. The purpose of the power is to impact spiritual and physical realities and bring about the desired changes.

The name 'solar plexus' can be a source of confusion and make people take this energy center for the energy center of the heart or 4th chakra or sacred heart. The reason is that both names evoke radiating energy from a center. This is what 'solar' suggests and this is how the sacred heart manifests and is represented. However, all chakras or energy centers of the spirit function that way each with some particularities.

So, the energy center of the solar plexus is distinct from that of the heart. It is located below it in the abdomen and is specifically linked to the stomach. That is why quieting the physical stomach through fasting allows perceiving better its manifestation.

As most teachings on chakras state and as Seeker has observed on himself, the energy center of the solar plexus is more related to physical strength than the energies of the 4th, the 3rd, the 2nd, and the 1st chakras.

When a powerful prayer is delivered, one can feel the 5th chakra in action. If a person cannot feel this, fasting more will help achieve that goal though there is a limitation to how long and the way one can and should fast. Perceiving this phenomenon while praying gives an extra boost of confidence which increases concentration and determination to fashion the change wished. Then the prayer is more efficient.

The most powerful prayers are those delivered when the praying person is in a state of perception of the manifestations of the chakras and also the manifestations of the psychic or electromagnetic network of the blood and the nervous system. This peripheral power has the tendency to come and concentrate in the palms and can leave the body and operate cures if the person has the knowledge of its use. Research in this direction is more than recommended.

Frequency of prayer

How often one should pray depends on needs. In the current state of humanity, Jesus is right to advice endless prayer [Luke 18:1].

First, it is important to pray to God at the beginning of the day in order to keep the soul or the mind focused on goals until they are realized. This strengthens the person to face the different situations that can occur during the day in the family, at the work place, or any other place.

Second, prayer before sleeping is important because the soul regains a certain freedom from the activities of this world and is more receptive to the teachings from God or other good spirits.

Third, one should say the particular blessing or consecrating prayers needed in particular situations such as birth, marriage, death, exams, academic semesters, meals, acquisition of new objects and houses, and so on. In case of deviation from the divine path, one should also sanctify the objects involved after repenting.

Now *there is another kind of prayer according to time which connects all sorts of prayers and help really pray without ceasing.* This is *continuous prayer, or mindfulness* described by Meister Eckhart, Thich Nhat Hanh, Rudolph Steiner, and many other religious and spiritual teachers.

Continuous prayer or mindfulness means a permanent positive attitude of observation; understanding; and good care of nature, oneself, and society. It is also permanent good intention or aspiration and having the right attitude or making correct decision in all activities as the Buddha taught. Continuous prayer like the other forms of prayer is gradually learned and mastered.

Depending on spiritual research, various days or dates or seasons or years etc…, could be the objects of particular attention during prayers. However, the advanced divine humanist transcends time and space like God and sees the bigger picture rather than the time and space under angelic influence.

Numerology and geometry in scriptures, the energy world, nature, time, and in prayer

Numerology is a science which ascribes particular meanings and usefulness to numbers. *Pythagoras* who received a lot of religious and spiritual instruction is said [34] to have been its inventor and best practitioner since the science has been lost a long time ago. Pythagoras alongside other prominent ancient, modern, and contemporary scientists also made outstanding contributions in the field of geometry.

In prayer, numerology and geometry manifest in the choice of the time and space of prayer and/or in the choice of the elements used to support it like candles. For example, some people attach particular values to numbers such as 1, 2, 3, 4, 5, 6, 7, 8, 9, 10, 11, 12, 13, 21, 24, 30, 33, 36, 40, 60, 72, 80, 120, 144, and so forth.

The *foundations of numerology* are religious and spiritual scriptures, revelation or special theology, and general theology which is divine teaching concealed in nature and time.

The energy world is influenced by geometry and numerology which are both mathematical sub disciplines. For example physical science teaches that the building blocks of matter are ultimately small blocks of energy associated in various quantities or numbers and in various configurations. Atoms vary according to the numbers of protons, neutrons and electrons.

Coming to nature, it is well known that man creates a lot by imitating it. Spiritual science should be open to learn from it. The way in which some elements of nature are arranged is truly amazing. Numbers and form intervene fundamentally in the identification of species of plants and animals. And they play a fundamental role in the richness, the usefulness, the beauty, and the harmony of nature.

---

[34]Manly Hall, *Secret Teachings of All Ages*, 206.

The influence of numerology and geometry on the natural order is so wonderful that it is better not to give examples in a book like this. A better thing to do is to watch documentaries on animal, vegetal, and mineral worlds made by eminent zoologists, botanists, mineralogists, crystallographers, astronomers, journalists, and so on.

Seeker feels however the need to mention his experiences about the *sun* which opens the discussion to numerology in time. Several times, he has observed the image of the sun in documentaries, movies, and cartoons or animes. Sometimes it has 4 rays, other times, 6, or 8. His direct observations of the sun showed him that 6, 8, and 12 rays often appear to the eye.

This could be one of the reasons of the 6 pointed star of Israel besides the association of two pyramids symbolizing heaven and earth, masculinity and feminity, and so forth. It could explain why the clock is divided into 12 main sectors besides the steps of the sun indicated by the ancient gnomon, why there were 12 tribes besides the signs of the zodiac in ancient Israel, and why the symbolic new city of Jerusalem which descends from heaven has 12 gates [Revelation 21: 12] also besides the signs of the zodiac. Furthermore, this could also be associated to the 24 thrones and elders surrounding the symbolic throne of God in heaven [Revelation 4: 1-4].

Another amazing phenomenon reported by astronomy is the presence of a perfect geometrical form [a hexagon] at the North Pole of planet Saturn. It was discovered in 1979 by spacecraft Voyager and its presence was confirmed by spacecraft Cassini in 2006. This reality mentioned in the eighth episode of the first season of the documentary *The Universe* [21min to 23min] is the first of its kind yet discovered in the universe. The hexagon is strange and mysterious even in the eyes of astronomers[35].

In the documentary, Kevin Baines working at the Jet Propulsion Laboratory of the American NASA [JPL/NASA] is astonished and wonders what

---

[35]The Universe, http://www.free-tv-video-online.me/player/megavideo.php?id=UJ2676HU (accessed April 19th, 2011).

this phenomenon is? Well, the answer is not complicated. Saturn's perfect hexagon is a bigger version of the perfect geometrical and numerical entities on earth.

Again, it makes more sense to ascribe these phenomena to intelligent design rather than blind and random evolution. What is also mysterious and astonishing about Saturn's Perfect Hexagon is that the figure is so big and marked by the number 6 at the same time when the planet is the 6th from the sun.

Coming back to the sun and time, it is important to remember the relativity of time according to its star of reference. The subdivisions of time as generally known to humanity are linked to the structural and functional system in which the sun and the earth exist. Especially the rotation and the speed of the rotation of the earth on its axis, its trajectory around the sun, and its speed on that trajectory determine the years, seasons, days, hours, minutes, seconds, and so on.

This is the rationale behind having 24 hours per day and 12 hours for the night and for the day in equatorial regions and during days of equinox in non-equatorial regions. This is why there are 60 minutes per hour, 60 seconds per minutes etc…

So, choosing specific hours and places for prayer is more about the convenience of human beings in their immediate and distant environments. This relativity of time and space makes understandable why God is said to be beyond time and space and why those who are advanced on the divine path are not really influenced by such things.

In reality, the seconds, minutes, hours, months, years, and so on could have been divided otherwise. For instance, 1 minute could have been considered 30 seconds. The current system is just one convention adopted among several possible.

Forms of prayer

Silent prayer and audible prayer

Some people wonder when it is fitting to pray silently and when it is good to make audible prayers.

Since God is the Universal Mind, it is sufficient and better to pray to him from one's own mind developing a telepathic relationship. But one can pray to God using physical voice in order to give a learner an example of how to conduct this sort of prayer.

Seeker has identified three circumstances in which prayer using physical sound from the vocal cords is recommendable.

The first situation is when an experienced person is teaching a beginner how to pray whether in classroom, during an internship, or in the course of everyday life. The second is when one prays to heal another person especially when that person can hear. The third circumstance is when one blesses objects and spaces. The reason is that physical vocal prayer uses sound vibrations which are closer to physical matter than thoughts. Sound impacts matter in a more concrete way than thoughts. However, further precision from research needs to be added.

Individual prayer and group prayer

Private individual prayer for the goals identified is important but group prayer too is necessary since a life in community is far more enriching than an isolate existence.

In occasions in which people gather, each person should silently bless the period of time, make internal preparation to fully participate for the fulfillment of personal and group objectives. This kind of prayer could be addressed to God or simply express the will of each person to engage in the meeting using the personal divine resources stored within.

This means that during encounters, one should take the flore to make good contributions in terms of reason, feeling, determination, creativity, and amusement when appropriate.

Divine humanism emphasizes both discipline and authenticity. But it prefers mistakes in attempts to be authentic and enjoy life to unproductive disciplinary silence. If a participant thinks another has made a mistake, he/she should respectfully and kindly say so and explain why in order for the entire group to benefit. If it happens that the correction is the mistake, the correcting person would have made a fool of him/herself and everybody can laugh about it.

Community life is one of the most important pillars of the happiest society. Therefore it should improve the sense of safety, the growth potential, and enjoyment possibilities. Community life should never be a place for gossip or to undermine people. It should never be a competing milieu where the least able is ridiculed.

Community life is the place where qualities are valued, appreciated, and enjoyed while shortcomings are corrected. No matter the level of development, community life should be a place where everybody can perceive potential and actual development with the understanding and support of others. Community is a place for genuine *cooperation*, not for competition. In that line there should be group prayers to *support community projects and for healing*.

Healing prayers should follow the rules of medical science especially the dosage and method of administration of medicines.

This is what Jesus taught when he told his disciples to use prayer and fasting at an occasion [Matthew 17: 21] though he did not say what kind of prayer and fasting and how long they should last. Nevertheless, research should help solve the issues of dosage and methodology. Reiki and traditional qigong can be of a great help in this domain.

It is not recommendable for people to gather and vocally pray when they do not know with proofs what they are doing. Negative consequences could result from too emotional uses of prayer like when the seven sons of Sceva got seriously beaten by a possessed man from whom they tried to chase a demon [Acts 19: 13-16]. This is collective hysteria. Other negative consequences can also be the waste of energy or the perturbation of other people's minds.

In group prayer, participants can gather in common place or set a time at which people start praying from different places. People can also pray in chain one after the other at predetermined times.

Meditation

Meditation is often associated with prayer because it can be part of prayer. But it is also an activity that can fully be conducted outside the context of prayer as a distinct activity of spiritual science or philosophy or theology or psychology.

It is the observation or contemplation of all sorts of phenomena, their analysis, and the formulation of explanations and possible explanations. It can be mental or verbal; conducted by one person or many; and it can use supports such as scriptures, teachings, and writings as well as nature, space, time, diagrams, art, technology etc….

Verbal meditation in group should be an important part of social life for the remembrance of uniting values and teachings, to strengthen social cohesion and the bonds between people, and to improve society through the outpouring of new contributions.

Music

The place of music in spiritual science cannot be sufficiently stressed in this volume. Countless individuals and organizations have understood its importance especially for spiritual development. That is why all religions and spiritual schools from all times and places have given it particular attention.

However it is good to remind readers of two things here: the impact of music in healing as emphasized by Rosicrucians and music therapy which is a very promising field [music heals and helps open spiritual doors] and its support for teaching and happiness.

Worship

In theology books, worship is described fundamentally as the attribution of worth or value to God and the expression of this through prayer, meditation, and music but also through preaching, rituals including sacraments, feasts, and so on.

This scholarly definition of worship is different from the idea that common worshippers have. Indeed, Seeker has found out that what most people consider as worship is adoration. This adoration is so developed that the content of the value mentioned almost disappears. According to his observation, worshippers in general are so respectful of God, so in awe that their individual sense of responsibility is weakened for the gain of a certain comfort.

The consequence is the abnormal dependence on ministers and religious founders, negligence in the development and expression of personal spiritual potentials, and finally the difficulty to deal efficiently with some issues of practical life.

In addition, ministers too are confused by this attitude which gives them an abnormal power over people that they manage with great difficulty. This pushes some ministers to live a life of pretense. They try to appear more knowledgeable, spiritually stronger, and more dependable while in reality they are not that different from the common people.

The main difference is that ministers have studied how to guide the spiritual lives of communities. However like each person of their congregation, they face the necessity to know the spiritual world from experience, to clear confusion on issues of marriage, sexuality, conflict resolution, and many other issues. In addition, their personal egos are constantly under the risk of becoming oversized because of their congregations.

Seeker thinks that there are so many problems related to worship that its reformation should be undertaken. In his opinion, Jesus displayed unusual wisdom when he refused to become king as wished by a group of people he had positively impressed in Galilee [John 6: 14-15].

What worship should aim for is to work for the realization of the dream, the vision, the wish, or prophecy of Jeremiah 31: 33-34 and Hebrews 8: 10-13: the establishment of a society in which all know God.

For this vision to become true, the preaching part of worship should be removed and the teaching part better emphasized. Indeed preaching gives the minister the opportunity to speak on behalf of God which is often untrue. Generally people speak on behalf of themselves except in direct encounters with God or his messengers.

So, giving a preacher the authority to speak on behalf of God about things he/she is unsure of is unwise. Teaching on the contrary is honest, offers the teacher the opportunity to impart his knowledge while maintaining a humble and open attitude that allows contradiction, debate, and possibly learning from students. Teaching protects both the teacher and the students against themselves and others in contrary to preaching.

In conclusion, worship as admiration and respect of the divine should not be undermined at the same time when individual responsibility is stressed. Teaching should supersede preaching.

In addition, rituals and sacraments should be administered only when scientific proofs of their necessity are available to all. Any ritual or sacrament should have a logical reason and an identifiable positive impact on people. This is where spiritual research, again, can be useful.

Worship should come to be seen not only as ascribing value or worth to God, but also to every human being and the rest of the entities of the cosmos. Worship should be the private and public arrangement of the activities of spiritual science in specific places and times as well as outside the official temporal and spatial coordinates.

The mountain, the roads, and the elephant

Students of theology, ministers, teachers of religion and spirituality, and other people interested in spirituality are familiar with the parable of the mountain, the roads, and, the elephant.

The top of the mountain symbolizes God who can be reached from the different mountainsides representing world religions and spiritual currents. So, all religions and spiritual schools lead to God they say. Each religion or school has a part of the big elephant that represents God.

These parable, as presented here, confirms the necessity of a universal philosophy, science, and spirituality which *Abode of Divinities* and the present book especially this chapter on spiritual science try to set while remaining open to other contributions.

Chapter 10

Sexuality, reproduction, and marriage

FOR millennia, human kind knew no mean to reproduce and keep peopling the earth other than sexuality. Even in the 21st century, almost 100% of babies are conceived that way; the exceptions being the very rare cases of test tube babies.

Test tube babies are children conceived through In Vitro Fecundation [IVF] in which the encounter between the eggs of women and the spermatozoa of a men are made possible in test tubes. One fecundated egg is then implanted in the womb of the donor of the eggs or another woman. IVF is used to help women who cannot have children because fecundation cannot take place within them or because their uterus cannot bear a fetus.

The American policy makers centered on a recommendation of the Food and Drug Administration [FDA] dating from January 2008 not only allow animal cloning but also authorize the consumption of meat and milk from cloned animals on the ground that they are as safe as the food derived from non-cloned animals[36].

Concerning human cloning, according to an official report to the American Congress from 2006[37]; there is a rich debate at all levels of the American society including the Senate but a decision has not yet been taken at the federal level. However, according to the same report, fifteen states have prohibited reproductive cloning. Six among them have also voted laws against human cloning for therapeutic ends while two have explicitly authorized it.

Besides its reproductive function, sexual activity is also a source of pleasure, joy, and happiness. Sexuality thus can be independent from reproduction. Additionally, historical and contemporary social observations show that human sexuality and reproduction take place within a kind of official relationship called marriage and also out of it. Though they can be linked, the three topics of sexuality, reproduction, and marriage will be considered separately in this chapter.

Sexuality

Society today is characterized by a wide variety of sexual behaviors; from people who choose not to have sex at all to those who have it abundantly including with animals. This observation makes some people think that they ought to be judgmental and consequently ascribe a value to their own sexual conducts as well as those of others. In the meantime, other people refuse to engage in such assessment accepting that everybody freely lives sexually as he/she pleases.

---

[36]http://www.fda.gov/AnimalVeterinary/SafetyHealth/AnimalCloning/default.htm (accessed April 30, 2011).
[37]http://fpc.state.gov/documents/organization/70307.pdf (accessed April 29, 2011).

Seeker thinks it is reasonable to have personal judgment about the different sorts of sexual behaviors not only for individual development but also to advance toward the emergence of the happiest society. Being judgmental in the sense of disagreement and criticism is acceptable. What is not is hypercriticism or condemnation in a pluralistic society.

A pluralistic society is one in which groups of people hold different opinions with different lifestyles and an advanced degree of coexistence. In the contrary, Hypercriticism or condemnation is philosophically justifiable in a monistic society. In other words if nobody defends a certain idea, people can strongly criticize it with no one feeling uncomfortable.

According to a well-researched and well written article on Wikipedia[38], having sex with animals while legal in some countries is considered illegal in others and in 31 states in the U.S. including the 16 which qualify it as a felony. A felony is a grave crime severely punishable by law.

Countries in which human-animal sexual intercourse is prohibited are Canada, Ethiopia, France, Ghana, Hong Kong, India, New Zealand, Norway, Turkey, Switzerland, the United Kingdom, and Zambia.

The American states against are Alaska, Arkansas, Arizona, California, Delaware, Georgia, Idaho, Iowa, Illinois, Indiana, Maine, Maryland, Massachusetts, Michigan, Minnesota, Mississippi, Missouri, Nebraska, New York, North Dakota, Oklahoma, Oregon, Pennsylvania, Rhode Island, South Carolina, South Dakota, Tennessee, Utah, Virginia, Washington, and Wisconsin.

Before the examination and assessment the various sexual behaviors known, it is important to take a look at the concept of the Tree of the Knowledge of Good and Evil mentioned in Genesis 2: 17 because it is believed by some interpreters to have sexual implications.

---

[38]http://en.wikipedia.org/wiki/Zoophilia_and_the_law (accessed April 30, 2011).

The Tree of the Knowledge of Good and Evil (TKGE)

Five different interpretations of the TKGE

Augustine, one of the most renowned Church Fathers who lived during the 4th and 5th centuries C.E, is often referred to for the meaning of the TKGE. He made his most direct and clearest declarations about this tree in the 6th chapter of the 8th volume of his first series of commentaries on the book of Genesis.

In the two chapters preceding this 6th chapter, Augustine succeeds in logically showing that the *Tree of Life* which was also in the Garden of Eden was both literal and symbolical. In the symbolic sense, the *Tree of Life* is wisdom as stated in the book of Proverbs of King Solomon. But to Augustine there must be a literal tree that represents wisdom. This argument is sound because in human language, animals, plants, and minerals are often associated with moral values or qualities according to the law of correspondences.

Surprisingly, concerning the TKGE, Augustine states that it was only a literal tree which contained nothing harmful but was given its particular name just because of the commandment not to eat of its fruit, the violation of which would lead to punishment. Through the punishment of their disobedience, Adam and Eve would then come to know what good and evil are.

In *The Secret Teachings of All Ages* that he published for the first time in 1928, Manly P. Hall expresses the opinion that the *Tree of Life* represents the spiritual point of balance, the secret of immortality while, the TKGE represents polarity and unbalance, the secret of mortality.

In the early 1950s, Sun Myung Moon, the founder of the Holy Spirit Association for the Unification of World Christianity also known as Unification Movement made public his interpretation according to which both the *Tree of Life* and the TKGE are symbolic and not literal respectively representing

Adam and Eve as the two trees put in the middle of the Garden of Eden [See *Divine Principle 1996 Chapter 2*].

To Moon, since the ultimate hope of humanity during the period of the Old Testament [Proverbs 13: 12] and the New Testament [Revelation 22: 14] was the *Tree of Life*; and since the path to this tree was blocked after Adam's disobedience; it symbolizes a man who has fully realized the ideal of creation.

For him, the original sin makes it impossible to humans to become trees of life by their personal efforts alone. That is why they need to be engrafted to a man who has come to earth and has realized the ideal of creation like Jesus.

Still according to Sun Myung Moon, the blockade of the path to the *Tree of Life* was removed on the day of the Pentecost when the flaming sword appearing as tongues of fire was moved aside enabling humans to receive the Holy Spirit, to approach Jesus the *Tree of Life*, and be engrafted to him.

However, continues Moon, Christians have been engrafted to Jesus only spiritually, that is why saints still have the original sin which remains transmissible to children; and that is why Christians await the Second Coming of Christ as the *Tree of Life* to be engrafted again and be freed from the original sin.

Since the *Tree of Life* symbolized the perfected man that Adam wanted to become, the TKGE which stands next to the *Tree of Life* must symbolize the perfected woman that Eve wanted to become through the fulfillment of the good purpose of that tree of the knowledge of good and evil.

Based on Jude 6-7, Genesis 2: 25, Genesis 3: 7, Job 31: 33, John 8: 44, Revelation 12: 9, Romans 8: 23, etc…, Moon argues that the sin of angels among whom was the serpent of Eden was illicit sexual relationship. Adam and Eve's sexual parts were the parts that were involved in the sin, that is why they realized their nakedness after their disobedience and covered it.

The serpent or Devil or fallen angel proposing the fruit to Eve first means he had sex with her through their respective spiritual bodies and Eve proposing the fruit to Adam means she tempted Adam, seduced him, and had sex with him thus making the sin reach the physical plane. Through the fall, humans have become the descendants of Satan and they must be redeemed through adoption by God.

A fourth original interpretation that Seeker's research has found is that of the twentieth century Gnostic teacher Samael Aun Weor. That interpretation was given in the early 1960s[39]. According to it, there was a Tree of Knowledge that gives Wisdom and a Tree of Life that gives Immortality through love.

Fifth, Kabbalah affirms that the *Tree of Life* is made of ten spiritual realms with beings of different characteristics. Centered on the Zohar, it adds, for example on www. Kabbalah.info, that the TKGE represents the good and bad qualities of a human who cannot become perfect.

Seeker sees good reasoning efforts in the ways Augustine, Hall, Moon, Aun Weor, and the Kabbalah tried to explain the meaning of the TKGE and also, that of the *Tree of Life*. Among these four explanations, only Moon associates The TKGE with Eve and its fruit with the sexual love of Eve. But Aun Weor is not far because he associates the *Tree of Life* this time to sexuality. These two explanations constitute the main reason why a section on the TKGE is developed in this chapter on sexuality, reproduction, and marriage.

Seeker's understanding of the TKGE and the original sin

Only the author of the story of the Garden of Eden could explain what he or she truly meant. All the other explanations including Seeker's are attempts to unlock the mystery using clues in scriptures and also reasoning.

---

[39] Aun Weor, *The Perfect Matrimony*, Chapter 20.

Augustine succeeds in describing well the *Tree of Life* as wisdom. Wisdom, the origin of the creation of all things [Proverbs 8] is equivalent to the Word [John 1] which is also at the origin of everything. According to Hermes Trismegistus, the Word is the son of Thought [Thoth] or son of the Mind and the origin of life. So Wisdom or Word truly is the *Tree of Life*.

The problem in Augustine's reasoning appears when he declares that the TKGE has no symbolic sense and simply points to the knowledge that Adam and Eve gain when they eat of its literal fruit by disobeying God. Nevertheless, by speaking in such a manner, Augustine without acknowledging it does give a symbolic meaning to the Tree of Knowledge of Good and Evil.

The existence of literal trees as emblems of spiritual realities or of soul qualities according to the law of correspondences is possible and admissible. However, the story of the Garden of Eden does not look primarily like a story about literal trees, and in this, Hall is right. So is Moon who also gives a symbolical interpretation.

While Moon's explanation on the Tree of life and the TKGE is too limited and includes incorrect statements that will be highlighted, Hall's is correct but too short except when he sees good and evil as a polarity. On that, he was wrong.

By overemphasizing that the *Tree of Life* is the perfect man, Moon led himself to makes important mistakes. His perfect man can come into existence only after eating perfectly of the Tree of Life; differently said after receiving all the wisdom necessary. He lost sight of Wisdom or the Word as the *real Tree of Life* of which humans must eat to become trees of life too. The origin of this mistake lies in the Christian understanding of Jesus as absolutely necessary as Messiah for the salvation of mankind.

By shifting attention from wisdom to a man, the door is opened for several other mistakes. Most of those mistakes are the misinterpretation of several other passages such as the ancient prophecies of Israel. Seeker has presented some of these errors in *Abode of Divinities*, in the section on deified humans, messiahs, and the meaning of godship. Moon's theory that in the Bible trees symbolize humans is limited because Ezekiel 31 clearly shows that nations too are called trees of the Garden of Eden thus making Eden equivalent to the earth. This limitation also explains partially why his explanation of the *Tree of Life* and the TKGE were limited to Adam and Eve neglecting the importance of Wisdom and Evil.

Christianity and Moon believe that it is the person of Jesus that is necessary for salvation, while in reality it is the divine wisdom or word which God imparted to Jesus that operates salvation. That is what appears after deep consideration of Jesus' sayings, the entire Bible, other scriptures, and reason.

Wisdom or the Word was saving people even before the birth of Jesus Christ. But Moon and Christianity do not mention this. Paul and Moon made the mistake believing that the Holy Spirit is given to humanity only because of Jesus while in reality, as presented in *Abode of Divinities*, the Holy Spirit was given in Ancient Israel at the time of Moses for example as well as in other societies. As a teacher, Jesus tried to improve the divine wisdom available to humans so that they can eat more of the *Tree of Life*.

Instead of saying like Moon that it was at the time of Jesus that the blockade of the *Tree of Life* was removed, Seeker advances that the removal of that obstacle began long before Jesus when the God of the Old Testament [a powerful angel] and his opponents were trying to recruit humans for their respective causes. The blockade of the way leading to the *Tree of Life* by angels means that the God of the Old Testament has decided not to let Adam [not humans in general] access important wisdom or word or teaching or knowledge since that tree symbolizes wisdom.

Latter, bad angels taught some kind of wisdom [the corrupted one] to humans while good angels tried to teach people like Abraham, Moses, and so on. That is why the tradition of Kabbalah and esoteric teachings in general have been and are still kept secret because to angels and demons, wisdom or knowledge can be a weapon. This explains why the God of the Old Testament who no longer trusted Adam decided not let him access important information that he could probably use against him and his system as Solomon will do.

Another difference between Moon's teaching and Seeker's is that the latter has made a clear difference between the God of the Old Testament [a powerful angel] and the true God who is All Pervading and Omnipresent. Anybody who reads the Old Testament carefully can see the limits of its God.

By clearly identifying the angelic nature of the God of the Old Testament and by considering the Holy Spirit as Divine Energy that good angels can use instead of calling it a feminine spirit like Moon, Seeker is thus able to present the unfolding of the events in Genesis and the Bible in a manner that sheds a different light on the behaviors of angels and demons toward humans, the manifestations of the Holy Spirit even before the New Testament, the true meaning of wisdom, the secondary importance of the Messiah or Messiahs, and the unnoticed work of the Universal Soul.

At first, the God of the Old Testament authorized Adam and Eve to eat of the fruit of the *Tree of Life*. As its name shows, it is a life giving and life preserving tree. Reason recommends agreeing that giving and preserving life is good. Since angels helped for the creation of nature which nourishes the physical body, it makes sense to admit that that they also helped for the nourishment of the spirit and the soul through spirituality and wisdom.

In ancient times wisdom encompassed both spiritual science or magic and ideology. That is why after each creation thanks to Divine Wisdom or Word, the God of the Old Testament in Genesis sees the creation as good or very good. Therefore, it is by eating of the *Tree of Life* that mankind *knows* Good. The *Tree of Life* can also be called *Tree of the Knowledge of Good*.

The "fear" of the God of the Old Testament for Adam and Eve was about Evil. That powerful angel knew there was a way for Evil to be created as Good is created. The means by which Evil is created is the Tree of Knowledge of Good and Evil. The God of Adam could have just said the Tree of the Knowledge of Evil, but by adding Good, he most probably wanted to teach that *any kind of Evil comes from creatures originally good*. That is why demons can disguise as agents of light.

Seekers of the world can see the reason why the Devil is presented in Ezekiel 28 as an angel [a cherub] originally full of wisdom before the corruption of that wisdom. Since wisdom gives life, corrupted wisdom would give corrupted life or death. So, corrupted wisdom is the Tree of the Knowledge of Good and Evil that can bring death as the God of the Old Testament warned Adam [Genesis 2:17].

The TKGE is a perverted *Tree of Life*; the appearance of Evil in Good elements like a cancer in a healthy body. Hence, the Devil who is also the serpent of Eden as many religious teachers have said approached Eve with his corrupted wisdom or TKGE.

Jesus calls the Devil 'father of lies' in John 8: 44 not because he is truly a father of humanity through a blood lineage as Moon says but because he was the *creator or father* of practical lie and deceit that corrupted the original nature of humans. There is no reproduction possible between an angel and a human. So, there is no way humans would be Satan's children via a blood connection. Humans are the blood descendants of Adam and Eve according to scripture and the children of God because he created them. Since humans have become something different from the original design because of Satan, the latter can also be called their *father or creator through bad education.*

Lie is the opposite of truth. Truth is 'Right Word' that gives life while lie is 'perverted Word' which brings death. The TKGE is Lie. The Devil, by lying to Eve brought her the death against which the God of the Old Testament warned her and Adam.

In TKGE, 'knowledge' means practice. Sometime in language, 'to eat' also means 'to practice'. That is the explanation of a phrase like: '*I don't eat of that fruit*' meaning '*this is not my nature, practice, or habit*'. The God of the Old Testament clearly asked Adam not to eat of the TKGE because it will bring him death [Genesis 2:17]. In other words, he wanted them not to bring the theoretical evil that anybody can imagine into concrete reality by practicing it. Manly Hall is extremely correct when he says that the *Tree of Life* is the way to immortality while the TKGE is the way to mortality. But again, in contrary to Hall, Seeker does not think that polarity which is part of the creation is the cause of mortality since in chemistry and physics, plus and minus are both necessary and good.

With his corrupted wisdom, the Devil approached Eve, not Adam. He certainly had good reasons for that. This explains why he succeeded in convincing Eve and why other creation myths in Zoroastrianism, Gnosticism, and Shintoism attribute a negative role to some female at the beginning of the world.

This also explains why the decision of the God of the Old Testament after the disobedience of Adam and Eve contains the following declaration to Eve in Genesis 3: 16: *'You will desire to control your husband, but he will rule over you.'* Indeed Eve decided to shape the future of Adam by giving him the fruit of Evil or corrupted wisdom or corrupted philosophy learned from the Devil; however Adam's wisdom was still better than Eve's not only because of Genesis 2: 18 which presents him as the principal figure of his couple but also because he was not the type to disobey first according to the serpent's calculation.

Additionally, the reason why the great majority of prophets, messiahs and rulers have been male is clearer. It is also very probably why women have a lesser role in Judaism and why several esoteric schools do not allow women in men's meetings. From a sociological standpoint, many believe that women in general are more emotive [less reasonable] than men, less strong, and easily believe seducers and liars. But there are some exceptions and the general inclination can change when the exceptions multiply to become the majority and then the whole.

The correct understanding of the *Tree of Life* and the TKGE also explains why the Gospels presents only masculine persons as the main disciples of Jesus and why Paul in several occasions was so severe toward women going as far as to state that they should remain silent in public, protect themselves from fallen angels, learn from their husbands, and be saved through them [1 Corinthians 14: 34-35, Ephesians 5: 25-26, and 1 Timothy 2: 11-15].

Seeker's opinion is that women are nevertheless awesome beings whose wisdom like men's can be restored. When this is done, women would no longer desire to control men who in turn would truly live as one with their wives and not as rulers as history has shown.

Moon's declaration that sex was involved in the story of Eden has many supporting elements such as the biblical passages he points to and the sociological analysis he made but also because of other passages such as Genesis 6: 1-8, sexual offense passages in Leviticus, the book of Enoch, and so on.

However, sexual misconduct is not the primary reason that explains the declaration of Jesus to some of his fellow citizens that the Devil was their father and it is not the prime reason of Eve's mistake.

Let us not be limited to physical nakedness and verify if 'Nakedness' like other words in the Bible can mean something different.

If the physical body can be naked and is in fact born naked, it would make sense that the spiritual body and to soul be naked and be born naked as well. *Soul or mind nakedness therefore is not only ignorance but also innocence.* There is good ignorance and bad ignorance and there is good wisdom and bad wisdom.

Good ignorance is compatible with age or parallels it while bad ignorance is not. So, the nakedness or ignorance of Adam and Eve at a young age was not a bad thing especially when the God of the Old Testament had a plan for the bad ignorance or bad nakedness not to occur. That plan was the progressive eating of the *Tree of Life* or Wisdom, the opposite of Ignorance.

But the serpent or the Devil for some reason that needs to be further researched decided to teach the immature and weak Eve something different. By showing Eve prematurely the attractiveness of some realities while the

God of the Old Testament was waiting for the right moment, the Devil displayed a twofold bad wisdom: choosing a bad time and telling a lie.

An important element neglected in the ideas of Moon is that Eve saw that the TKGE was desirable to make one *wise*. So, that tree has more to do with wisdom or teaching than with sex. When Adam ate of the fruit of the TKGE and told the God of the Old Testament that he was afraid of him because he was naked, that God immediately asked him who *told* him he was naked. This means that the way for Adam to know he was naked was to be told by someone; *in other words to receive a teaching* and not necessarily and primarily through the sexual act. So, the damage inflicted by Eve to Adam was to make him accept [tell him] and follow a bad teaching, philosophy, or guidance.

So, the Devil taught Eve and Adam at that time that being naked or ignorant about some subjects was not in their interest. Then they made clothes with fig leaves to cover themselves. At this point of his thinking, it hit Seeker's soul that Jesus cursed a fig tree [Matthew 21: 18-19] not simply because it had no fruit and only leaves but also to teach the person who has the right eye and the right ear lessons about the fig tree leaves. One lesson is most probably related to the story of Adam. Whether Jesus actually cursed a fig tree or whether that was the best way to teach is another question.

So, the fig leaves represent the result of the work of the Devil which is prematurity and deceit that is why the God of the Old Testament replaced them with animal skin.

The fact that priest, prophets, and kings were anointed in the Bible has always intrigued Seeker. His personal experience with the Holy Spirit and its manifestation with Moses and the 70 elders as well with Jesus and the disciples at the Pentecost made him consider that the olive tree which produces oil for anointment is a symbol of the *Tree of Life*. But a passage such as Ezekiel 47:12 shows that others trees too contribute to life; which makes sense. But the oil of the olive tree that connects it with the Holy Spirit makes that tree an important or central one. That is why the God of the Old Testament allowed Adam to eat of all the trees except one, the TKGE.

Adam and Eve at their creation had common attributes but they were also made different in some ways. By uniting as one, each of them gains what is lacking and becomes whole. One relies on the other concerning certain things of life. So, the secular humanist Jeaneane Fowler, the Unificationist Sun Myung Moon, and others are right when they advocate complementarity between man and woman.

It looks like concerning certain matters of wisdom and spirituality; wives would do well to rely on their husbands until a certain time. This was most probably Paul's view, but the way he conveyed it can appear harsh to many women today.

Seeker was not there when Adam and Eve committed their sin. So he cannot say for sure if sexuality was involved or not. What he can say without hesitation is that a sexual offense is a possibility and if it did occur, it could only be secondary to the main problem which had to do with the nakedness or ignorance of young souls and their corruption by the deception of Satan.

Through a physical sexual relationship, matter, substance, or energy is exchanged. Based on the definition of the term 'spirit' proposed in chapter 4, it is conceivable that two spirits have sex and exchange energy as Moon explains. In case there is a negative energy from one partner, this could make the spirit and the physical body of the other partner sick and the sickness could be inherited by future generations.

The notion of disobedience is far more fundamental than sexual misconduct. Whether it comes to be proven that illicit sex between Eve and the fallen angel and then between Eve and Adam happened and whether clear proofs that such a thing did not happen exist, the fact remains that the purpose of Eve by eating the fruit was the wisdom it would give her. This brings the discussion back to Wisdom and the *Tree of Life*.

Eve, thanks to the serpent saw that the TKGE was beautiful and its fruit looked delicious. But she was just tricked to believe so. If she had properly done her homework she would have seen through the lies and perceived the ugliness of the TKGE and sense the bitterness of its fruit or practice.

For a moment, the TKGE disguised appeared to Eve as a better provider of wisdom than the *Tree of Life* [Wisdom itself]. In Africa 'long eye' is a phrase often used to described abnormally ambitious people; those who want a great benefit that they have not worked for. Eve must have found God's method for gaining wisdom more difficult than that of the serpent. But the rest of the biblical story and the current state of the world show that the TKGE is ugly and its fruit bitter at taste.

Sexual misconduct is one of the most dangerous outcomes of the corruption of wisdom or of the eating of the fruit of the TKGE. But it is the restoration of the place of Wisdom, the *Tree of Life*, and obedience to it that will save people and give them total resurrection and true freedom including from sexual misconduct. Cleansing the blood as Moon suggests may be compared to treating some of the symptoms of a disease while restoring Wisdom can be considered as the treatment of the cause of the disease. However, both the methodology and efficiency of the treatments should be clear.

As long as the cause of a disease remains, the problem is not solved. *Women in particular should be encouraged to eat from the Tree of Wisdom to prevent social destruction since it looks like they are the privileged target of deceivers.*

This interpretation of the *Tree of Life* and the TKGE is another reason besides the historical meaning of the term messiah and the meaning of godship which confirms to Seeker that the "Messiah" in Christian and Unificationist understanding results from a misinterpretation.

It shows that Arius was correct while his bishop Alexander of Alexandria was not. Pelagius was right to encourage every human being to put efforts in personal development and happiness while Augustine, Paul, Luther, and Calvin who emphasized the Grace of God too much were not. It would have been better for God to create robot human beings who do not sin rather than let free people create ugliness and suffering and then save them with His-Her Grace. It is reasonable to affirm that freedom should always be associated with responsibility.

The grace of God so dear to many already manifested In the fact that the human being was endowed with a mind. What remains is to put that mind into good use. Asking for an additional grace from God is like the situation of a child who does not want to become adult preferring to always receive things from the parents instead of working. Some passages of the writings of Paul such as Romans 2: 13; 1 Thessalonians 5: 19, 21;and 2 Thessalonians 2: 2 show that he understood this.

But his desire to justify the messianism of Jesus and his crucifixion has often led him to faith and grace. Nevertheless, human history clearly shows that the human beings remains free to choose between good and evil according to the analysis of his/her mind.

Why would listening to the Devil and behaving badly be a human sin while the same person who do good by listening to the word of God or the teaching of Jesus would not be credited for the success? Bringing death or protecting life is the responsibility of humans and they should be honored or dishonored accordingly.

Aun Weor's description is erroneous for two reasons. First he shortened the name TKGE to TK [Tree of Knowledge] to give a chance to his interpretation. Hence, he was able to connect knowledge to wisdom. If he had maintained the full name given by the scripture, it would have been difficult for him to make the connection with wisdom and justify how the knowledge of evil *really* gives wisdom.

Second, since he has already wrongly associated the TKGE with wisdom, he made another error changing the true meaning of the *Tree of Life* [Wisdom] into immortality *through sexual love*. But it is evident for who has understanding that it is wisdom which is to be linked to immortality. This second mistake is not isolated from the first since it enables Aun Weor to introduce the notion of sexual love and justify his perfect matrimony.

There are problems with the interpretation of Kabbalah as well. If the TKGE were truly the good and bad qualities of a human who cannot become perfect, as some kabbalists affirm based on the Zohar, it would not have been written not to eat of that tree[Genesis: 2: 17 and 3:1-2]. That would be impossible since no one lives alone unless mentally sick or traumatized. And living alone is in contradiction with living with a spouse as recommended in Genesis 1 and 2.

The creation of Adam and Eve was qualified as good in Genesis, not good and bad. Also, let's not forget that Jesus asked humans to be perfect like their heavenly father [Matthew 5: 48]. So, humans were created good and should grow in goodness. But corruption or evil or sin or crime is a possibility that they should vanquished as it was advised Cain [Genesis 4: 6].

At this point an important problem that seems to appear with Genesis 3: 22 must be solved. In almost all biblical versions, it is rendered: *'And the LORD God said: The man has now become like one of us, knowing good and evil. He must not be allowed to reach out his hand and take also from the tree of life and eat, and live forever.'*

With this way of rendering the verse, a serious contradiction in the message of Genesis appears. If the verse were to be taken as it is formulated above, this would signify that God and other beings had already eaten of the TKGE and knew good and evil. Hence, forbidding man to eat of the TKGE portrays a malicious and tyrannical God. It would mean that God did not really want human at His-Her image as said in Genesis 1: 27. It would mean that the serpent was right while God was wrong. It would also mean that the God knowing good and evil is different from a purely benevolent God.

With the verse thus phrased, not only is the biblical message contradictory and confusing; but in addition, no serious interpretation of the TKGE including Seeker's can be made.

Fortunately, one biblical version, the *Young's Literal Translation* [YLT] saves the interpreter from simply declaring the verse incorrect and from asking for a new translation. The YLT was made by Robert Young during the second half of the 19th century with the declared purpose to respect the tense of original Hebrew and Greek texts.

Thus he rendered the verse as followed: *'And Jehovah God saith, Lo, he man <u>was as one of Us</u>, as to the knowledge of good and evil; and now, lest* *he send forth his hand, and have taken also of the tree of life, and eaten, and lived to the age.'*

By correcting the tense of the first part of the declaration according to original texts, Young succeeds in opening a way for this verse to fit in the rest of Genesis and the entire Bible. Hence this rendition reaffirms that man *was* [Genesis 1: 27] at the image of God knowing good and evil the same way God did meaning 0% evil or innocence. So, now [in Genesis 3: 22], man is no longer the image of God which is why he has to be chased away.

The rest of the verse and all the other judgments pronounced by the God of the Old Testament do not necessarily need his actual intervention. They are the logical [Reasonable] consequences of the practical knowledge of evil and corruption of wisdom. *Corrupted wisdom is a "natural" or logical obstacle to true wisdom.* Without wisdom, life and immortality cannot be; which means death. In order to regain access to the *Tree of Life* or Wisdom, humanity must get rid of corrupted wisdom, lies, and false teachings and connect with teachings that can give life as Jesus said: '*My word is life and resurrection*' [John 5: 20-30/John 6:63].

It is thanks to the restoration of wisdom to a certain level that the following assessments of various sexual conducts will be introduced.

Examination and assessment of various sexual behaviors

No sex at all?

Several groups of people in history have advocated celibacy but the two main groups that immediately come to the mind today at the mention of this concept are Buddhism and Christianity especially in its Catholic form because the two groups have the most elaborated doctrines on monasticism and the greatest number of monks and nuns.

At the opposite, Muhammad in the Qur'an [57: 27] speaks against celibacy and monasticism saying that it is a human invention and not a command from God. However, Muhammad went as far as to authorize people to marry up to four wives because wars made too many male victims with many female orphans to take care of [4: 3 with note in Yusuf Ali's version]. An analysis of polygamy will be made later in this same chapter.

In Buddhism, the most fundamental reason why some choose not to engage in sexual relations is because of the example given by the founder of that religion, Gautama Buddha[40]. At the beginning of his quest for enlightenment, Buddha left his wife and son for an ascetic life.

Buddha believed celibacy was necessary to reach the high levels of enlightenment of non-returner and arahant and that his own enlightenment required renouncing all sexual activity. He thought sexual desire was a serious obstacle to attaining the Nirvana or heaven.

However, apart from the sexualdomain, it was not pure ascetic life which made him succeed. It was the "Middle Way" which he described as a moderation in everything. In principle, this conclusion should have led Gautama Buddha to also engage in moderate sexual activity. But no record of that sort figures in Buddhist teachings.

One can say without the risk of making a mistake that the level of enlightenment Buddha reached, though high, was not the highest. A human wisdom that cannot see the Divine Wisdom in natural phenomena such as sex still has some way to go.

Jesus too lived without having a wife according to the New Testament and taught that people can choose not to marry for the sake of heaven [Matthew 19: 12]. He added that those who will resurrect will not marry but will live like angels in heaven [Matthew 22; 30]. Paul recommended to people who are not married not to seek marriage [1 Corinthians 7: 27] unless they cannot control sexual desire [verse 9].

---

[40] Christopher W. Gowans, *Philosophy of the Buddha* (New York, NY: Taylor and Francis Group, 2005) pp 170 and 177.

There is a paradox in the teaching ascribed to Jesus in Matthew 19 because before verse 12 where he speaks of being eunuch for the sake of heaven, he has previously said in verse 5 like in Genesis 2: 24 that spouses leave their parents to unite as one. With verse 12, there is no longer a general sexual law for all mankind because some can now choose not to have a wife.

More troubling is the reason of this choice: 'the sake of heaven' as if by creating Adam and Eve and finding it very good, the God of the Old Testament did not intend that the couple goes to heaven united as one. However, there are two ways to understand this teaching which is in harmony with Jesus' whole message.

First, because of their disobedience in Eden which made them know evil in practice, it became possible that the relationship between Adam and Eve prevents them from accessing heaven, a world of Good. So, Jesus is teaching that it is acceptable that a person chooses to remain single in order to avoid such handicap like in the case where he taught to cut any part of the body that pushes to sin and not be condemned to hell [Matthew 5: 29-30]. Nevertheless, it is better for humans to keep every part of their being and avoid sinning. It is because this was difficult for the people of his time that Jesus taught as he did.

The second way the teaching of Jesus about celibacy can be comprehended as Moon taught is that people can remain single until they are ready for marriage. But the teaching of Jesus is so short in this matter that one cannot say for sure if Jesus held such an idea. The advantage of this second interpretation is that the teaching about being single would be in harmony with the divine decree for spouses to become one.

Swedenborg and Moon taught in contrary to Jesus that there are marriages in heaven and consequently sex life.

When Genesis presents the creation of Adam and Eve, it does not say whether their union was temporary, just for their earthly lives, or for eternity even after the shedding of the physical body.

No other biblical passage to the knowledge of Seeker tackles such a matter except Matthew 22: 30 where it is mentioned that in Jesus' opinion, there is no marriage after resurrection and people live like angels. Here the seeker faces three choices: a- Jesus was right, b- the passage about eunuchs is not from Jesus and is wrong, and c- Jesus was wrong.

In any cases, one major argument appears to be completely against the declaration in Matthew 22: 30. A human being has a spiritual body in the likeness of the physical body. Based on dream experiences and numerous scriptures, one can say that the spiritual body has a sexual organ which is used for sexual relations.

This is what Genesis 6: 1-2 and Jude 6-7 teach. If spirits have sexual organs according to God's law of creation, those organs must have a purpose which they serve at least according to scripture and dreams. If sex has a purpose, it is better that its fulfillment be within marriage than outside it.

Hence, the union in Genesis 2: 24 is not temporary but eternal. With the disobedience in Eden, all sorts of complicated relationships emerged which explains for example the law of Moses about divorce. That law though given in the line of the punishment of the woman in Genesis 3 also opens the way for abuse.

This law of Moses was a circumstantial law, not an original or eternal one. It corresponds to a level of human spiritual development that is not supreme. It was a law to manage the troubles created in Eden. When humankind develops, it will come a time when people would want and would be able to establish everlasting marriages.

In that époque, marriages would be so well prepared that divorcing would be a pure evil act. However, if humanity continues to create situations in which people are legitimately unhappy in marriages or have been tricked into marriages full of problems, divorce should remain a way to limit the damages.

Nevertheless, the best thing to do is not to be satisfied with divorce laws, but use Divine Wisdom, the *Tree of Life*, the most precious treasure of the philosophy of divine humanism to create educational programs that teach scientifically about sexual and marital lives based on physical and spiritual realities.

To have sex with animals?

Logically people who engage in sexual relationships with animals cannot honestly say that they follow God [Lev 18:23]. If they do then their "God" cannot be the One described in *Abode of Divinities*.

Beyond the acceptance of the existence of God, there are reasons that many atheists agree with which can also explain why so many countries and so many states of the U.S.A. have pronounced themselves against sexual relations between animals and humans. These arguments come from the efforts of reasoning and can be accepted by both religious and secular morals.

Among the arguments brought forth by the adversaries of zoosex as reported by the article previously cited, two appear to be the most receivable by secular philosophy. The first is the possibility of birth of monsters. The second non theistic argument is animal abuse which needs to be further explained.

Most of the proponents of this argument explain that zoosex is an animal abuse because animals cannot give their *consent*. Seeker agrees but thinks there is a better justification than that of the consent. Pedophilia is condemned worldwide even when a child willingly gets involved in it. The reason of the condemnation of pedophilia even with child consent dwells in the immaturity of children who have not yet developed the mind set and the body that would make sexual activity with adult humans harmless.

If children do not know everything that is good for them, the case of animals who cannot even think as humans do is worse. Before to give a consent or not, one needs a well elaborated opinion which animals are incapable of having. Therefore zoosex is a total abuse.

The argument that zoosexuality involves mature animals is not receivable because mature animals are even less mature than children from a psychological point of view. Pedophilia is not rejected solely on the base of the immaturity of the human body, but more importantly on the ground of the immaturity of the human psyche in children.

However an important counter argument of the advocates of zoosex should be considered. To them, if having sex with animals is an abuse, killing them, eating them, and using them for various purposes are abuses as well. This argument can appears sound at first; but a deep analysis reveals it is not.

This is where the third argument against zoosexuality should be advanced. It is the argument of *historical utilitarianism*. This argument has three components: a- all human sexual desires and need of sexual pleasure can be satisfied within a couple of husband and wife [within the human race], b- humans are superior to animals and can please better sexually, c- eating animals has been and still is a need, a use rather than an abuse.

if societies in the past have refrained from killing and eating animals, many people would have died and several people in today's world [their descendants] could not have come into existence the way they did; many animals kill and eat other animals, they are designed to do so; however what is good for animals is not necessarily good for humans. Therefore humanity should develop ways of living and living well without necessarily eating animals.

That a human being is incapable of finding sexual satisfaction within the human population is not only an individual failure but also the failure of the entire human race both historically and contemporarily. With some effort of wisdom, love, and compassion people can easily solve the problem of zoosexuality and nobody would need to go look for sexual pleasure in the animal realm.

Zoosexuality is a result of the psychological, philosophical, and spiritual weakness of the human race considered as a whole. Having sex with animals is unlawful according to the divine standard and should be unlawful according to the secular standard as well. But law alone is not sufficient. Wisdom, love, and compassion are important tools to be used in well designed and well popularized educational and health programs.

To be lesbian, gay, bisexual, transsexual, or transgender [LGBT]?

It is public knowledge that the main argument that the religious opponents of homosexuality use comes from the Bible particularly from passages such as Jude 7 and Genesis 18 and 19. However, some religious people accept the Bible as a fundamental scripture and nevertheless defend homosexuality. They try to show that each biblical passage used against it in fact does not clearly and specifically condemn this sexual behavior.

However, the attempt to forcefully bend the scripture to make it *not look unfavorable* to homosexuality is very difficult and biased especially when one considers Lev 18: 22/20:13 and Rom 1: 27].

If Seeker thinks that the scriptural arguments against homosexuality are unbreakable, he is also of the opinion that arguments beyond scripture should be added. These arguments strictly follow reason or wisdom. By proving homosexuality wrong, one can also demonstrate the wrongness of bisexuality, transsexualism, and transgender people.

The best way to show the wrongness of homosexuality without using the Bible is to prove that despite the claims of homosexuals, this sexual practice is not only unnatural, but more importantly harmful and unjust.

One of the most influential books if not the most influential that the supporters of homosexuality use today to prove that it is a natural sexual behavior is *Biological Exuberance: Animal Homosexuality and Natural Diversity* of the biologist, linguist, and author Bruce Bagemihl[41].

---

[41]Bagemihl, Bruce. *Biological Exuberance: Animal Homosexuality and Natural Diversity*. New York: St. Martin's Press, 1999.

The book is indeed rich in describing homosexuality in the animal realm. However, as one can expect, it offers more evidences for male-male homosexuality than for female-female sex. *It would be interesting to have a documentary that shows images of female animals displaying sexual behaviors towards each other and compare them to how female human homosexuals behave.*

It will not surprise to notice that animal male-male homosexuality better parallels gay behaviors than female-female animal sexual behavior resembles lesbian attitudes. The reason of this postulate dwells in human intelligence and creativity that women possess. Most lesbians in their sexual relationships do not neglect penetration using a phallic instrument to replace the masculine sexual organ.

This shows an unconscious attempt to introduce a "natural" element into an "artificial" [or created, or cultural] sexual behavior. Hence, lesbianism demonstrates that the body of a woman or a female animal is not *naturally* equipped to satisfy the sexual needs of another.

Most lesbians use a phallic instrument in their sexual acts but female animals which are not that intelligent or creative do not. Hence, one can say that lesbians try to fill the "natural" void they have created in preferring a woman to a man creating an instrument to serve the same purpose even though in a very incomplete way. For example no instrument can produce sperm and make a lesbian desiring a child pregnant. Animal "lesbians" must somehow be frustrated since they cannot even create a phallic instrument.

On the other hand, gays and male animals engaging in the sexual act with other males do not have to be so inventive. The phallus is intended for the vagina in heterosexual relationships. In contrary to fingers which are not very similar to the phallus, the anus has more in common with the vagina in terms of their capacity of reception of the phallus. So gays and male animals have almost a "natural" replacement for the vagina and do not need to invent an instrument specifically for that purpose.

However, similarly to phallic instruments which do not produce sperm, the anus is not connected to an internal female genital apparatus that gays do not have anyway. So, gays too cannot satisfy their "natural" need of children exclusively through the sexual choice they have made.

The reader must have noticed that the term 'natural' in this section has not yet been defined since it has been put between quotation marks. This was purposely done so that the issue be tackled once more after chapter 4. Indeed since advanced creativity is part of human nature, one must be careful as to what is natural or not. *That is why in this chapter, 'unnatural' would qualify something that even human creativity, reason, intelligence, or wisdom in last consideration cannot accept as valid.*

The words issued so far have shown that homosexuality poses a problem of *anatomical and physiological incompatibility*. The fact that homosexuals want things or have desires that their anatomy or body cannot satisfy proves that this sexual behavior is *unnatural [from the anatomo-physiological standpoint]*. This type of sexual life is also *unjust* and brings *inequality*.

Thanks to the IVF method of reproduction, practitioners of homosexuality could have children, but at an expensive cost that all cannot yet afford. So the inequality and injustice persists. Additionally, homosexuality like zoosexuality is historically unjust and unequal because IVF was not available to assure the survival of the human race if all humans had decided to use their "freedom" and have chosen to be gay or lesbian.

If this had happened, humanity would have disappeared in one generation. On the contrary, all human beings could have chosen to be heterosexual at any time of history without risk of annihilation of the human species.

Historically, the existence of homosexuals is impossible without that of heterosexuals while the contrary is not true. Without heterosexuality, homosexuals cannot exist to claim any right like trying to adopt children produced by heterosexuals. This is unjust for both heterosexual parents and the adopted children. *There is no way to historically satisfy gay and lesbian rights and "freedom" without violating those of heterosexuals after rigorous philosophical analysis.*

In case a "purely homosexual" society decides to have generations that follow one another in the course of history, they can try to have gays temporarily mate with lesbians for the sole purpose of producing children. This will only show again that homosexuality cannot exist without heterosexuality.

So homosexuality brings anatomo-physilogical troubles, generates inequality and injustice, and proves to be a result of a lack of wisdom or reason and also a lack of control or body restraint. In medical language, this called a psychosomatic disorder.

What is presented as occurrence of homosexuality in the animal realm might well be a psychological or soul or mental disorder as well. If animals like humans are known to be able to be physically sick and if humans can develop various mental diseases [including the lack of reason], what scientist would seriously declare that *animals* are incapable of displaying *psychological disorders*? This would invalidate the argument that homosexuality occurs naturally among animals and would confirm its unnatural character.

Animals sometimes behave strangely. One day, Seeker has witnessed a cock mounting a female duck. This case of cross species sexuality could be a justification for zoosexuality despite Lev 19: 19.

But what do animals know? An animal is animal. To which extent should humans justify their choices of life centered on the animal population? Many homosexuals declare that the human race is just another animal species. However, several of the previous chapters have shown that humans are superior to animals in many ways and that their nature is more sophisticated.

Of course human can imitate animals and build airplanes and so on. But animals cannot imitate humans especially their reason. So, humanity must know the border not to cross in imitating animals and keep in mind that there is no other species like humans on earth which can use advanced wisdom or divine wisdom or divine humanism to manage the planet in the most efficient way.

Limiting oneself to the animal world to speak of the natural or unnatural character of homosexuality would be a mistake. Further proof of the unnatural character of this sexual behavior can be found in the worlds of animals, minerals, and quantum physics.

Seeker has never heard of homosexual plants and knows that atoms and molecules do not result from a relationship between two positively or negatively charged elements, but from one plus and one minus. This is how the world develops. If homosexuality were to be exclusively applied to the world of subatomic particles, there would be nothing else than those particles since they will not associate in a way that enables atoms and molecules to appear. *So homosexuality is antidevelopment and anti-existence.*

Since *it has been shown that homosexuality is unnatural, unequal, unjust, and harmful compared to heterosexuality*, engaging in sexual relationship with a partner of the same sex knowing all this would be similar to what medicine and psychology call OCD [Obsessive Compulsive Disorder] a kind of nervous unbalance. In case a homosexual rejects the arguments that make his/her choice invalid; this would be comparable to a denial of reality and should be treated as a psychosis.

However, whether a neurosis or a psychosis, homosexuality does not appear to be too harmful because of the existence of heterosexuality which hides some of its consequences.

Since society is still trying to shape itself so that the greatest happiness emerges *it is wise at this time of history to give homosexuals the right of existence and association without compromising the freedom and rights of heterosexuals especially strict heterosexuals who want to avoid unwanted educational influence through example on their children.*

Human beings in general appreciate being among likeminded people. So, those who consider homosexuality as valid despite all the arguments presented should be allowed to form communities. *Those homosexuals should not be hated. They deserve the respect of their rights as well as help and support against physical and mental diseases, against economic breakdown, against violence, and so forth.* Homosexuals who want help in order to become hetero should also be supported.

Sexuality in the happiest society can only be strict heterosexuality because of all the arguments given in this section.

To fornicate? To cheat? Group sex or orgies? Multiple spouses?

Fornication designates a sexual intercourse between two persons not married while adultery or cheating characterizes a sexual relation between a married person and an unmarried one. The common denominator to all these sexual behaviors is that they are condemned by the great majority of the religious world. However, there are non-scriptural reasons that are against these practices as well.

Fornication between two unmarried persons who are too young is comparable to the consumption immature fruit which can prove harmful not only to the body through sexual diseases and difficulties to procreate later but also through disturbances of the powers of the mind or soul which are intelligence, emotions, the will, creativity, etc....

As the development of a body is disturbed by premature sex, so is the development of the mind. Several good books and articles have been published on the subject. By preventing fornication, one authorizes the body, the spirit, and the soul to reach the level of maturity necessary for sexual activity be fully enjoyed and for a long time. It is good to remember here the advice in the Song of Songs 2: 7 not to awaken love before the time is right.

Fornication between two adults is the result of lack of wisdom or lack of security. If two adult partners love each other they should marry. But some can refuse this way in order to be able to "taste" as many partners as possible. But this is still a lack of wisdom because there is nothing another partner would offer more than the right one. Moreover, fornication between adults is only the creation of more social disturbances.

People must strive to find their right partners rather than trying each other. Besides, there is something in most humans that makes them unappreciative of the previous sexual life of their partners. To avoid all the troubles related to this fact, an appropriate educational system must be designed to help people marry. This is to say that the social sexual disorders observed nowadays and in the past are matters of both individual and collective responsibility.

In addition to the negative elements already shown, fornication makes it difficult to genetically and spiritually trace and improve mankind. A disciplined sexual life helps identify genetic and spiritual disorders when they occur at the same time when it helps control and eradicate them. A good matching between partners is a way to solve many health and social issues and foster happiness.

If fornication is not good for all the reasons presented, adultery and group sex are worse. Having several wives or husbands might have been accepted in history and be adopted today even by some religious people. But the problems polygamy or polyandry tried to solve can be better tackled today through the culture of peace, medicine, education and so on.

For example, if there are no more wars that massively kill male soldiers, a source of unbalance between the male and the female populations will be eliminated and the Islamic justification for marrying up to four wives will be no more.

In addition medicine has developed the methods necessary to always maintain a balance between males and females. It is the collective responsibility of human kind to improve those methods, upgrade the educational system, and put medicine at the service of all.

Pedophilia?

For several reasons discussed in the sub section on sexual relation with animals, pedophilia is not a good thing even its form that involves only children trying to love one another. How can a person who does not know what love and sex are have a sexual relation? How can a child give birth to another child!

These are things that should not be. Theoretical knowledge of love and sex should be completed by the time biological maturity and economic stability are reached. Hence, many related social troubles and individual mental sickness will no longer appear.

Masturbation?

Masturbation is a technique employed by a person to obtain sexual pleasure without intercourse with a partner. It has advantages as well as disadvantages.

The advantages are: the evacuation of sexual urge, a psychological satisfaction or boost, and the avoidance of troubles that attempted or actual sexual relationships with another person can cause and do cause.

The disadvantages are: a less than effective reproduction mean and the acceptance of a low form of sexual life in comparison to what one can experience in a monogamous heterosexual marriage.

Viewed globally, masturbation should not be recommended. Rather, emphasis should be placed on supporting people and preparing them for a good marriage. A good way to prevent masturbation is to dream on marriage while actively gaining scholarly knowledge, wisdom, and financial means with the help of prayer, music, meditation, sport etc…

Through a well-designed program that includes these elements; sexual urge can be suppressed efficiently to enable the individual to start a family. *Good experiences, the concrete positive impacts [physical and spiritual] of a life of sexual control, and hope are of paramount importance in this enterprise.*

Pornography?

Porn, whether made or viewed has even less advantages and more disadvantages than masturbation. However, one of its least negative forms in which cartoons instead of real people are involved can help support sexual education on sexual positions to please the partner.

The disadvantages are so overwhelming that anybody could identify several of them. Hence, it is not vital to list all of them here. What is vital is that the anti-masturbation measures can perfectly work against pornography as well.

Abortion?

The only acceptable form of abortion is when it is done because of medical reasons. All the other reasons can be prevented. The advance of science will also help significantly reduce abortions done for medical reasons.

To be married to and be faithful to one spouse?

Yes, for all the reasons developed in the preceding sections and others including statistical evidences that the number of men worldwide equals approximately that of women.

It is true that a man or a woman alone is an incomplete being. Since there are billions of men and billions of women on earth, it is not easy for people to find the right partner for life. Consequently, a marriage program that will solve that problem most directly must be created.

Such a marriage education should offer teachings and activities that allow those who will marry to learn a lot both in theory and practice about life and people. By gaining significant multidisciplinary knowledge and by interacting with many people in their immediate and distant environment while cultivating virtue, a person can make a better choice concerning his/her life partner.

Marriage education should not replace an individual's right and duty to have the last word in identifying the future spouse. He/she knows him/herself more than anyone else. Moreover, he/she is the one taking responsibility to honor the marriage.

In addition to creating encounter opportunities and helping people study a variety of human beings of the other sex, a marriage preparation should encourage people to be sensitive, not only to physical attraction, but also to spiritual and soul attraction.

Physical attraction can be assessed pretty quickly. Most of the time a few seconds is enough. Sometimes minutes or days maybe months or years are necessary for someone to find out if another person is beautiful in his/her eyes or not.

Then, magnetic attraction or sex-appeal or "chemistry" comes. *Soul-appeal* is the attraction between two souls of opposite sex. The state of a soul at the time of attraction is the product of inborn inclinations combined with a theological, psychological, or philosophical education of some sort plus culture which is equivalent to practical history.

People have several common criteria while trying to determine beauty; but each individual also has his/her sensitivities. That is why it is commonly said that beauty is relative. A person might describe another as beautiful or handsome but find no operational magnetism between them. A person can also stop considering another for marriage after discovering significant differences in terms of vision of life.

Of the three levels of compatibility, the soul level is the most important because the philosophy or view of life of an individual determines his/her actions which nourish joy. The soul is the center of eternal life. That is why the wisdom teaching of divine humanism should be the fundamental element in preparation for marriage.

With a conjunction of minds, people can work to harmonize the physical and the spiritual. The harmonization of souls comes first. When there is soul conjunction and when physical and spiritual criteria are almost harmonized at the time of encounter between two people, they spend less time and effort to get along and the marriage celebration is quicker.

A marriage between two lovers should be scheduled as soon as a minimum condition is gathered. As said a few paragraphs above, the first condition is soul education and the second is experiential knowledge of people. These two conditions are important for finding the marriage partner but also to make sure the union is viable.

The other conditions for the viability of the marriage are: a discussion involving future parents in law, a financial preparation, medical examinations to avoid unnecessary surprises and suffering, a review of biology courses on reproduction, the drafting of a detailed marriage ceremony, a knowledge of the responsibilities of each spouse and that of the children who will be born, a minimum age etc....The marriage contract should bear the signatures of the two spouses, their parents, the religious or philosophic officer, a state judiciary officer, and the mayor in societies in which those categories of people exist.

Early bloomers can seriously identify a marriage partner as early as adolescence. In that case, a betrothal ceremony or a marriage can be envisaged. The minimum age of 16 years with parental authorization is judicious.

A good matching should make sure that a premature death of one of the partners will not happen. Hence, the medical test must be conducted with this additional purpose. The marriage contract should also contain an article that none of the future spouses will engage in irresponsible activities that can shorten life. Consequently, the notion of remarriage will disappear.

A few words on reproduction, the concepts of family and friendship, and child adoption

Human life is a wonder and is necessary for a good standing of the earth and the universe. Therefore, there should always be humans in the visible world. This is one reason humans should reproduce. Another reason is that reproduction allows the birth of children who are amazing beings in many ways. That is why most adults like taking care of them.

In the happiest society, there would be no medical problem preventing from having children. A better management and planning of natural resources and the creation of new resources will always match the human population. In these circumstances, each adult could freely appreciate the joy of taking care of children.

However, even before this ideal situation, adoption is a good solution. The reason dwells in the fact that human beings need others who care for them. This is the meaning of friendship which is superior to the concept of family. Having relatives as enemies makes no sense. Genes are just a mean to organize human society. All people, parents or not, must strive for friendship. Understanding friendship deeply is a powerful way of preventing conflicts at all levels from the nuclear family to the universal society

If friendship is truly understood, adoption appears as a better intermediary philosophical solution than in vitro fecundation and even cloning. It saves money, time, and pain. However, society should always be able to trace the biological origin of children for social health surveillance. So, on the way of making everyone able to have children through education, medicine, and global strategy, adoption is the best solution for people to experience the joy of raising children.

Chapter 11

Recreation, arts, sport, media, politics, and economy

 society cannot be truly happy without relaxation and recreation. Amusement positively influences health by contributing to the nourishment and balance of the human soul, spirit, and body. However an incorrect use of the arts, sport, and media can be a source of damage, unbalance, and unhappiness rather than a way to happiness. This is also the case for politics and economy.

The philosophy of divine humanism cannot be fully elaborated without a reassessment and an amendment of these fields of life. Many have followed this path before Seeker and have helped human society through their wisdoms, discoveries, faiths, loves, knowledge, and so forth.

In the history of America and in the religious field, Puritans are known to have made several moral proposals for example concerning the commerce and consumption of alcohol. Seeker's desire is to find a way to explain why Puritans, Islam, and other schools of ideas are correct in advising for instance for a decent dress code paying attention however not to violate individual freedom and right. He also wants to acknowledge the contributions of political systems such as democracy and those of economic models like capitalism and get rid at the same time of the problems they cause.

Arts, sports, and the media

There are three kinds of arts: the visual arts [painting, architecture etc…], the literary arts [fictional like poetry and non-fictional like philosophy], and the performing arts [music, theatre, dance etc…]. Arts should be used for educational purposes as well as for recreational ones.

The intellect can always develop thanks to the arts because they can be the vehicle of important knowledge or information necessary for the soul. Through the arts, one can learn more about beauty and awfulness, joy and sadness, pleasure and discontentment, and so on.

Arts, particularly music have been well described by Rosicrucians and Theosophists as strengthening the will power which has a lot to do with sound power. Seeker remembers that after listening to a great song, watching a good movie, or reading a good fictional or non-fictional book, he feels in himself a power able to make him transcend his limitations and make a reality the things that appear at first sight to be difficult or impossible. Through the arts, education is so empowered that the learner becomes quickly a creator in any field of life.

Like the arts, sport provides entertainment and fosters human development by always giving examples of broken performance records. For example Carl Lewis demonstrated the first that a man is able to run a 100 m race under 10 s and Celine Dion has amazed the world with her great vocal performances.

Media including newspapers, radios, TVs, the internet, and so forth serve to popularize education and the arts. So, they increase the potential either of the good or of the harm that education and arts can generate. A few more words concerning the possible negative influence of arts, sports, and the media will now be written.

Wisdom, the *Tree of Life* can be corrupted; so are the arts, sports, and the media. Since they are powerful and have great influence on the soul, harm and unhappiness are caused in a greater extent when they are corrupted. This happens when immoral ideas are expressed. Being able to increase the exploration and consumption of the fruits of the *Tree of Life*, arts, sports, and the media can also sustain a fast expansion of the knowledge of evil in the human sphere.

A song propagating an immoral sexual conduct is more dangerous than an unfaithful farmer not only because it attacks human intelligence, but because it impacts emotion, hypnotizes the will better, at a great scale. The design of clothes that leave the body more naked than covered is another example.

If the French legislators are correct in trying these days to implement a law according to which no one should entirely cover the face in order to remain identifiable; Islam and other groups are also partly correct. So, in this matter, it would be wise as the Buddha taught to have a moderate attitude: to wear decent clothes while remaining identifiable.

Human beings have the potential not to be negatively influenced by nudity. But so far, most have not yet reached the level of maturity necessary not to be negatively influenced by it display. The culture of the *"sexy"* have proved more harmful and damaging than beneficial to human society. Numerous illustrations can be given.

There is a difference between the *"sexy"* and beauty. The *"sexy"* is beauty used as an instrument for purposes that in the end corrupt and harm humans. It is temptation, therefore an act of bad intention or an attempt to destroy goodness and morality in people. The "sexy" is beauty oriented toward sexual attraction and consequently should be kept private. It should not be public before the time when collective reason, will, and morality are strong enough to prevent emotions and passions from dragging human beings down.

Though human emotions are important and beneficial, when reason is lacking, they have the tendency to make human beings similar to beasts and even worse because as Helena Blavatsky has said, corrupted super intelligence is more dangerous than uncorrupted low intelligence.

Since divine humanism wants to avoid any knowledge and behavior harmful to human kind, its teachings on the arts, sports, and media stresses their positive effects and seeks to remove and prevent the negative ones.

Arts, sports, and the media should be at the service of Wisdom, Reason or the *Tree of Life* rather than strengthen evil ideas and behaviors. If humanity seriously tries to do this, it will get more experiential evidences that several ways of doings things in these domains of life are unnecessary and harmful and that there are better and healthy ways.

Politics and economy

Politics

Among the definitions given by the Merriam-Webster dictionary online to the word 'politics', two in particular appeal to Seeker and contain the seed of his thoughts about it. The definition 1a presents politics as the art or science of government and definition 3c introduces it as a bunch of artful and dishonest practices.

The same dictionary offers several meanings to the verb 'to govern' among which two parallel those of 'politics' mentioned above. Definition 1a says that to govern is to control and direct the making and administration of policy and definition 1b affirms that to govern can be understood as to rule without the authority to determine basic policy.

Seeker has been surprised to see that the second definitions of both terms actually figure in a dictionary. Before consulting that dictionary, he has always thought that this definition was only popular among the people of his village who have come to no longer trust politics defining it as *'the art of telling lies.'* A politician even took on himself the pain to explain to his potential voters that *'those who believe in electoral promises are fools'*. Nevertheless, this fact is also known in the western world to the extent that it figures in the Merriam-Webster dictionary and certainly in other volumes.

The second definition is a proof that the science [or wisdom] to govern can be corrupted and be a tremendous instrument for the Tree of the Knowledge of Good and Evil because politics in that sense enables evil to be forced upon people and make them miserable or shape them so that they can mistreat others. This is why phrases such as *'to eat or be eaten'* or *'the law of the jungle'* have been officially or unofficially pronounced here and there.

However, the law of the jungle is only valid for animals which humans, again, are not. What happens in the human sphere is worse than the law of the jungle because *with the exception of extremely rare cases of some carnivorous, animals do not eat the members of their own species.* This is why several spiritual people and philosophers have declared that a human can lower him/herself even under the level of the beast.

Coming back to the first definition of 'politics' and 'to govern' as the science of directing the making and administration of policy, Seeker is not entirely satisfied because it always means a pyramidal system in which a few people control, rule over, or tell others what to do. To him this kind of system can only be temporary until all human beings become responsible enough for equally to fully manifest.

Politics even in the best case is not compatible with full equally and cannot be eternal. Even democracy, the most beautiful offspring of politics has been proven to generate injustice, inequality, and suffering. Atilio Boron, an important sociologist and political scientist showed an in article in the *Socialist Register* of 2006 that none among *electoral democracy, participa-*

tory democracy, social democracy, and economic democracy is entirely acceptable or reasonable[42].

That democracy is the best offspring of politics so far does not mean that humanity is incapable of finding a better way of organizing itself and managing resources to meet peoples' need. This is what the philosophy of divine humanism proposes to attempt.

As long as there are adult people who are too ignorant, make significant mistakes, or are evil, politics and democracy well-polished would be necessary. However, when everybody knows the Divine Laws in the mind and the heart as stipulated in Hebrews 8: 10-11*, even the best form of democracy will not be necessary.* It will no longer be necessary for a person to teach another those laws or to govern him/her.

What this means is that practical divine humanism has the duty to popularize divine laws through teachings and social service in order to quickly reach the ideal desired. In the meantime, democracy can be improved in such a way that only truly wise people are elected to "serve" the community and not to "rule" over it. Truly wise people are those able to deeply understand the origin of social and individual problems in the soul, the spirit, and the body and bring answers to them.

When the people of ancient Israel decided to have a king as in the neighboring nations [Samuel 8: 4] bigger troubles began. But this choice of the people was an attempt to find a solution to the corruption of the oldest sons of Samuel who replaced him as judges of Israel [verse 1 to 3].

The reader can see here a repetition of history. Again, a good thing that the God of the Old Testament has made became corrupted. Saul the king chosen could not set up a wise government and the task was passed on to

---

[42]Boron, A A. "The Truth About Capitalist Democracy." *The Socialist Register.* (2006): 28-58. Print.

David. Though Saul and David had some connection with the divine, that connection was not as strong that of Samuel and Nathan who held prophetic offices during their respective reigns. Nathan probably in return was not as skilled as David in managing secular affairs.

The separation of *"Church and State"* which is the current situation of most democratic systems originated probably from that time. Through King Solomon, an attempt was made by divine providence to unite again divine wisdom and government. However, after a brilliant beginning, Solomon failed to fulfill this task. If Adam disobeyed God because of one woman, Solomon's failure says the Bible [1 Kings 11:1-10] was due to his love for several women whose cultures and spiritualities were corrupted.

Since Solomon, *"Church and State"* remained divided. Rulers became more and more incapable of divine wisdom and prophets though they knew a lot about the divine were not able to use this knowledge and wisdom for social betterment. Sometimes they even caused social chaos by irritating or provoking kings who could not understand them.

Even Jesus did not reunite politics and religion or spirituality. Though he seemed to be inclined to do so at the beginning of his public ministry by asking people to repent because of the nearness of the *Kingdom* of God, he refused to be king teaching that his kingdom was not of this world and prepared his disciples for the afterlife.

After Jesus, Christianity's influence remained limited to the religious sphere for a while, but it quickly crossed the borders of the religious sphere to the point to make the Pope a person that exercises political authority.

However, according to history, the rule of many popes has not been beneficial to humanity in contrary to what was said about Abraham, Jacob, Moses, and Samuel. Instead of seeing Christian rulers as allies, people perceived them often as corrupted and supporters of corrupted secular powers exactly as the corrupted sons of Samuel. All ruled with what they pretended to be divine wisdom but which were not as the results showed.

So, the unhappiness generated by centuries of Christian domination led to atheism and many revolutions. Several philosophies such as those of Nietzsche and Marx emerged to discredit God, spirituality, religion, and divine wisdom. At the same time politics became more secularized.

The predictable result of such choices is the return of the animal man in politics and the persistence and aggravation of human misery. The rate of hunger, crimes, injustices, and suicide today says a lot despite the fact that many secular nations advocate the values of equality and justice. It would have been better to make ways for the divine man in politics, but since some who pretended to be divine men have failed, divinity was banished and an attempt to find true divinity was not made.

Sun Moon's solution to bring a religious council in the United Nations will not do either because this will maintain the social division between those who know the divine and those who do not. What is needed is not this kind of inequality contrary to the ideal of Hebrews 8 but that every human being be knowledgeable and skilled in philosophical, spiritual, and physical matters and that the best be put to serve in strategic positions while they sincerely prepare their successors until all adults of human kind reach a high level of competence at least in theology, philosophy, spirituality, and a few disciplines of physical science.

Those with a lot of divine wisdom and knowledge of spiritual science should teach secular people and secular people who are more skilled in societal technical management and physical science should teach those who have only specialized in religion and spirituality. It is capital that leaders who are already managing public affairs be infused with divine wisdom.

A great era of prosperity came upon ancient India when the Emperor Ashoka the Great [304 – 232 B.C.E] decided to use Buddhist teachings. Today, with the globalization of civilization, divine wisdom must be globalized as well.

Since the human soul, spirit body, and physical body are not separate, it is not wise to separate the management of social life called state from wisdom and spiritual affairs. It is because of the troubles caused by religion that *Church and State* have been separated. The restoration of Wisdom and the improvement of spiritual science should be able to demonstrate to people why wisdom, spirituality, and physicality should be united in one global social system.

This was the objective of *Abode of Divinities: Toward a Universal Philosophy, Science, and Spirituality*; this is also the purpose of the present volume on *Divine Humanism or the Creation of the Happiest Society*. If politicians were to decide to be inspired by these volumes, Seeker has no doubt that a truly amazing era of happiness will befall.

Economy

Democracy emerged out of history victorious as the world's main political system. The victory of capitalism which is the economic system often associate with it in the West is even more remarkable. Almost all the countries of the world are involved in the market economy. The majority of the countries of the former communist bloc have now adopted this model of economy.

If politics is the art of management of resources including the economic one, economy is the system that generates the latter. To many scholars, capitalism is an economic system that has many flaws. Communism and socialism have not been successful because they have not been able to elaborate a social equality and justice that fully integrate individual potential, creativity, equality, and freedom.

Chapter 12

Human beings and their futures

Individual and collective futures

THOUGH the question of the origin of humanity is very important, the eschatological one is even more important because human beings cannot affect their origin which is in the past while they can determine to some extent what future will unfold on them thanks to the exercise of free will. Furthermore, by taking eschatology seriously, thinkers can end up finding detailed answers about the origins of human kind.

The reality of *Physical death* for every single human being renders necessary to distinguish two kinds of eschatology or future of humanity: the future of an individual on earth and what happens after death; and the global future of the earth population at a given time and beyond it the ultimate future of humanity after a great number of generations.

Individual future

Every human being has an immortal soul shaped by the use of free will in personal choices. While the soul develops, the physical body and the spirit body develop as well. The growth of the soul and that of the physical body are often quickly perceivable in contrary to that of the spirit. At death, the physical body is destroyed, but the soul and the spiritual body continue to exist as demonstrated.

According to how the soul and the spiritual body had been nurtured and taken care of; they arrive in the spirit world able to conveniently live in it or not, like when a fetus is able normally or not to live on earth after sometime in the waters of the mother.

The difference with the fetus is that individual will, reason, emotions, and so on have contributed greatly to determine what or who the person is at the entrance of the spiritual world. People who are unable to live in the "natural" environment of the spiritual world because of criminal record issues and or/health issues go the equivalent of prisons and hospitals for a short period or for a very long one like people who sinned at the time of Noah [1Peter 3: 19-20].

Collective future or eschatology

On Earth

Influential factors

The earthly future of a generation of human beings depends on its theological, philosophical, spiritual, religious, political, economic, judiciary, and psychological, situation which is both the result of history [choices made by past generations] and of contemporary life [choices made by the members of that generation].

Elements of change

The future of a generation is slow to change because of the weight of its history and the systems it inherits. The time necessary for a single person to change the course of his/her future is much shorter than when an entire generation is considered. Relatively fast social changes occur when particular individuals emerge in various fields of life and succeed in mobilizing the others persons around ambitious projects.

When the visionary person is right, an era of collective well-being follows; but when he/she is wrong social catastrophes happen. Though money is important in the current states of affairs, it should not guide politics, philosophy, and religion. Jesus knew that. That is why he asks in Matthew 6: 33 to look first for the kingdom and justice of God and everything else will be received in addition.

Because some religious people have tarnished the image of religion, other people have made the mistake to put earthly things in the first place. What this generation needs is a powerful spiritual and religious philosophy supported by right actions and right behaviors. When those who have placed their trust in economy see the good results of the philosophy of divine humanism, the seed of wisdom and spirituality which has never died in them will bloom and they will bring their expertise to create a happier society.

Ultimate fate of humankind on earth and beyond earth

This is where theories about the end of the world appear. These theories are of two kinds: the apocalyptic theories characterized by destructive events which kill the great majority of the population before a new era of general welfare and the non-apocalyptic ones.

Apocalypticism

The biblical book of Revelation or Apocalypse has contributed without doubt to greatly popularize the apocalyptic concept. But the notion existed well before the writing of that famous literature and it has been further developed after it.

Within the Bible, the first occurrence of apocalyptic phenomena involving massive destruction and human physical death appears in Genesis 6-9 where the God of the Old Testament sent a universal flood to destroy rampant evil and start a new history of good with the family of the patriarch Noah.

The second case of biblical apocalypse manifested at a lesser scale, a national level, when the same God of the Old Testament caused a lot of destruction and human death in Ancient Egypt and beyond to free and establish the people of Ancient Israel guided by Moses and Joshua.

The books of Judges, Kings, and Chronicles also narrate several mini apocalypses sent to reeducate the people of Ancient Israel when it displayed too much signs of unfaithfulness. These are *scripture-based historical apocalypses*. The destruction of Jerusalem by soldiers of the Roman Empire during the 1st century is also a historical apocalypse.

Many historical apocalypses have been prophetic at first. The flood at the time of Noah is one of them. The characteristic of prophetic apocalypses is that powerful spiritual beings warn humanity before sending catastrophes. *Prophetic apocalypses can become historical or not.*

A good example which demonstrates that a prophetic apocalypse does not necessarily become historical appears in the book of Jonah. In Jonah 1: 1-2 and 3:1-4 the intention of the God of Jonah to destroy the city of Nineveh in Assyria [Mesopotamia] because of its wickedness clearly appears. But when the King of the City and its population changed they behavior, that God decided not to bring about the collective judgment he had threatened them with [Jonah 3: 10].

If today's political leaders and people of the world were to follow the example of Nineveh instead of that of Sodom and Gomorrah, the numerous prophetic apocalypses of Jesus, Nostradamus, Merlin, Mother Shipton, and every destructive event predicted will not happen.

The new era of universal positive change in consciousness often spoken of in spiritual talks is not tied to a particular date. It has already begun and will continue. Human beings are still free and only the choices they make will determine close and distant futures.

If negative energies, pain, suffering, ignorance, violence, crime, sexual misconduct, addictions of all sorts, and so on continue as they are, no doubt that the earth will continue to undergo a catastrophe one after the other. But if people decide to value wisdom, love, cooperation, justice, harmony, equality, ecology and so on, there also is no doubt that good things will happen to humanity one after the other.

Cosmic cooperation, harmony, equality, beauty, health, justice, and happiness

Happiness occurs in society when the needs of each of its members are met. This presupposes that no individual builds personal happiness on the suffering of others which allows speaking of harmony, equality, and justice.

These values cannot be fulfilled through competition but through cooperation.

For people to truly cooperate, one essential condition should be realized: the understanding, knowledge, or wisdom of how it is possible for every person to get the most pleasant things according to individual taste without others having to lose anything.

As mentioned in chapter 4, the soul or the mind has the power to transform the physical world and the spiritual one thanks to a good appliance of knowledge which can require time to be completed. This is the way for the perfection of beauty. Since the soul is eternal, patience will bring any problem to an end.

Most of the ugliness and diseases on the face of the earth are the results of mistakes and evil accumulated over millennia. When a person takes seriously the path of goodness, he/she allows the soul to function at its best, have a good picture of beauty, and find the way to transfer that vision from to noumenal [soul] world to the phenomenal worlds [physical and spiritual].

Beauty and harmony are often companions and can be found at four levels: the soul, the spirit, the physical body, and their environment. Ecology should be valued in order to construct a harmonious and beautiful world.

There is no true justice without true equality and through equality cannot emerge without cooperation and mutual support. According to the Temple of the People, jealousy is an important cause of evil. Pride and ignorance are others. If knowledge or wisdom is advanced in a society, people will truly come to admit that there is nothing to be proud of or jealous of comparing to others. Only victory over possible personal negativity is worth boasting about.

Consequently, it appears that Socrates was right when he stated that the solution of evil dwells in education. Jesus used other words to say the same thing stating that truth sets free. When an individual's wisdom is developed he/she truly realizes that anything done to harm another individual harms oneself and also that anything desired can be obtained through cooperation.

Many people indulge in harmful behaviors because they did not get the chance to know something else. When they do get that chance, guilt can overwhelm them and sincere repentance and change can follow. Hermes and Jesus were great opportunities for mankind. Prison is a temporary and partial solution to evil. True justice prevents crimes. So, education must be a tool to foster justice.

Through education, especially theology, philosophy, and spiritual science negative habits and cultures as well as many diseases will be eliminated. These three kinds of education can help make a difference between *positive and negative discrimination*.

Positive discrimination is the art of avoiding truly harmful and unpleasant experiences. Negative discrimination is to see harm where there is none. But even in that case, the problem can be minimized with likeminded getting together respecting others' freedom of opinion and organization. There is no reason to force someone to eat apple when the person would rather take a mango and vice versa.

The human soul is such that when it is not confined in evilness, madness, injustice, and oppression, it shines transforming both the physical and the spiritual worlds. Hence, some might come to start appreciating people they previously did not hold in great esteem. A person who likes apple today might come to like mango as well tomorrow; when he/she overcomes the fear of the mango while seeing how it can participate in invigorating the body.

Seeker is convinced for example that one day, people all over the world will come to fully comprehend that the concept of nationality is meaningless and suppress it opening a new era for more cooperation, equality, justice, beauty, and happiness.

Based on the $E = MC2$ law, people should realize the incredible amount of energy available in the universe to be used for the creation and management of all kinds of technologies including those that improve bodily [physical and spiritual] and environmental beauty.

If human beings were to decide to deeply think about cooperation now, wise people will bring their wisdom, scientists [physical and spiritual] their knowledge, and rich people their economic power in a melting pot to produce a satisfying outcome for all. No one would need to hide anything anymore. All will have the power of divine law in their minds and hearts as said in Hebrews 8. The appendix at the end of this volume is a tool designed to help in the transitional period toward that ideal.

Imagine a society in which everyone is wise, considerate, powerful, knowledgeable, and wealthy.

Conclusion

If at the end of this volume the reader comes to think that the philosophy of divine humanism has been clearly described; then its primary goal would have been reached. To sum things up, divine humanism is a new philosophy with new ideas that acknowledges in addition previous philosophies and counts on ideas coming from people all over the world living now and in the future in order to overlook no aspect of truth, reason, or wisdom that could positively transform society lastingly.

It is a dream dreamt by humanity as a whole whether consciously or not. As formulated here, it is a proposal that will develop thanks to collective participation. This philosophy is fundamentally based on reason that so many sages, philosophers, spiritual teachers, scientists, and even some religious people value.

The reason spoken of is not ordinary reason that hides selfishly behind personal or small group desire while trying to appear unselfish. It is the transcendental reason mentioned by Immanuel Kant, John Locke, Hermes Trismegistus, and Paul brought to a new level. It is the reason shared by God and the human who accepts as reality both the natural and the supernatural knowing that it is difficult for the natural to perceive the supernatural if a solid bridge is not built.

Like Nietzsche and Taoism, reason in divine humanism stresses the superhuman potential hidden in the ordinary person. But unlike them it agrees with Hermes Trismegistus to say there is a cause for everything including reason called God who is transcendental and supports the human journey from the ordinary to the extraordinary. As Rosicrucians say, it is not because a "phenomenon" [God here] is misunderstood or not well explained that "it" does not exist.

Divine humanism is not a rejection of atheism or skepticism; to them it says: *'let's investigate seriously and honestly together and see if there is nothing as amazing as described by spiritual teachers beneath the veil of materiality that the physical eye is akin to.'*

Seeker is grateful to Hinduism, the Jehovah Witnesses, the Unification Movement, and Secular Humanism which among the exoteric traditions have sufficiently formulate ideologies of human nature, condition, and happiness and have made them available so that he could find and meditate upon them.

From the Freemason Manly Hall, the Theosophist Helena Blavatsky, the Teachings of the Temple of the People, and from the Rosicrucian Manual, he has gathered invaluable information that helped him broaden his knowledge and trigger more accuracy in his thought.

Seeker's gratefulness also goes to physical scientists of all fields particularly those who developed quantum physics and medicine because thanks to their effort, the bridged from the natural to the supernatural is getting stronger. The numerous individuals and organizations working sincerely for justice and equality whether in the United Nations or not deserve his respect and encouragement.

Above everything else, he is thankful to the source of the philosophical and spiritual inflow, namely *God the Universal Thinker that allows him to think thoughts that he would never have thought he would think so that other thinkers too enrich their ways of thinking thoughtful thoughts.*

In divine humanism the scientific aspect of everything particularly theology, philosophy, spiritual and physical science, and education is of paramount importance. Faith is treated similarly to a hypothesis which is not knowledge and therefore cannot be the foundation to create the happiest society.

Science and reason are universal and transcendental while faith is limited to the opinions of individuals and small groups of people. Attempts to build society based on faiths can only result in oppositions, conflicts, and wars. The happiest society can emerge only when spiritual and religious people give teachings that are sound with practical results reachable by all like when everyone agrees on the usefulness for all of computer science.

Divine humanism does not negate the importance of religious traditions such as prayer, meditation, teachings, celebrations and so forth. What it looks for is the logical or scientific justification for those activities. That is what chapter 9 tries to accomplish leading however to a reconsideration of the concept of worship that prefers teaching to preaching and emphasizes prayer, alchemy or positive magic or spiritual science, numerology, and so on.

The purpose of reason in divine humanism is not solely to strive for super humanism, but for super morality as well. Only super morality can generate and handle super humanism. Both are generated by reason and support one another. Through the understanding and development of spiritual power and the respect of just laws, the path is created for love to be experienced at a greater level generating a greater happiness.

It would be a mistake to think that the world can jump from its current state and make manifest the vision, the dream of divine humanism. That is why education should be boosted and upgraded. To do this; all good wills of all fields and regions of the world would be necessary. The world should undergo a collective development of consciousness so that the whole favors the full development of the individual.

Many souls are aware that this has already started. What people should avoid is to let individual or group's unreasonable pride and lack of knowledge create a worldwide philosophical and moral failure. All should unite based on the motto: *'respect to me and my dignity are not synonymous of selfishness.'*

In the transitional phase before all human adults become super powerful, super moral, super lovers and super enjoyers; the fields of sexuality, reproduction, and marriage should become more reasonable and less harmful.

Also, the teaching of the philosophy of divine humanism associated with other activities should generate more wise and compassionate people available for the sectors of politics, economy, media, arts and sport, justice, the military, the health system, the educational system, beauty care, and so on.

All people of good will in the world as well as organizations sincerely working for good should unite to have more efficient actions. As a person who has sworn the oath of Hippocrates to protect life and not harm people whether good or bad, Seeker knows that a transition to the happiest society requires healing a great number of souls, spirits, and bodies bringing the medical science to a global level. This is why cooperation with people who are already making efforts in each domain is necessary.

It would be wise to create a new organization for this unprecedented common effort and make it as inclusive as possible in order to generate good life in abundance. Seeker already has a name, bylaws, and programs of activity ready and awaits those that other people can propose so that a final collective design comes into existence. The contributions of individuals and existing organizations to this enterprise will be made public at all times and recorded in history for future generations.

May the less reasonable becomes more reasonable

May the weak becomes empowered

May the discouraged knows hope again

May the lonely finds real friends

May the less loving and less loved be regenerated through transcending love

CONCLUSION

So be it.

References

Adler, Alfred, and Colin Brett. *Understanding Human Nature.* Center City, Minn: Hazelden, 1998.

Alapini, Frank. *Abode of Divinities: Toward a Universal Philosophy, Science, and Spirituality.* New York, NY: Cosmic Harmony Pub, 2011.

Amir-Aslani, Ardavan. *La guerre des dieux: géopolitique de la spiritualité.* Paris: Nouveau Monde éditions, 2011.

Augustine, and Marcus Dods. *The City of God, Translated <And Edited> by Marcus Dods.* 1949.

Aun Weor, Samael. *The Perfect Matrimony.* Australia: The Gnostic Movement, 1998.

Bagemihl, Bruce. *Biological Exuberance: Animal Homosexuality and Natural Diversity.* New York: St. Martin's Press, 1999.

Blavatsky, Helena Petrovna. *The Secret Doctrine: the Synthesis of Science, Religion, and Philosophy. Second Edition,* 1888.

Boron, A A. "The Truth About Capitalist Democracy." *The Socialist Register.* (2006): 28-58. Print.

Browne, Sylvia, and Lindsay Harrison. *Phenomenon: Everything You Need to Know About the Paranormal.* New York: Dutton, 2005.

Edwards, Paul. *Reincarnation: A Critical Examination.* Amherst,

N.Y.: Prometheus Books, 2002.

Fowler, Jeaneane D. *Humanism: Beliefs and Practices.* Brighton [England]: Sussex Academic Press, 1999.

Gowans, Christopher W. *Philosophy of the Buddha.* New York, NY: Taylor and Francis Group, 2005.

Hacker, P. M. S. *Human Nature: The Categorial Framework.* Malden, MA: Blackwell Pub, 2007.

Hall, Manly P. *The Secret Teachings of All Ages: An Encyclopedic Outline of Masonic, Hermetic, Qabbalistic, and Rosicrucian Symbolical Philosophy : Being an Interpretation of the Secret Teachings Concealed Within the Rituals, Allegories, and Mysteries of the Ages.* New York: Jeremy P. Tarcher/Penguin, 2003.

Jung, C. G. *The Archetypes and the Collective Unconscious.* Bollingen series, 20. [Princeton, N.J.]: Princeton University Press, 1968.

Kurtz, Paul. *Embracing the Power of Humanism.* Lanham, Md: Rowman& Littlefield Publishers, 2000.

Lee, Sang Hun. *Essentials of Unification Thought: The Head-Wing Thought.* Tokyo: Unification Thought Institute, 1992.

Lewis, Ralph M., and H. Spencer Lewis. *Rosicrucian Manual.* San Jose, Calif: Supreme Grand Lodge of AMORC, 1987.

Loptson, Peter. *Theories of Human Nature.* Peterborough, Ont: Broadview Press, 2006.

Moon, Sun Myung. *Exposition of the Divine Principle.* New York: The Holy Spirit Association for the Unification of World Christianity, 1996.

Ouspensky, P. D. *In Search of the Miraculous: Fragments of an Unknown Teaching.* New York: Harcourt, Brance & World, 1949.

Rosen, Steven. *The Reincarnation Controversy: Uncovering the Truth in the World Religions.* Badger, CA: Torchlight Pub, 1997.

Rouner, Leroy S. *Is There a Human Nature?* Notre Dame, Ind: University of Notre Dame Press, 1997.

Salaman, Clement, and Hermes. *The Way of Hermes: Translations of The Corpus Hermeticum and the Definitions of Hermes Trismegistus to Asclepius.* Rochester, VT: Inner Traditions, 2000.

Schopenhauer, Arthur, and T. Bailey Saunders. *The Essays of Schopenhauer. Book VI, On Human Nature.* Start, Kan: De Young Press, 1997.

Sprawls, Perry. *Physical Principles of Medical Imaging.* Rockville, Md: Aspen Publishers, 1987.

Stevenson, Leslie Forster, and David L. Haberman. *Ten Theories of Human Nature.* New York: Oxford University Press, 2004.

Temple of the People. *Teachings of the Temple.* Halcyon, Calif: The Temple of the People, 1948.

Trigg, Roger. *Ideas of Human Nature: An Historical Introduction.* Oxford, UK: Blackwell Publishers, 1999.

Watch Tower Bible and Tract Society of Pennsylvania. *Vous Pouvez Vivre Eternellement su rune Terre qui Deviendra Un Paradis.* Brooklyn, New York, U.S.A., 1989.

Index

Abode of Divinities, 53-54, 58, 60, 62, 64, 67, 76, 83-85, 97, 101-102, 111-112, 127, 130-132, 135, 157, 176, 183-184, 198, 220

Abraham, 96-97, 121, 131, 152, 184, 218

Active evilness, 162

Adam, 22, 24, 26-27, 62, 92, 107, 114-115, 122, 152, 180-190, 193, 196, 218, 225

Adler, Alfred, 18, 71

Akasha, 34-35, 83

Alzheimer, 87

Angel, 6-7, 26, 33, 62, 65, 79-80, 85, 96, 98, 105-108, 113-115, 121, 136, 152, 159, 162, 164-165, 167, 181-182, 184-186, 188, 190, 195, 197, 203

Amir-Aslani, Ardavan, 9-10

Annunaki, 114

Aquinas, Thomas, 14-16, 70, 83

Alchemy, 91, 155, 163, 231

Aristotle, 14, 74, 83, 85, 117

Ashoka The Great, 219

Astral, 31-35, 38-39, 42, 55, 57, 66-69

Astrology, 8, 106-109

Astrotheology, 8, 30, 100

Atman, 22

Atonement, 152

Augustine, 18, 83, 93, 180, 182-183, 191

Aun Weor, Samael, 36, 100, 105, 135-138, 141, 142, 182, 192

Aura, 35

Bagemihl, Bruce, 200

Baines, Kevin, 169

Balaam, 152

Bergson, Henri, 74

Besant, Annie, 87

Blavatsky, Helena, 28, 30, 69, 148, 215, 230

Blood, 33, 40, 52-53, 60-61, 65, 142, 186, 191

Book of life, 35, 99

Borderline state, 43

Brahma, 22

Brain, 18, 29, 32-34, 41, 43, 53, 71-73, 76, 120, 122, 131

Browne, Sylvia, 108

Buddha, 5-9, 167, 195, 214

Buddhi, 31, 34-36

Buddhism, 30, 56, 91, 113, 155, 194-195

Chakra, 10, 32-33, 53, 56, 139-141, 151, 163, 165-166

Christian, 25, 53, 61, 65, 86, 89, 93, 102, 127, 135, 148, 180-181, 183-184, 191, 194, 218-219

Church and State, 218, 220

Cloning, 177-178, 211

Community, 9, 105, 122, 127, 165, 171-172, 217

Compassion, 17, 35, 82, 88, 123, 134, 199-200, 232
Comte, August, 119
Confucius, 18
Consciousness, 16, 20, 22, 26, 30-31, 36, 38, 41-43, 54, 57, 69, 72-73, 103, 105, 133, 136-137, 225, 231
Constantine, 148
Correspondence, 38-39, 58, 180, 183
Creation, 3, 11, 23, 46, 110-111, 113-114, 122, 136-137, 181, 183, 185, 187, 190-193, 196-197, 205, 211-213, 220, 227
Creationism, 111
Creativity, 16, 20, 57, 83, 89, 122, 134, 155, 161, 172, 201-202, 205, 220
Creator, 1, 9, 31, 38, 114, 186, 213
Crucifixion, 7, 61-64, 66, 192
Cultural, 19, 122, 136, 201
Culture, 10, 18-20, 106, 109, 132, 206, 209
Darwin, Charles, 16, 84
Democracy, 122, 213, 216-217, 220
Descartes, René, 18, 69
De Spinoza, Benedict, 18, 71
Destiny, 14, 19, 106
Determinism, 106-107
Devachan, 34-36, 39
Devil, 85, 182, 186-189, 192
Dion, Celine, 213
Divine humanism, 2, 5, 10, 14, 22, 34, 74-75, 82, 103, 116, 118, 126, 128, 130-131, 133-134, 142-143, 148-150, 172, 197, 203, 210, 212, 214-215, 220, 223, 228-231
Divine principle, 25-26, 29, 63, 92, 181
DMT, 59
DNA, 47, 71, 75-76

Dream, 2, 38-39, 54-55, 75, 77-78, 82, 132-133, 155, 157, 175, 187, 207, 229, 231
Education, 10-11, 19, 60, 65, 84, 86, 107, 122, 132, 140, 142, 144-147, 149-150, 154-155, 165, 186, 197, 200, 204, 206, 208-211, 213, 226-227, 231
Edwards, Paul, 71, 73, 76
Ego, 16-17, 22, 35-37, 41, 43, 68, 69, 109, 120, 159, 175
Egypt, 115, 117, 128, 153-155, 224
Einstein, Albert, 41, 46, 58-59
Eisler, Riane, 20
Electric, 2, 31, 33, 35, 39, 47-47, 52, 57
Electromagnetic radiations, 49-50, 57
Electromagnetism, 51-53, 142
Emotion, 14, 20, 32, 70, 103, 121, 173, 205, 214-215, 222
Energy, 2, 6, 10, 31-35, 39-40, 43, 57, 59-60, 65-67, 69, 106, 113-114, 132, 135-136, 138-139, 141-142, 151-154, 157, 160-161, 165-166, 168, 175, 185, 190, 227
Enlightenment, 195
Equality, 18, 84, 122, , 125, 132, 202-203, 216, 219-220, 225-227, 230
Esoteric, 13, 28-32, 93, 98, 128, 131, 184, 187
Ether, 31-32, 34-35, 38-39, 42, 52, 56-57, 63, 83
Euthanasia, 122, 132
Eve, 24, 27, 114, 152, 180-191, 193, 196
Evil, 2, 6, 14, 20, 25-27, 30, 35, 37-38, 60-61, 64, 72-73, 79-80, 82-86, 92, 94, 98, 102-103, 106, 124, 134, 160-165, 179-189, 192-194, 226-227
Evolution, 9, 19, 33, 110-111, 113, 123, 127, 133, 136-137, 170, 219

INDEX

Expiation, 152
Faith, 18, 24, 33, 38, 83, 125-126, 129, 161, 192, 208, 212, 214, 224, 231
Family, 84, 88, 120, 125, 132, 167, 207, 211, 224,
Fall, 26, 182
Fourth dimension, 44
Fowler, Jeaneane, 119-124, 190
Free, 6-7, 15-16, 18-19, 28, 32, 38, 42, 64-65, 83, 86, 107-108, 122, 124-125, 128, 130, 148-149, 155, 160, 167, 169, 178, 181, 191-192, 202, 204, 211, 213, 220-222, 224-225, 227, 230
Freud, Sigmund, 16, 18, 70, 84
Fruitful morality, 155
Garden of Eden, 136, 180-184
Gehenna, 23, 94, 97
Geometry, 38, 101, 168-169
Gnomon, 169
Golden light, 34, 56
Good, 3, 5-6, 8-9, 17, 20, 23, 25-26, 30, 38, 43, 60-61, 65-66, 72-73, 78-80, 82-83, 85-86, 88-90, 92-93, 97-99, 103, 106-108, 122-123, 132, 139-140, 142, 147-148, 152, 157-158, 160-162, 164-165, 167, 171-172, 174, 179-188, 192-194, 196, 198-199, 205-207, 210-211, 213-214, 216-217, 223-226, 231, 232
Grace, 18, 121, 191-192
Gravitation, 32, 47-48, 51, 58
Hacker, Peter M. S., 20, 84, 103
Hades, 23, 94, 97-98
Hall, Manly, 28-29, 53, 70, 86, 98, 147-148, 168, 180, 187, 230
Heaven, 18, 23-24, 26, 34-37, 39, 57, 69, 83, 86, 90, 92-93, 95-96, 99, 102, 121, 137, 169, 193, 195-196
Hedonism, 123
Hell, 23, 26, 86, 90, 94, 97, 102, 196
Hereditary, 18, 71
Heredity, 90, 106, 109

Hermes Trismegistus, 2, 5, 64-65, 83, 103, 106, 112, 128, 153, 158, 183, 229-230
Higher astral, 31, 33-34, 38-39, 57, 68-69
Higher etheric, 39, 57, 68
Higher self, 31
Hinduism, 21-22, 30, 56, 86, 113, 115, 230
Historical apocalypse, 224
Hobbes, Thomas, 15
Holograms, 54
Hume, David, 15-17, 71, 73, 76, 84
Hypnotic regression, 87
Ibn Sina, 70
Immortal, 5, 14, 1829, 34, 43, 67, 104, 120, 123-124, 131, 180, 182, 187, 192, 194, 222
Inertia, 47
Instinct, 15-16
Intellect, 14, 17, 29-30, 72, 136, 213
Intelligent design, 111, 170
In Vitro Fecundation [IVF], 177, 211
Islam, 9, 80, 86, 91-93, 206, 212, 214
Israel, 2, 6, 34, 52, 89, 100, 117, 152, 169, 183-184, 217, 224
Jainism, 30, 134
Jesus, 2, 5, 7, 9, 23-24, 26-27, 36, 52-53, 60-65, 87, 89-90, 92-93, 95-99, 102, 105, 112, 127, 135-138, 147-148, 152-153, 155, 158-159, 161, 164, 167, 172, 175, 181, 183-184, 186-189, 192-197, 218, 223, 225-227
Judgment, 23, 71, 76, 78-80, 156, 178-179, 194, 225
Judgmental, 178-179
Jung, Carl, 18, 71
Justice, 6, 9, 11, 37, 71, 79-82, 123, 132, 202-203, 216, 219-220, 226-227, 230-232
Kant, Immanuel, 15, 70, 83, 124, 229

239

Karmic, 37
Krishnamurti, 87
Kurtz, Paul, 123-125
Lake of fire, 23, 67, 94, 97-98
Law of the jungle, 216
Leadbeater, Charles, 87
Lee, Sang Hun, 70-71
Lewis, Carl, 213
Light, 1, 3, 5, 7, 26, 31-35, 38-40, 50, 52, 56-57, 73, 76, 83-84, 87-88, 90, 148, 165, 183, 185-186, 195
Locke, John, 15, 70, 83, 87-89, 181, 229
Lorentz, Hendrik, 49, 58
Love, 15-16, 25-27, 32, 34-35, 37-38, 60, 67, 72, 76, 83-86, 89, 106, 108-109, 111-112, 123, 125-126, 129, 133-134, 136-141, 143-146, 155-156, 161, 182, 192, 199-200, 205-207, 210, 212, 218, 225, 231-232
Lower astral, 31-32, 35, 38-39, 57, 66-67, 69
Lower etheric, 39, 57
Lower self, 31
Lucifer, 26
Marx, Karl, 219
Memory, 35, 37, 41, 43, 57, 59, 70, 77-79, 87-88, 96, 98, 121
Melchizedek, 152
Mesmerism, 32
Middle Way, 195
Mind, 1, 3, 5-8, 14-16, 18-20, 25-26, 28, 31-37, 40-43, 46, 53, 59, 67-76, 83, 85, 89, 92, 97-98, 103-105, 107-109, 112-114, 119-122, 127, 131-138, 149, 153-154, 157, 160, 162, 165, 167, 171, 173-174, 183, 188-182, 194, 198, 203-205, 210, 217, 226-227
Mohammad, 152
Moksha, 22
Monasticism, 194-195

Moon, Sun Myung, 25, 48, 63, 180-186, 188-191, 196, 219
Moral, 59, 82-86, 91, 102-103, 108-109, 124, 134, 155, 180, 198, 212, 214, 231-232
Morrison, Toni, 55
Moses, 2, 5-9, 34, 53, 60, 64-65, 80, 86, 112, 152-153, 164, 184, 189, 197, 218, 224
Mummified, 32
Music, 40, 155, 157, 173-174, 207, 213
Mythology, 117
Natural selection, 16
Nibiru, 114
Nervous note, 40
Newton, Isaac, 48, 113
Nguemadon, Patrick, 55
Nietzsche, Friedrich, 16, 19, 38, 134, 219, 230
Nirvana, 36, 39, 67, 195
Non-theistic religion, 119
Original sin, 18, 92, 136, 152, 181-182
Parekh, Bhikhu, 19-20, 103
Past-life therapies, 87
Passive evilness, 162
Paul, the apostle, 18, 62, 64-65, 90, 92-93, 99, 102, 107, 128, 160, 165, 184, 187, 190-191, 195, 229
Peace, 3, 9-10, 122-123, 132, 206
Pentecost, 2, 34, 138, 181, 189
Petrarch, 119
Plato, 14, 69, 71, 73, 83, 117
Pelagius, 18, 191
Photon, 49-51
Pineal gland, 2, 34, 56
Pluralistic society, 179
Poimandres, 5, 68, 128
Practical morality, 155
Prana, 31-33, 52, 69

INDEX

Predestination, 106
Prototypes, 68, 71
Psyche, 14, 18, 34, 53, 68-69, 71, 84, 109, 120, 132-133, 199
Psychic, 29, 32-34, 38-40, 42-43, 57, 70, 166
Puritans, 212
Pythagoras, 64, 117, 168
Rational, 29, 52, 73, 123, 170, 209
Reason, 3, 5-8, 10, 14-18, 20, 26, 29, 30-33, 43, 55, 57, 61-62, 64, 70-71, 73, 80-81, 83-86, 89, 91, 94-95, 97-99, 102-103, 105-106, 109, 112-113, 118-119, 121, 123, 126-135, 137, 141-142, 148-149, 155-156, 159-161, 164, 166, 169, 171-172, 175, 179, 182-189, 191-192, 194-196, 198, 200-203, 205-208, 211, 214-215, 217, 222, 227, 229-232
Renaissance, 119, 127
Resurrection, 23-24, 26, 35-36, 62, 64, 86-87, 90-96, 98, 101-102, 194, 197
Röentgen, Wilhelm, 112-113
Rosen, Steven, 88
Rousseau, Jean Jacques, 134
Runco, Mark, 20
Sartre, Jean Paul, 19, 124
Satan, 26, 27
Saturn's Perfect Hexagon, 170
Scheol, 23, 94, 97
Schopenhauer, Arthur, 17, 83-84
Scriptural argument, 89, 97-98, 112, 200
Sitchin, Zecharia, 114
Seven sons of Sceva, 173
Silver cord, 42
Smart, J.J.C., 71, 76
Socrates, 71, 80, 117, 226
Solomon [King], 180, 185
Sound, 25, 32-33, 39-40, 44, 52, 67, 71, 76-77, 122, 150, 157, 171, 180, 199, 213, 231

Soul, 1, 3, 14-15, 18, 20, 23, 31-40, 41-43, 53-55, 57, 60, 62, 65-80, 82-83, 85-86, 88, 91, 03-94, 96, 103, 109, 112, 120, 123, 131-133, 137, 139-141, 145-146, 154-155, 157-159, 161-164, 167, 183, 185, 188-190, 203, 205, 209-210, 212-214, 217, 219, 222, 226-227, 231-232
Soul-appeal, 209
Spark, 31, 33, 52
Spirit world, 26, 60, 65, 67, 90, 92-93, 95-96, 104, 129, 154, 158, 164, 22
Steiner, Rudolph, 87, 167
Stevenson, Ian, 73
Strong nuclear force, 50-51
Superman, 16
Superhuman, 134-136
Swedenborg, Emmanuel, 56, 102, 196
Tatwa, 32-33
The Four Noble Truths, 7
The Noble Eightfold Path, 7
Theoretical morality, 155
Theory of relativity, 44, 57-59
Theosophy, 30, 33, 36-37, 52, 57, 67, 69, 72, 83-84, 86-87, 128
Third eye, 33, 56
Time travel, 58-59
Tolerance, 119, 123, 129
Transmigration, 34, 41, 103-104
Transmutation, 35, 91, 93
Tree of Life, 61, 66, 180-194
Tree of the Knowledge of Good and Evil, [TKGE], 180-184, 186-193
Trigg, Roger, 6, 14-15, 17, 53, 230
Ussher, James, 110
Utilitarianism, 122, 150, 199
Vibration, 34-35, 38, 43-44, 72-73, 76, 171
Vital force, 23
Von Daniken, Erich, 113
Weak nuclear force, 51

Wisdom, 3, 7-8, 14, 17, 30, 34, 37-38, 102, 128, 130, 134-135, 137-139, 142, 155, 162, 164, 175, 180, 182-192, 194-195, 197, 199-200, 202-203, 205, 207, 210, 212, 214-216, 218-220, 223, 226, 228-229

Worship, 124, 132, 152, 174-176, 231

X-rays, 20, 122
Yoga, 56, 113, 128, 155
Young, Robert, 193-194, 205
Zodiac, 30, 100, 169

Appendix

The philosogram

The philosogram is a questionnaire designed to help an individual determine his/her place in the universe of minds and a corresponding place in the universe of energy bodies [spirits] as well as in the universe of physical bodies.

Indeed, reason, ideas, wisdom, knowledge, truth, feelings, emotions, love, laws, determination, will, creativity at the mind level condition relationships including marriage and social service.

It is easier for a person who has précised his/her philosophy of life having taken the time to think about important matters to establish healthier and lasting relationships with other humans and the rest of the universe avoiding painful and useless mistakes. The purpose of the books *Abode of Divinities: Toward a Universal Philosophy, Science, and Spirituality* and *Divine Humanism: Creating the Happiest Society*, is to help the reader summarize and sharpen everything he/she has learned for an improved individual and social wellness.

This philosogram can serve as a sociogram or a tool to analyze and advance society. Centered on the past, it helps compare the philosophies of the previous generations and the level of individual and global wellness they have achieved in order to draw lessons for the present and the future. Centered on the present, it helps take a picture of contemporary society and indicates what kind of society is to be expected [aspirations] in a given future [a few days or several years afterward].

By determining in a standard way their positions, likeminded people can easily find each other especially with the help of the internet to build strong families and societies. The philosogram will help establish federations of blocks of convictions and social design with bridges between them.

For example a straight person might want to join similar people both philosophically and geographically but be willing to participate in health programs for homosexuals if the latter need and want them.

When people change their minds, they can move to different societies that accept transfers with or without probation periods.

By arranging living places according to ideas, the possibility of individuals to hurt one another will be significantly reduced and happiness will increase. This vision of a federation of ideas can be costly seeing the current state of the world in which all kinds of people are mingled.

But a new beginning is necessary to finally correct the mistakes of history and offer a better chance of expression to future generations. The current estate can be reoriented with the moving of many from their present places of living to the ones they long for. There are also enough non populated places around the world for the project to be successful especially if the population growth is mastered. If enough thinking is mobilized, the process will not be too costly and the benefits immeasurable.

When only likeminded good people live in the same geographical area, there will be a tremendous development in particular for the societies with the best intentions which then can generate resources to help other societies.

The philosogram is intended for people who are 16 years or older with parental consent when necessary. Those unable to accomplish their wishes should be helped. It is good that the reader fills the questionnaire before and after reading the two books above mentioned and keeps the record for future updates. So, he she can have enough blank copies available before starting.

The following is the first draft of that philosogram which can be improved.

God is	A-Universal Mind		B- Powerful Spiritual being with human form	C-There is no God	D- I do not know [DNK]
	A1-With Intelligence	A2-Without Intelligence			
I want to live in a social group in which people have other ideas of God	No			Yes A1- A2- B C- D-	
Human beings who can rule others should do so forever	No			Yes	
Human beings who can rule others should rather consider them as equal in thoughts, words, and actions and help them improve	No			Yes	
Some people	No			Yes	

should preach speaking in the name of God						
People should teach about their knowledge and convictions, accept respectful criticism, and avoid saying they represent the voice of God	No			Yes		
Spiritual beings call gods should be served	Angels			Demons		
	No	Yes	DNK	No	Yes	DNK
Spiritual science or magic should be pursued with measures to avoid harm	No			Yes		
Trinity is the Universal Mind, the Universal Energy [Holy Spirit], and the physical universe	No			Yes		
Trinity is God the Father, Jesus Christ, and the Holy Spirit and Jesus is different from	No			Yes		

a pure human		
I can live where Jesus is considered a pure human without harassing people to change their minds	No	Yes
A Messiah is a person who should be above other people forever	No	Yes
A Messiah is anybody who can help or save others being fully considered as their equal	No	Yes
Only good should prevail	No	Yes
The existence of good and evil in a society [a form of dualism] is ok	No	Yes
Family is the place to start social life but a family member should not be favored over others	No	Yes
Friendship is the prime relationship	No	Yes

Belief and faith should be private and shared without harassment	No	Yes
Only proven facts should primarily regulate social life	No	Yes
A disease is the malfunction and/or distortion of the mind or the energy body [spirit] or the physical body, or two of them, or the three	No	Yes
The medical body is made of any person who can recognize, treat, and prevent a disease and its size can be the entire population that can express ideas	No	Yes
Part of education should be hidden and only those considered worthy by its	No	Yes

possessors can be initiated		
The entire human knowledge should be part of public education with equal access to all and special programs to gifted and sick people	No	Yes
People should be allowed to accumulate wealth even if other suffer elsewhere	No	Yes
The human population should match the available natural and artificial resources	No	Yes
Nature should be protected, renewed, or improved, not destroyed	No	Yes
A person should be allowed never to have sex	No	Yes
A person should have only one spouse	No	Yes
A person can	No	Yes

have many spouses		
Fornication is ok	No	Yes
Adultery is ok	No	Yes
Homosexuality is ok	No	Yes
Only pornography based on cartoons with adult human characters should be allowed	No	Yes
All forms of forms of pornography should be authorized	No	Yes
No form of pornography should be authorized	No	Yes
Only masturbation based on cartoons is ok	No	Yes
All forms of masturbation are ok	No	Yes
No form of masturbation is ok	No	Yes
Sodomy is ok	No	Yes
Abortion should be authorized only for medical reasons	No	Yes
Sex with	No	Yes

animals is ok		
The public dress code can be beautiful but not sexy [not excite sexual desire in other people] and should leave the face recognizable	No	Yes
I Can live with people who have a different sexual orientation in the same social group	No	Yes
The greater good should always prevail	No	Yes

www.ingramcontent.com/pod-product-compliance
Lightning Source LLC
LaVergne TN
LVHW051545070426
835507LV00021B/2425